ACTING ON HOPE

World War II
Black and Minority Veterans

Items from ACES Veterans Museum

A. V. HANKINS MD FACP MSEd MPA

DEDICATION

For Kedan.

TABLE OF CONTENTS

Acknowledgments

William Broyles Jr Archivist

Dr. Aaron Wunsch of the University of Pennsylvania, "Thanks for the Parker Hall Project"

Forward

Dr. A.V. Hankins' book "Acting on Hope" is a timely and important testimonial to this country's many Black, Latinx, Asian, Jewish, Indigenous and Women veterans of World War II. As the founder and Director of ACES Museum, with locations in Philadelphia, PA and Pontiac, MI, Dr. Hankins promotes the dual mission of preserving their histories and of supporting the wellbeing of living veterans who have sacrificed much in service to the United States, and its democratic ideals and institutions.

Employing objects, artifacts, documents, and oral histories from the museum collection, Dr. Hankins brings to life many less well known people and events from the time period. The stories she relays of the courage and sacrifices made by individuals who faced racism and sexism at home even as they supported the Allied movement to defeat fascism, is both important history as well as an urgent reminder that their work represents an ongoing struggle that resonates today. The book urges us not to take the work of this generation for granted, but to rediscover this history, and pay it honor through our present day actions.

Tuomi Joshua Forrest
Executive Director
Historic Germantown
Philadelphia, PA

Introduction

ACTING ON HOPE

Black and Minority Veterans and World War II

Items from ACES Veterans Museum

History is important, it tells you the about the lives that have been lived, their value, and that what we do has consequences. The Hebrews have special schools to preserve their heritage. The Japanese pay their elders both respect and money to make sure that their culture stays alive. We have those among us that feel that history is a waste of time and that the only things that matter are what you get right now. This is a silly and shortsighted philosophy. History can help to offset the depression and feeling the hopelessness that we find in young people right now. When they can understand the struggles that happened to make the world progress, it might motivate them into positive actions of their own. The study of personal endurance, love of mankind, and personal grace can be reflected in the study of history. It is like a cross to a vampire and defuses the drug dealer. That selfish "get mine only", way of looking at the world is very small when compared to individuals that deliberately put themselves in jeopardy so that the future could be better for perfect strangers. They acted on hope.

World War II is important because as a major event it changed how people around the world lived. Women could come out the house and work in atypical jobs because of necessity. They proved both their skill and devotion. Blacks and other minorities had to face discrimination and fascism, but they did it with honor, self-sacrifice, and hard work. The result was that America went from a Supreme Court that legalized Jim Crow, separate and unequal, to the legal desegregation of the military and the equal awarding of unbiased government contracts.

World War II began an escalation of human rights. Blacks fought Double Victory Campaigns against fascism overseas and racism at home and were successful. Veterans and their families became 1/3 of the members of the civil rights movement. Noteworthy, World War II veterans that fought for voting rights including Medgar Evers and Floyd McKissick. Champions for the right of one person one vote. Joe Louis was successful in desegregating the buses in the Army, boxing programs, and saving Jackie Robinson from being court martialed. He continued the civil rights struggle and become the first black baseball player in the major baseball leagues.

Senator Inouye championed human rights as a Japanese veteran whose family was placed in internment while he served in World War II. The Japanese were not to receive due process for years later when the law was passed that they had to be compensated for the loss of liberty and property.

Cesar Chavez would form a union for migrant workers. He helped to address the plight of the migrant worker and the need for basic human decency: the right to work in a safe environment, fair compensation, and due process before penalties.

Tommy David Hankins would struggle to help form the United Auto Workers. This union was the basis of fair treatment for the working class and to assist in the development of a middle class. Workers could directly benefit from the production of the auto industry. Medical care, workman's compensation when injured on the job, and a living wage, were some of the things they had to fight for.

Manuel Lorenzo, the first Hispanic commandant, was a Puerto Rican that was among thousands that were recruited to fight in World War II but could not receive benefits because they were not in Spanish. He fought and won the victory for all literature to also be prepared in Spanish.

All women volunteered for service during World War II. Black, Native America, Hispanic and Asian women, would face racism as well as sexism.

World War II was a war against the superiority of one group of people over others. One group, the Axis powers, believed that there was only one type of person that deserved respect, everyone else was expendable. The Allied forces verbalize the concept: all men mattered.

Germans as the leaders of the War, had developed governmental forced brutality against anybody different in Germany. Jews, Gypsies, protesters, and intellectuals that questioned authority were brutally exterminated. Books were banded and independent thought criminalized.

The concept was fascism. Fascism is where the government dictates, usually in the form of an individual, how the society must work. It limits the economy and the opportunities for any the controller does not support. How you dress, where you go, what money you can make, when you can talk, and what you can say, are all regulated under law. The laws are broad and the power of the controller absolute. The chance for trial in which evidence can be presented, free speech, and protest, are nonexistent. The police military, what is supporting branch of this form of government, has total authority to kill as they "arrest". They have authority to torture, inflicting pain and distress, until the person tortured agrees with them. The crime against the state is any crime the state says it is.

In this backdrop, the Blacks in the United States were, experiencing full scale discrimination, lynching, other atrocities because of the color of their skin and the racist policy's that had been enacted against them since slavery's reconstruction. There was, a difference between The United States and the fascist governments. The Constitution of the United States had said , " all men are created equal." In the word of the Tommy D Hankins World War II Army veteran special forces, "Our goal was to make sure that the constitution was followed. This could not be done if Hitler were also ruling America. This is why we fought, and this is why we won both battles."

Although African Americans have been victims of racial oppression throughout the history of United States, they always supported the nation, especially during wartime. It was during World War II that the legal integration took place in the armed forces even though there were also segregated units. Segregated black units fought with distinction including the Tuskegee Airmen 99th Fighter Squadron. For their heroic feats throughout the war they received a distinguished unit citation, several Silver Stars, 150 flying crosses, 14 Brooks Brown stars comp, and 744 air medals.

The 761st Tank Battalion fought in the European Theater of Operations. It was the only all black unit which received the Presidential Unit Citation. They fought for 183 continuous days, conducted over 30 major assaults, held the Germans at bay, and saved civilians.

ACES Veterans Museum was created at the site of the historic Parker Hall. Parker Hall was a functioning USO during World War II for black veterans and their families. The USOs and support systems were segregated so that Blacks and other minorities had to have other places where they could go for support. The Germantown Historical Society certified Parker Hall is being historic and in 2000 ACES Museum was formally created.

ACES Museum gets its name from a child's simple question, "Is it true they used to call you spades?" "Yes." "Well if you had to be a Spade, I know you were the Ace!"

The items selected from the Museum are meant to address the object itself and the possible social impact during World war II. In keeping with training from Harvard University, museums are meant to have relevance and not just be storage warehouses for pieces of interest.

ACES Museum was created not only to reflect the black veterans' role in World War II but to be one of the first places that would celebrate all minorities of World War II. Telling a comprehensive story of the men and women that fought for democracy at home and abroad. They believed in the concept that all men are created equal and that the United States America was special because the constitution had that premise. It just had to be expanded to truly include any race, sex, and creed. These people were acting on hope.

MAJOR CHARITY ADAMS

Major Charity Adams 6888th Postal Battallion

The Women's Army Corps (WAC) of the U.S. Army was created by a law signed by President Franklin D. Roosevelt in 1943. The WAC was converted from the nonmilitary Women's Army Auxiliary Corps which was created in 1942. First Lady Eleanor Roosevelt and civil rights leader Dr. Mary McLeod Bethune successfully advocated for the admittance of black women as enlisted personnel and officers in the WAC. The black 6888th Postal Battalion was given the assignment to correctly process 1 million pieces of back logged mail that was stored in England. They created a new tracking system and processed an average of 65,000 pieces of mail per shift clearing the six-month backlog of mail in three months. The women adhered to the motto of, "No mail, low morale,". The 6888 provided essential support for the U.S. military in the European theater by linking service members to back home [1]

Major Adams was the head of the battalion and she stood her ground protecting the troops. When a general threatened to replace her with a white first lieutenant to "show" her how to command she said, "Over my dead body sir".[1] The general rescinded court martial when he realized how efficient the 6888 were. They were so successful in England; the 6888 was sent to France.

Major Charity Adams was promoted to Lieutenant Colonel upon her return to the U.S. The accomplishments of the 6888th in Europe encouraged the General Board of the United States Forces European Theater, to acknowledge the Women's Army Corps vital role in the service.

---

https://history.army.mil/html/topics/afam/6888thPBn/index.html

AIRPLANE INSTRUMENT

1940 Airplane Salvage – Women Airforce Wasp

In 1942 a need for World War II pilots left the door open for experienced women pilots to fly noncombat missions. The Women's Airforce Service Pilots (WASPs), was created from other civilian units. The WASPs were civilian women pilots who were attached to The United States Army Air Forces to fly military noncombat missions.

Women Airforce Service Pilots (WASP), had 1,100 civilian women with flight duties during World War II. The Women Airforce Service Pilots (WASP) were the first women to fly U.S. military aircraft. In addition to ferrying, and delivering supplies, they also performed check flights, put flying time on new engines, towed targets for gunnery practice, flew tracking missions, and instructed male pilot cadets.[1]

The WASP were part of the 350,000 females that served with the Armed Forces in America and abroad during World War II. The WASPs existed from 1942 to 1944. They flew over a million miles in service of the war and used 12,000 military planes.[2]

The WASP arrangement with the US Army Air Forces ended on December 20, 1944.

There were recognized as Veterans for their service to the Country in 1977.

www.britannica.com/topic/Women-Airforce-Service...
https://waspmuseum.org/

AFRICAN TROOPS

African Troops in World War II generally fought under a British banner. For Africans World War II started in 1935 not 1939. Italian dictator Benito Mussolini ordered troops into Ethiopia. People of the country were instructed to turn on their Emperor Haile Selassie. The Italian army was overwhelming because they used hundreds of tons of chemical weapons upon the Ethiopians.[1]

Black African soldiers fought in the army, and in air and naval forces. They joined the East African campaign was mainly fought by Allies of World War II, mainly from the British Empire. The British India, Uganda Protectorate, Kenya, Somaliland, West Africa, Northern and Southern Rhodesia, Sudan and Nyasaland participated in the War effort.

The African troops suffered the loss of at least 50,000. With the invasion of Ethiopia, during which chemical weapons were used, the number of loss including civilians would be between 300, 000 and 600,000.

Under the coordination of U.S. General Dwight D. Eisenhower, the combined British and American forces pressed the fight and after the fall of Tunis, the Axis forces in North Africa surrendered on May 13, 1943. 275,000 German and Italian soldiers were taken prisoner.

1 allthatsinteresting.com/african-soldiers-world-war
2. n.wikipedia.org/wiki/East_African_Campaign...

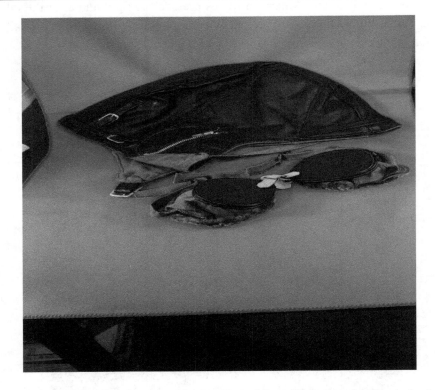

Willa Brown was a pre-World War II Aviator. She earned a Bachelor's degree from Indiana State Teachers College and A Master's degree in business from Northwestern University.

In 1935 she earned a Masters Mechanic certificate from Curtiss Wright Aeronautical University, and in 1937 she was the first African American in the U.S. to earn a commercial piolets license.

Ms. Brown and her husband Cornelius Coffey, a flight instructor, cofounded the Cornelius School of Aeronautics, the first black owned private flight training academy.

Brown also founded the National Airmen's Association of America.

By 1941 Ms. Brown had trained hundreds of men and women, including the Tuskegee Airmen.

In 1941 she became the first African American officer in the U.S. Civil Air Patrol (CAP).

Brown remained politically active fighting for racial and gender integration in the U.S & Army Air Corps.

In 1972 in recognition of her contributions to aviation, Ms. Brown was appointed to the Federal Aviation Administration (FAA) Women's Advisory Board.[1]

https://pioneersofflight.si.edu/content/willa-brown-

JOSEPHINE BAKER

Josephine Baker was an American that became a French citizen because of prejudice in America. She started as a talented dancer and became a stage singer, international star, the first black woman to star in a feature film, a recording artist, and a headliner in New York's Ziegfeld Follies. She was not accepted at the Follies.[1]

Ms. Baker was also a spy for the Maquis during World War II. This was a group of freedom fighters against German domination. She was crack shot, but her primary job was to deliver information. The information was written in invisible ink and she would carry it across boarders while touring. Ms. Baker was arrested several times but was able to maintain a haven for members of the Resistance. In addition to her work as a spy, Baker volunteered for the Red Cross as a nurse. She was also a pilot, delivering supplies for the fighters in her private plane. She entertained French and Allied troops. Ms. Baker was awarded with multiple medals from France for her dangerous work in World War II.[2]

Ms. Baker returned to America and marched for Civil Rights with Dr. Martin Luther King in the 1960s.

1https://selfrescuingprincesssociety.blogspot.com/2017/06/josephine-baker-world-war-ii-spy.html
2https://historynewsnetwork.org/article/170603

BARRAGE BALLON MANUAL

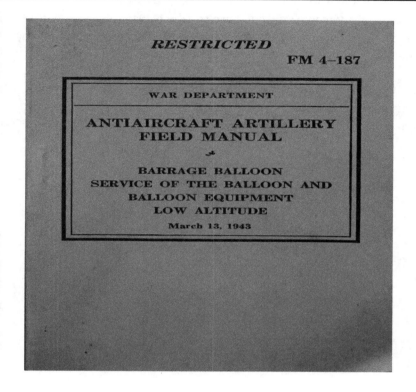

THE 320 BARRAGE BALLOON BATTALION

When the United States entered the war there, was the requirement to train the men 18 to 65 years of age. Over 10 million men were inducted into the military while the elective Training and Service Act was in effect from 1940, to 1947. Volunteers came from a variety of sources and male volunteer registration was at 37%. All women that served volunteered. Individualized instruction had to be completed on a mass level. Data was originally presented in book form, and there were several manuals. One of the manuals is above. They soldiers were trained for 4 weeks then sent into individual additional training depending on assignments [1]

The 320 Balloon Battalion was educated to go overseas. The Battalion was one of several Battalions trained to handle massive balloons. These balloons were used to stop planes from landing because they could not fly close enough to their targets. The 320th BB was sent to Europe and served on the Omaha and Utah beaches, the D Day invasion, and were in France 150 days. The 320th protected the ships, soldiers, and supplies from German aircraft.

For their work on Omaha beach, the battalion received a commendation from Supreme Commander of the Allied Expeditionary Forces in Europe General Dwight D. Eisenhower [2]

1 https://msu.edu/~sleightd/trainhst.html

2 htps://airandspace.si.edu/stories/editorial/protecting-beaches-balloons-d-day-and-320th-barrage-balloon-battalion

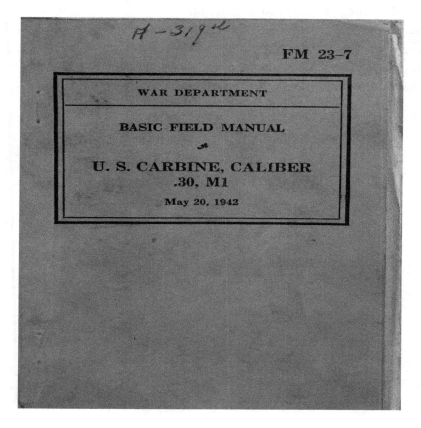

WAR DEPARTMENT

BASIC FIELD MANUAL

U. S. CARBINE, CALIBER .30, M1

May 20, 1942

FM 23–7

761 Tank Battalion

The 761-Tank Battalion became the first black tank battalion to see combat in World War II. They were called the Black Panthers and fought in France, Belgium, and Russia. Their actions allowed George S. Patton's troops to enter Germany.

The 761st Tank Battalion was formed in the spring of 1942 had 30 black officers, six white officers, and 676 enlisted men. This majority-black military unit was known by the nickname "Black Panthers" in reference to the panther patches they wore on their uniforms and their fierce fighting ability. While other units fought for weeks, the 761st Battalion served for over 183 consecutive days. The Panthers were also part of the Allied forces who liberated a concentration camp. The Army awarded the unit with four campaign ribbons. In addition, the men of the 761st received a total of 11 Silver Stars, 69 Bronze Stars and about 300 Purple Hearts. Back at home, though, the surviving members of the 761st returned from Europe to a still-segregated nation.

history.com/news/761st-tank-battalion-black-panthers-liberators-battle-of-the-bulge

BENJAMIN BERRY

Benjamin Berry was a black soldier of the Battle of the Bulge and an ACES Board member.[1]

It was the first time an integrated Army was legally sanctioned. The 761st Tank Battalion, the original Black Panthers were at the major German offensive of the War.[1] Additional Black units to serve in the Battle of the Bulge were the 614th Tank Destroyer, 333rd, 378th, and 969th Field Artillery Battalions, and the 3418th Trucking company (Red Ball

Express). Additionally, more than 2,500 Blacks from service units - quartermaster, engineers, cooks- answered the call for infantrymen.[2]

Benjamin Berry answered the call and continues to fight for civil rights. His most recent accomplishments include the placement of a marker for the colored soldiers of the Civil War at Philadelphia National Cemetery and helping to preserve Parker hall from unnecessary destruction.

1.https://www.history.com/news/761st-tank-battalion-black-panthers-liberators-battle-of-the-bulge
2.www.dogonvillage.com/.../battle_of_the_bulge.htm

BETTY BOOP

Betty Boop was a cartoon character of the 1930s popular in the 1940s. In the 1930s she was black and danced with Popeye the sailor man.

The black Baby Ester was a popular act at the Cotton Club in Harlem. She sang "boop-boop-a-doops" and other scat sounds.

Initially, Betty Boop was black and danced with Popeye in the Sailor Man series. In the video of the cartoon series it illustrated an integrated dance scene.

Ms. Boop was transformed into a white woman, by the "discoverers". She became a million-dollar enterprise, and Baby Esther was not acknowledged, nor compensated.

Ms. Esther and her legendary way of singing is remembered with the Harlem Renaissance, the preserved videos of Popeye, and through the Betty Boop in dress.

https://www.blackhistory.com/2018/05/real-betty-boop-black-woman-baby-esther-whitewashed.html#:~:text=The%20Real%20Betty%20Boop%20Was%20a%20Black%20Woman...,sin
https://www.britannica.com/topic/Betty-Boop

BLACK MEDAL OF HONOR WINNERS
WORLD WAR II

BLACK MEDAL OF HONOR WINNERS WORLD WAR II

Picture from the Pentagon Washington, DC
Medal of Honor Recipients

In 1997, after legislation, President William Clinton, presented Medals of Honors to African American Veterans that had been denied due to racial disparity in World War II.

The awardees summary of events includes:

- **First Lieutenant Vernon J. Baker**-attacked machine guns and protected wounded personnel.

- **Staff Sergeant Edward A. Carter, Jr.**-Lead against a tank and received valuable information,
- **First Lieutenant John R. Fox**-Stayed in a town in Italy to direct fire against the Germans.
- **Private First-Class Willy F. James, Jr.** -Drew fire exposing enemy fire, then lead the assault.
- **Staff Sargent Ruben Rivers**-Wounded, he advanced his tank against a German one and protected the soldiers.
- **Captain Charles L. Thomas**-Remained in command while wounded making sure antitank guns were in place.
- **Private George Watson**-Drowned while saving capsized soldiers.

http://www.history.army/moh.html#FOX

BLACK NURSES

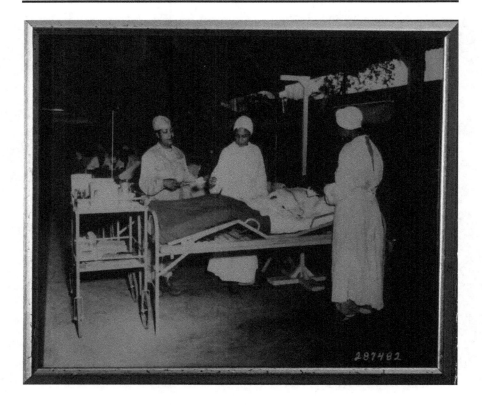

National Archives

Black nurses served in the Army Nurse Corps when the opportunities became available. In World War II from 1941 to 1944 they were in segregated units. Their recruitment was limited until there were civilian outcries and a personal plea from First lady Eleanor Roosevelt.[1]

The black nurses duties were restricted to serving black soldiers and German prisoners of war. These prisoners were sometimes granted privileges the nurses couldn't enjoy.[2]

Black nurses cared for troops in 1943 in Liberia, Burma, and England. By the end of the war, black nurses had served in Africa, England' Burma, and the Southwest Pacific.

In 1945 there were 300 black nurses. Now African American make up 17% of the Army Nurse Corps.[1]

1 https://blackthen.com/black-nurses-serving-in-the-military-during-world-war-ii/
2 https://history.army.mil/books/wwii/72-14/72-14.HTM

BLACK ROSIE THE RIVETERS

Many men had mandatory military service, which led to a shortage of available laborers, thus the demand for women workers. Black and minority women were also part of these corps of fabled "Rosies." An estimated 600,000 African American women fled oppressive and often demeaning jobs as domestics and sharecroppers. They chose instead to help build airplanes, tanks and ships, fueling America's "arsenal of democracy."

Noted Philadelphia historian and filmmaker Gregory S. Cooke noted that pressure applied on the government by Mary McLeod Bethune, A. Phillipa Randolph, Eleanor Roosevelt, and others moved the President to sign for fair hiring practices.

https://www.phillytrib.com/lifestyle/black-rosies-of-wwii-opened-doors-for-others/article_007f433b-c4d5-5359-8d58-7214c8d70069.html

HUMPHREY BOGART

The Hollywood Canteen was started by John Garfield and Betty Davis. Garfield had a heart condition and could not enlist in the Armed Services. The Canteen operated in Los Angeles and offered food, dancing and entertainment for servicemen of all races.[1]

The Hollywood Canteen operated from 1942 and 1945 as a free service for allied servicemen and women in the service. The movie The Hollywood Canteen made in 1944 was integrated. The East Coast counterpart was the New York City–based Stage Door Canteen. It featured Broadway stars and was also had a film, Stage Door Canteen.

At the time the canteen closed its doors, it had hosted almost three million servicemen.

In a time of a segregated military service, restrictions on blacks in America, and limitations on blood for black people at the Red Cross, the canteen and its integrated and fair policies was democracy in action.

---

https://en.wikipedia.org/wiki/Hollywood_Canteen

BOOKS

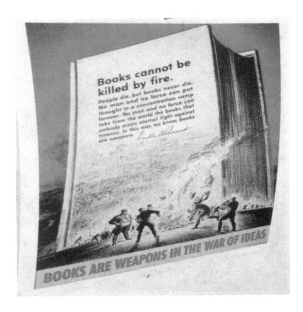

Historical Poster Recreation

The first target of Adolf Hitler and his Nazi organization were books. This began in 1933, shortly after Hitler seized power in Germany. He ordered any book that did not support his thoughts confiscated and destroyed.[1]

Independents who thought questioning why actions occurred and who benefitted from government contracts were considered dangerous to dictators.

Modern day equivalents would be those that want to suppress or have restricted internet access in their countries. The worse countries that prevent the freedom of electronic interchange include Turkmenistan, North Korea, Eritea, China, and Vietnam.[2]

---

1 http://totallyhistory.com/nazi-book-burnings/
2 Internet Censorship 2020: A Global Map of Internet ...

BOX ARMY WORLD WAR II

Tommy D. Hankins Special Forces

Tommy D Hankins Dawud Muhammed served four tours of duty during World War II which was unusual at that time. He was part of black special forces sent to Japan after the bomb to test its effects. A patriot, he was questioned as to how he could be committed to a country that abused him in such a manner. He said, the United States Constitution states that "all men are created equal." Here we have an opportunity to turn that into truth. That is not the case around the world. Individual rights, a private vote, the right to read, and business opportunities are only available to the people at the top and they choose. Here we may, we must, get the right to choose. In the box was hope. He helped to form the UAW, United Auto Workers.

Gwendolyn Broyles Hankins was a Neighborhood Mayor, Rosie, and a Civil Rights advocate. When ask how she could marry a Muslim she said, Faith is what you do.

They died within months of each other.

BUFFALO PATCH

BUFFALO SOLDIERS 1866-1951

Buffalo Soldiers were formally formed in 1866 as a peacetime "colored unit". Their motto: We can, We will." There were 4 different regiments. The nick name came from the Native Americans because of the black's troops strength, courage, and wooly hair. The soldiers served in major military conflicts. The Buffalo soldier units served in the Spanish-American War, World War I, and the Italian campaign of World War II, when elements of the 92nd Division were among a handful of black units in that war to serve in combat.

World War II in 1944, after pressure from the black community, the African American soldiers were sent to combat in Italy.

The Buffalo soldiers had an impressive record with that opportunity. Of 12,846 Buffalo soldiers who saw action, 2,848 were killed, captured or wounded. The Buffalo Soldiers broke through the G Line in Italy. They reached their objective, captured or helped to capture nearly 24,000 prisoners and received more than 12,000 decorations and citations for their gallantry in combat. The soldiers of the 92nd Division had proved their worth through months of bitter combat in the Italian campaign.[1]

Blacks would fight with distinction during the War in other areas, including in combat in the Pacific.

https://www.militarytimes.com/military-honor/black-military-history/2018/02/14/how-the-buffalo-soldiers-helped-turn-the-tide-in-italy-during-world-war-ii/

CAMP MACKALL NC PAPERWEIGHT

Paperweights are solid objects from2.5 and 3.5 inches in normal standard. These domes are used to accent the enclosed items and are generally used as collectibles. Camp Mackall is located in North Carolina. It began as a separate U.S. Army training base during World War II. There were three airborne divisions formed and trained there from 1943 to 1945.

Initially named Camp Hoffman, the facility was renamed Camp Mackell in honor of private John Thomas Mackall, a paratrooper. The camp was a marvel of war time construction completed in four months.

https://arsof-history.org/articles/v3n4_camp_mackall_page_1.html 1
https://www.glasspaperweightfoAbout
Paperweightsundation.com/all_about_paperweight.

CANTEEN   SHOVEL

Quartermasters Troops and the Red Ball Express

The US Army Quartermaster section is its oldest logistics branch. It was established in 1775. Quartermaster means master of quarters-one who goes ahead to provide lodging. Their job is to provide the support needed for the Army.[1]

More than 32,000 officers, officer cadets and key enlisted personnel received their training at the Quartermaster School between July 1, 1940 and December 3, 1945. The physical conditioning of entrants was emphasized along with rigorous military training. They had to shovel foxholes.[2]

The Red Ball Express was a series of truck convoys that carried supplies for Patton's Third Army. Through a span of 82 days in 1944, the black soldiers delivered more than 400,000 tons of war materials over 700 miles to the front in a route marked with red balls. Their efficiency prompted a British infantry brigade commander to note: "Few who saw them will ever forget the enthusiasm of the Negro drivers, hell-bent whatever the risk, to get Gen. [George] Patton his supplies." Some also participated in armed combat.[3]

Private George Watson was a black Medal of Honor winner that was a quartermaster that gave his life saving others.

1. https://quartermaster.army.mil/history/u-s-history.com/pages/h1714.html
2. https://qmmuseum.lee.army.mil/WWII/qm_school.htm
3. https://www.dav.org/learn-more/news/2015/black-history-month-2015-remembering-red-ball-express/#:

CHRISTMAS BOX

**1940s Christmas Boxes and Christmas with the
92nd Infantry Division**

The Buffalo soldiers had to fight and, the black community protest, for them to get a chance to fight and represent themselves as equal citizens and men during World War II. They proved their qualification on a special Christmas Day.

On Christmas Eve the Fifth Army, had called off its Christmas Day assault in Italy. The Buffalo Soldiers were deployed on both sides of the Serchio River and were forced to advance. They faced German mortar and artillery rounds as they moved through more of northern Italy's mountain towns.

Before sunrise on the day after Christmas, the Germans attacked the villages just north and east of Gallicano. Many of the Germans were dressed as partisans, making the situation even more confusing and dangerous. Just before noon, the platoons were ordered to evacuate the village, but they were trapped. They managed to hold out until nightfall, but of the 70 Americans involved, only one officer and 17 men managed to fight their way out of the village that night as ordered. fighter-bombers roared into the valley and hammered Sommocolonia, Gallicano and other front-line areas, and by January 1, the Allies had re-established their original positions.

The village was not overtaken due to the determination of the 92nd Infantry, and their refusal to surrender, during that Christmas, or any other, period.

COON CHICKEN

COON CHICKEN POSTER

Segregation and Black Codes

Jim Crow laws began as early as 1865, immediately following the ratification of the 13th Amendment, which abolished slavery in the United States. These codes were strict and detailed a legal way to keep black citizens in servitude.

The codes appeared throughout the South as a legal way to control how they lived, worked, traveled and were treated in Court. They made it legal and to seize children for labor purposes.[1]

The post-World War II era saw an increase in civil rights activities in the African American community, with a focus on ensuring that Black citizens were able to vote. This ushered in the civil rights movement, resulting in the removal of Jim Crow laws.

Specifically:
- In 1948 President Harry Truman ordered integration in the military.

- In 1954, the Supreme Court ruled in *Brown v. Board of Education* that educational segregation was unconstitutional.

- 1964, President Lyndon B. Johnson signed the Civil Rights Act, which legally ended the segregation that had been institutionalized by Jim Crow laws.

https://www.history.com/topics/early-20th-century-us/jim-crow-laws

DUKE AND WING AND A PRAYER

Music had several roles in World War II. 96.2 % of American families had radios so music was a universal commodity. American music featured jazz which was banned by Germany. Music was a source of inspiration, motivation, and civil rights updates. Some of the music was directly written for the war, as above. Music helped people cope with the stress of the war and grieve for their losses.[1]

Popular artists included Frank Sinatra, Ella Fitzgerald, the Andrew Sisters and Duke Ellington.

Duke Ellington was special. Band leader Edward Kennedy "Duke" Ellington was a musical genius. He composed over one thousand works, traveled all over the world with his band and was featured in motion pictures.[2]

In 1943 Duke Ellington and his band made their debut at Carnegie Hall during the height of World War II. He used his music to promote respect and racial harmony with his longest composition, Black, Brown, and Beige. [3]

1.wikipedia.org/wiki/American_music_during.world war II.
2.www.bartleby.com/essay/The-Role-of-Music-during..world war II.
3.lvphil.org/2020/06/the-music-plays-on-duke-ellington-black-brown-and-beige-by-donato-cabr

EAR WARDENS

HEARING PROTECTIVE DEVICES DEVELOPED WWWII ARMY

Ear warden are hearing devices known as HPD worn in or over ears to protect from hearing loss. There was a 10-20% hearing loss from WWI.

A study by the U.S. Army in the 1940s caused the recommendation that gun crews and others exposed routinely to gunfire be provided with hearing protection. The Ear Warden V-51R were developed during the end of World War II. They were produced in different sizes-an innovation of the time period. Hearing rehabilitation was also started in the newly re-organized Veterans Administration.

Hearing loss has become so significant that 17 percent of young people between 12 and 19 have some degree of noise induced hearing loss. They may not realize the issue is permanent and fail to seek help. Noise induced hearing loss is the leading cause of the decrease. Any hearing change should be investigated, regardless of age.

Decrease loud noise exposure, use earplugs on noise-cancelling headphones. Each can reduce sound intensity by 30 decibels. Stop smoking to decrease damage to ear hair cells.

1.www.ishn.com/articles/106961-tracing-the-origins-of-hearing-protection#:~:text=A%20landmark
2.https://asa.scitation.org/doi/abs/10.1121/1.1917477

FIELD COMMUNICATIONS TELEPHONE –

MARINES

Marines are part of Naval wing of armed forces performing combat

From 1798 to 1942 blacks were denied entrance into the Marines. After Executive Order 8802 forbid racial discrimination, Howard Perry and others joined the Marines and trained at Montford Point, North Carolina. The black USMC recruits would form the 51st and 52nd Defense Battalions. In total, 19,168 African Americans joined the Marines, about 4% of the USMC's strength. 75% of them performed their duties overseas. About 8,000 black USMC stevedores and ammunition handlers served under enemy fire during offensive operations in the Pacific.

In 1944 the 7th Marines needed help to get their wounded to safety. The segregated companies of the 16 Marine Field Depot, and the 17th Special Seabees volunteered to assist. The counteract was repulsed and the black troops received written commendations for their heroic actions.[1]

Following the June 1944 Battle of Saipan, USMC General Alexander Vandegrift said of the steadfast performance of the all-black 3d Marine Ammunition Company: "The Negro Marines are no longer on trial. They are Marines, period."[1]

Women were part of the Marines since 1918. The Marine Corps Reserves had 20,000 women in 225 different jobs in World War II.[2]

There were 874 Native American Code talkers in the Marines during World War II. Only white Hispanics were admitted to the Marines at that time.

The Marines would not become fully intergraded until 1960.

https://en.wikipedia.org/wiki/Desegregation_in_the_United_States_Marine_Corps
https://marineparents.com/marinecorps/women

FOUR FREEDOMS – BILL OF RIGHTS

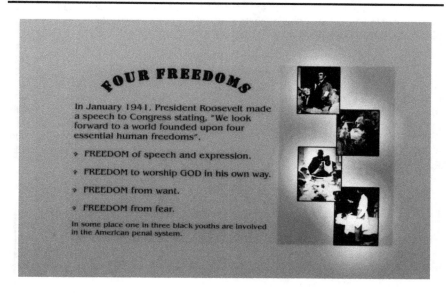

Four Freedoms were a state of objectives formulated by United States President Franklin D Roosevelt. They were delicvered to Congress in 1941. [1]

Constitutional Bill of Rights, the first 10 Amendments to the Constitution.

Amendment 1
- Freedom of Religion, Speech, and the Press

Congress shall make no law respecting an establishment of religion or prohibiting the free exercise thereof, or abridging the freedom of speech or of the press, or the right of the people peaceably to assemble and to petition the government for a redress of grievances.

Amendment 2
- The Right to Bear Arms

A well-regulated Militia being necessary to the security of a free State, the right of the people to keep and bear Arms shall not be infringed.

Amendment 3
- The Housing of Soldiers

No soldier shall, in time of peace, be quartered in any house without the consent of the owner, nor in time of war but in a manner to be prescribed by law.

Amendment 4
- Protection from Unreasonable Searches and Seizures
The right of the people to be secure in their persons, houses, papers, and effects against unreasonable searches and seizures shall not be violated, and no warrants shall issue but upon probable cause, supported by oath or affirmation, and particularly describing the place to be searched and the persons or things to be seized.

Amendment 5
- Protection of Rights to Life, Liberty, and Property
No person shall be held to answer for a capital or otherwise infamous crime unless on a presentment or indictment of a grand jury, except in cases arising in the land or naval forces, or in the militia, when in actual service in time of war or public danger; nor shall any person be subject for the same offense to be twice put in jeopardy of life or limb; nor shall be compelled in any criminal case to be a witness against himself, nor be deprived of life, liberty, or property without due process of law; nor shall private property be taken for public use without just compensation.

Amendment 6
-Rights of Accused Persons in Criminal Cases
In all criminal prosecutions, the accused shall enjoy the right to a speedy and public trial by an impartial jury of the state and district wherein the crime shall have been committed, which district shall have been previously ascertained by law, and to be informed of the nature and cause of the accusation; to be confronted with the witnesses against him; to have compulsory process for obtaining witnesses in his favor; and to have the assistance of counsel or his defense.

Amendment 7
- Rights in Civil Cases
In suits at common law, where the value in controversy shall exceed twenty dollars, the right of trial by jury shall be preserved, and no act tried by a jury shall be otherwise reexamined in any court of the United States than according to the rules of the common law.

Amendment 8
- Excessive Bail, Fines, and Punishments Forbidden
Excessive bail shall not be required, nor excessive fines imposed, nor cruel and unusual punishments inflicted.

Amendment 9
- Other Rights Kept by the People
The enumeration in the Constitution of certain rights shall not be construed to deny or disparage others retained by the people.

Amendment 10
- Undelegated Powers Kept by the States and the People
The powers not delegated to the United States by the Constitution, nor prohibited by it to the states, are reserved to the states respectively, or to the people.

---

1 https://www.britannica.com/event/Four-Freedoms

2 https://nccs.net/blogs/americas-founding-documents/bill-of-rights-amendments-1-10

FUR AND HATS 1940

Women, that were rich and upper middle class, were prevalent in the Special Operations Executive. They left a life of privilege to assist the French resistance and fight for freedom from German occupation. S.O.E. was a network of spies and amateurs that wrought havoc on German-dominated Europe. Scores of female operatives worked for the S.O.E. These women were trained to handle guns and explosives, memorize complex codes, organize munitions and supplies drops, endure harsh interrogation, and, in some cases, supervised thousands of men. They went from 39 volunteers to organizing D-Day in occupied France.

Especially noteworthy: Nancy Wake, used her wealth to buy ambulances, while she helped allied soldiers and political prisoners by setting up an "underground railway". *Virginia Hall* was an American and British spy. She mapped drop zones for equipment and soldiers. *Inayat Khan* was a princess that became the first female radio operator to be sent from the United Kingdom to France in the summer of 1943. Her work as a secret agent became crucial to the war effort communication. Her last word was "Liberty".

https://www.thevintagenews.com/2016/10/03/top-five-female-spies-world-war-ii/
https://time.com/5892932/a-call-to-spy-real-history/

The American West was settled by many freed slaves that came for the work opportunities and a less segregated environment. Of the 35,000 cowboys in 1880s 25% were black. The name "cowboy" was meant to be a derogatory form of cowhand. Over time the contribution of blacks was removed from history, and cowboy referred to white males only. [1, 2]

In the 1930s and 1940s there was a thriving independent black owned cinema industry. Blacks were drawn to the independence and success of the black western experience. The Harlem western experience mixed two worlds.

The "Bronze Buckaroo" Herb Jeffries, was a jazz singer and actor who had performed with Duke Ellington and in a series of all-black 1930s Westerns. He was known as the only black singing cowboy in the movies.[3]

1https://allthatsinteresting.com/black-cowboys#:~:text=%20The%20Forgotten%20Black%20Cowboys
2https://atlantablackstar.com/2015/07/24/forgotten-story-americas-black-cowboys/
3https://www.fesfilms.com/public-domain/black-heritage.html

HELMENT

Induction by Race in World War II

One million African Americans induction as of December 31. 1945:

1. 885, 945 went into the Army (10.9 %),
2. 153, 224 into the Navy (10.0%),
3. 16,005 into the Marine Corps (8.5%), and
4. 1,667 into the Coast Guard (10.9%).

Other racial and nationality groups:

1. 13,311 Chinese.
2. 20,080 Japanese.
3. 1,320 Hawaiians.
4. 44,000 American Indians.
5. 11,506 Filipinos, and
6. 51,438 Puerto Ricans.

https://www.history.army.mil/documents/WWII

HOMECOMING WORLD WAR II

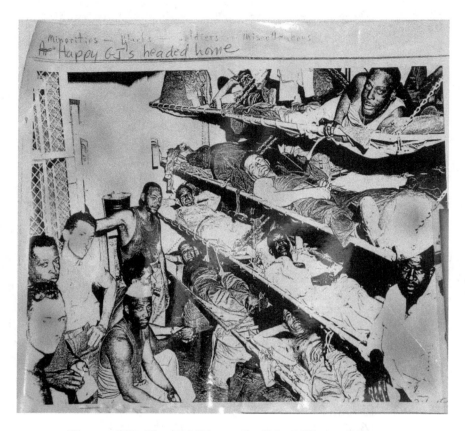

Happy GI's Headed Home Carlisle Military Library

There were different reasons for being in the military in World War II. Some men were drafted and had no legal choice. Others volunteered for the love of country. Some minorities fought for the right to fight in the War in order to prove that they merited equal rights and could meet the responsibilities that came with them. They believed that a victory against overseas fascism could help defeat the racism in America. They took a strategic approach hoping that serving as veterans would do away with racial discrimination and segregation and help to increase their financial opportunities.

Women also enlisted. They shared the same motivation as the men, patriotism, opportunity, and chance to change the limited perception of female capabilities.

Whatever the reason, minorities faced further discrimination in the U. S. armed forces during World War II. At the start, all branches of the military were segregated, and women's role severely restricted. Their valor however, changed people's minds. Women's opportunities were expanded, and they were able to serve directly with the armed forces rather than being auxiliary. The Executive Order 9981 in 1948 signed by President Harry S. Truman, ordered the end of military segregation.

There were veterans that did not need a legal document specifically; in the Pacific, during the Battle of the Bulge, with the Tuskegee Airmen, and others, to end segregation. They realized they were all Americans and deserved to fight and go home together.

https://en.wikipedia.org/wik/Ethnic_minorities_in_the_US_armed_forces_during_World_War_II

The Office of Civilian Defense was a United States federal emergency war agency set up in 1941, by Executive Order 8757. It coordinated state and federal measures for protection of civilians in case of war emergency. It supervised blackouts, fire protection, and special war services including child care, housing, health and transportation [1]

The Civil Air Patrol and the Coast Guard Auxiliary used civilian spotters. All exterior lighting was extinguished, and black curtains placed on the windows.

Fear of attack in United States helped Americans accept a sacrifice economy. In 1942, a rationing program was established. This set control on the amount of gas, food and clothing you could receive. Limits were set on the amount of gas, food and clothing consumers could purchase. Ration stamps were used to control supplies. Families used stamps to buy meat, sugar, fat, butter, gas, tires, clothing and fuel oil. The United States Office of War Information released posters in which Americans were urged to "Do with less—so they'll have enough" ("they" referred to U.S. troops). Meanwhile, individuals and communities conducted drives for the collection of scrap and purchased war bonds to pay for the war. A concept of reuse rather than discard or recycling was born.[1]

---

https://www.history.com/topics/world-war-ii/us-home-front-during-world-war-ii

HONOR FLAG

White minority participation in the US Armed Forces during World War II [1]

Latino-Americans

    Mexican-American   500,000

Jewish-Americans   550,000

Polish-Americans   1,000,000

Italian-Americans   1,500,000

Arab-Americans   30,000

Armenian-Americans   18,500

The back part is American.

---

http://en.wikipedia.org/wiki/Ethnic_minorities_in_the_US_armed_forces_during_World_War_II

CHAMPION JOE LOUIS

Joseph Louis Barrow (May 13, 1914 – April 12, 1981), known professionally as Joe Louis, was an American professional boxer who competed from 1934 to 1951. He reigned as the world heavyweight champion from 1937 to 1949 and is one of the greatest heavyweight boxers of all time. He enlisted in the Army during World War II and fought multiple promotional fights to assist with military morale.

As world champion, he used this status to help with desegregation during World War II as a "goodwill ambassador". Specifically: fighting to aid the Army and Navy Relief funds, refusing to fight for segregated audiences, integrating Army buses, helping Jackie Robison to prevent court martial from the service, and promoting enlistment and promotion in the service.

He received the Legion of Merit Award.

https://www.sunsigns.org/famousbirthdays/d/profile/joe-louis/

MARCH ON! 1943 MOVIE "WHERE'S MY MAN TONIGHT"

There was a thriving black independent film industry during the 1930s and 1940s.

Marching On! Is a 1943 black film that follows a soldier in boot camp after being drafted in the Army in World War II. His family has a tradition of military service. The soldier becomes a hero when he locates the Japanese saboteurs that were operating a radio station outside of the military base.

It was written and directed by Spencer Williams. Sequences were filmed at Fort Huachuca, Arizona. The film was later rereleased with additional musical sequences under the title Where's My Man To-nite?

---

https://www.fesfilms.com/public-domain/black-heritage.html

MILITARY TRENCH COAT - FEMALE

Wool coats offered great utility. Warm in winter, cool in summer.1

Women served in the military in World War II. Women were in or near combat zones, especially nurses, but they did not have direct combat positions. Many used their nursing expertise in the war effort. There were Red Cross and military nurses. About 74,000 women served in the American Army and Navy Nurse Corps in World War II.

Women also served in other military branches, often in traditional "women's work"—secretarial duties or cleaning, for instance. Others freed men for combat by performing their duties.

Figures for each branch of the American military are:

- Army - 140,000
- Navy - 100,000
- Marines - 23,000
- Coast Guard - 13,000
- Air Force - 1,000
- Army and Navy Nurse Corps - 74,000

https://military.wikia.org/wiki/United_States_Army_uniforms_in_World War 2.

2.https://www.ibiblio.org/hyperwar/USA/ref/FM/index.html

DORIS MILLER (DORIE)

"above and beyond the call of duty"

Doris Miller, known as "Dorie," was born in Waco, Texas, in 1919. After high school, he enlisted in the Navy as mess attendant (kitchen worker) to earn money for his family. At that time, the Navy was segregated so combat positions were not open to African Americans.

On December 7, 1941, when the Japanese attack occurred, he immediately reported to his assigned battle station. Miller was an athletic, so his job was to carry any of the injured to safer quarters; this included the mortally wounded ship's captain. Miller returned to deck and saw that the Japanese planes were still dive-bombing the U.S. Naval Fleet. He picked up a 50-caliber Browning antiaircraft machine gun on which he had never been trained and managed to shoot down three to four enemy aircraft. He fired until he ran out of ammunition. He received the Navy Cross for his heroic act.

Miller returned to service after selling war bonds. He was on a new ship that was torpedoed in 1944.

americacomesalive.com/dorie-miller-1919-1943

AUDIE MURPHY

Most decorated veteran of World War II and invisible wound sufferer.

Audie Leon Murphy was an American soldier, actor, songwriter, rancher, and veterans' advocate. He was one of the most decorated soldiers of World War II. He received every military combat award available from the US Army, and French and Belgian honors.[1]

Audie Murphy suffered from Post-Traumatic Stress Disorder known in World War II as Battle fatigue. To help returning veterans, he spoke out about his problems including difficulty sleeping and not feeling safe and the need for mental health support if needed. [2]

Now invisible wounds like post-traumatic stress disorder, military sexual trauma, and other post-traumatic and exposure mental challenges, are recognized as possible consequence of military service. To help prevent veterans' suicides, organizations like ACES Veterans Museum and ACES Veterans Annex try to boost morale and provide referral services. The staff and Board are also requested to undergo education by the federal program pschyarmor.org, and others.

1https://www.biography.com/military-figure/audie-murphy
2http://www.americans-working-together.com/post_traumatic_stress_disorder_ptsd/id15.html#:~:text=Audie%20Murphy%20sufferred%20from%

PAMELA "PAM" ARCHER MURPHY

Pamela Murphy was the widow of Audie Murphy actor and hero, but she had her own career serving Veterans full time for 35 years at the Sepulveda Veteran's Administrative Hospital.

She paid off his debts and raised her sons in a modest apartment.

Ms. Murphy was such an affective veterans' advocate, that when budget cuts were proposed they demanded she remain. She was known to treat each veteran as special and would make sure their needs were met. She considered each soldier or Marine to be a hero like her husband.

Audie Murphy died broke in a plane crash in 1971, squandering millions of dollars on gambling, bad investments, and yes, other women. "Even with the adultery and desertion at the end, he always remained my hero," Pam said.[1]

Pamela Murphy represents the family members that are devoted and support the veterans, even with difficult circumstances.

https://www.findagrave.com/memorial/51117433/pamela-opal_lee-murphy

DAISY MYERS

DAISY MYERS: A Rosie The Riveter With Big Shoulders
A small town woman took courage to change her life and left home to work for the war effort.
Daisy Myers used the same courage to travel to the World War II Monument Program in
Washington in 2004 by herself after her husband died.

ROSIE THE RIVETERS

Rosie the Riveter was an allegorical cultural icon of World War II, representing the women who worked in factories and shipyards during World War II. They produced munitions and war supplies. These women sometimes took entirely new jobs replacing the male workers who joined the military. From 1941-1945 there were 20 million women added to the labor pool.[1]

Daisy Myers was a Rosie the Riveter that met Dr. Hankins at the dedication of the World War II Memorial. Her husband had recently died but she showed courage to support him and the Country. First, by leaving her "little town "to work in a factory while he was overseas during the War. Second, she came to Washington DC to represent them both at the memorial. She stated they would be forgotten. Dr. Hankins assured her they are part of the ACES Museum.

There were 310,000 women or 65% of the aircraft industry in 1943. This was compared to 1% female employees prior to the war. [1]

---

www.history.com/.../world-war-ii/rosie-the-riveter

NATIVE AMERICANS PATCH 1940

NATIVE AMERICANS WORLD WAR II

From 25,000 to 44,000 Native Americans fought actively in World War II. They were in intergraded units, in the Army, Navy, Marines, and Coast Guard. 800 Native American women served as nurses and joined the WACs, Women Army Corps. Over one third of able-bodied Native American men aged 18 to 50 enlisted making them the highest percentage ethnic group. The military population was as high as 70 percent of the population of some tribes. [1]

The idea of using American Indians who were fluent in both their traditional tribal language and in English to send secret messages in battle was started in World War I. In World War II there was a specific policy to recruit and train code talkers.[2]

General Douglas MacArthur met with Navajo, O'odham, Pawnee and other native troops on December 31, 1943, to formalize the Code Talker Program. Navajo and other code talkers helped relay military secrets in the Pacific. They established an unbreakable code. [2]

The program was removed from a secrete status and formally awarded in 1982.

1.en.wikipedia.org/wiki/Native_Americans_and_World_War_II
2.www.intelligence.gov/.../453-navajo-code-talkers

ACES Veterans Annex was discovered and created by Commander William "Bill" Maxey United States Army Retired USAF. ACES Veterans Annex was dedicated in 2019 as a permanent testimony of the Black and minority veterans that served in World War II and the love, respect, and support that their community gave them.

ACES Annex follows the template of the parent, ACES Museum, and functions as a VSO, Veterans Service Organization. They also provide food and other services for the community at large.

The staff also encourages veterans sensitivity, and participates in the psycharmor.org education program.

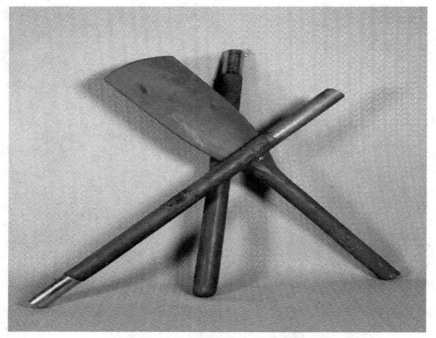

THE COAST GUARD

This official Oar represents the blacks that served in the coast Guard during World War II.

In the 228 years of Coast Guard history, blacks have been an integrated minority group in their history. In the early years of the U.S. Revenue Cutter Service, many African American cutter men both slaves and free, served with white shipmates.

In World War II, the Coast Guard undertook the federal government's first program in desegregation. African American Coast Guard candidates started in the Reserve Officer Training Program. In 1943, the Coast Guard began sending African American officer candidates through its Officer Training Program. 50 black officers were assigned to the USS Sea Cloud and other sea vessels. By 1945 there were several black commanders.

In addition, there were five African American women that enlisted in SPARS. The United States Coast Guard Reserve were known as SPARS. SPARS started in 1942.

Alex Haley was a well-known journalist and Coast Guard member. He joined the Coast Guard in 1939 and retired 20 years later. He started the "Mail Call" article to address the need for mail for the men. He was promoted to enlisted journalist. For his promotion and support of the Coast Guard, Haley was honored. He had a Cutter named for him, a special award named after him, and a honorary degree from Coast Guard Academy.

https://www.history.uscg.mil/Browse-by-Topic/Notable-People/Women/SPARS/https://coastguard.dodlive.mil/2018/02/tlbl-african-americans-in-uscg-combat/https://www.pacificarea.uscg.mil/Our-Organization/Cutters/cgcAlexHaley/

SEA BEES PAPERWEIGHT

The Naval Construction Force, known as the Seabees, was created in 1942 to address the need for construction in combat zones during World War II. They are deployed around the world to provide engineering and construction.

African Americans were accepted. They endured Japanese bombing raids and lost five men killed and 35 wounded in their first deployment. Their work in the Solomons garnered numerous commendations and citations for exceptional service. In Trinidad, the 80th constructed a massive airship hangar and other airfield facilities in defense of the Caribbean from German U-boat operations. First Lady Eleanor Roosevelt, and other dignitaries visited the unit to inspect their progress.

The black members of the battalion had to stage a hunger strike in 1945 because of unfair duties and promotions. Thurgood Marshall and the NAACP were also involved in securing basic rights in the Navy Seabees. The Southern officers were replaced with fair officers that were screened for racial prejudices.

The U.S. Navy Seabee Museum as a plaque from World War II that states "Proving Our Worth" for the 20th NSBs. It was a description of men fighting against fascism and racism. More than 12,500 African American men served in the Seabees in the Atlantic and the Pacific. In 1944 the Pacific units were integrated. By late 1945 the black and white Seabees where the Navy's first fully integrated units.

https://www.history.navy.mil/browse-by-topic/communities/seabees1.html

PARATROOPERS SUPPORT POSTER 19240

TRIPLE NICKELS

The Triple Nickels was the nickname of the 555 Parachute Infantry Battalion, the nation's first black paratroopers. The battalion would be folded into the 82nd Airborne Division. They were composed of "exceptional men" college educated, professional athletes. It existed from 1944-1947. The 555th would refine special operations that are still in use today.

The 555th were involved in a secret mission to fight the attacks the Japanese sent to American soil in the winter of 1944-45. There were 9,300 Fu-Go balloon bombs that were sent and 1000 reached America. The Nickels had to find, detonate and remove these bombs. They also had to shut out associated fires that resulted from the explosives. The 555th worked on twenty-eight fires in 1945.The paratroopers jumped into 15 of these fires. They lost one trooper. The 555th were part of the "colored test platoon" from the 92nd Infantry (Buffalo) Division.

https://www.opb.org/news/article/triple-nickles-pendleton-oregon-history-smokejumpers/

PARKER HALL ACES MUSEUM

Parker Hall was certified as a functioning USO for Black soldiers in World War II by Germantown Historic Society in Philadelphia, PA. Due to segregation in the 1940s, blacks had to set up independent support systems. Parker Hall was one of those places that was formed.

Although Parker Hall was black, the decision was made by ACES founders to create a museum that reflected the minorities stories that were often left out of World War II, and history in general. ACES Veterans Museum has been dedicated to the preservation of Parker Hall and the history of Black and minority Veterans of World War II and their families. There has been continuous programing since 2001.

ACES was certified as a VSO, Veteran Support Organization, by the City of Philadelphia in 2009 for our help referral network. Staff is encouraged to get training by psycharmor.org. This federal program encourages education to assist in improving Veterans support. In 2016 ACES was awarded the 800-pound Vietnam Memorial Plaque for our commitment to Vietnam Veterans. Motto: "Every Day Is Veterans Day at ACES". The items in the book are from AVM.

ACES Annex, Pontiac was formed to preserve the Native Kings paintings, and the history of black and minority Veterans in Pontiac, MI.

For further information: acesmuseum.online. and aces museum You Tube videos.
https://psycharmor.org/

GENERAL PATTON MEDAL

NATIONAL ARCHIVES AND PARKER HALL

General George S. Patton, U.S. Third Army commander, pinning the Silver Star on Private Ernest A. Jenkins of New York City in the liberation of France, 1944.

In 1944, the all black 761st Tank Battalion became the first African Americans assigned to General George S. Patton's Third Army in France. Patton said, "You're the first Negro tankers to ever fight in the American Army. I would never have asked for you if you weren't good. I have nothing but the best in my Army. I don't care what color you are as long as you go up there and kill those Kraut sons of bitches. Everyone has their eyes on you and is expecting great things from you ... Don't let them down and damn you, don't let me down!"[1]

history.com/news/761st-tank-battalion-black-panthers-liberators-battle-of-the-bulgue

PLASTER

NISEI TROOPS

The Nisei were second generation Japanese that served in the military while their families were placed in camps because of racist fears that netted the passage of Executive Order 9066. While German prisoners of war were going to movies, the Japanese lost their homes, their businesses and their freedom.[1]

When allowed to serve, 33,000 Japanese Americans entered the service. 20,000 joined the Army. The segregated Nisei troops, the 100th Infantry Battalion, was composed of men from Hawaii. They entered combat in Italy and suffered such horrific casualties that they became known as the Purple Heart Battalion. The 1st Battalion of the 442nd had to send replacement troops to join the 100th in early 1944. The 2nd and 3rd Battalions shipped out on May 1, 1944, joining the 100th in Italy in June 1944. For its size and length of service, the Nisei unit was the most decorated in U.S. military history.[2]

The Japanese were sent for Allied Language Training and worked in noncombat roles translating enemy documents and interrogating prisoners of war. They helped translate 18,000 enemy documents, created 16,000 propaganda leaflets and interrogated over 10,000 Japanese POWs. As servicemen, they were present at every major battle against Japanese forces. They sometimes suffered under friendly fire from U.S. soldiers unable to distinguish them from the Japanese troops.[2]

Japanese American women volunteered for the service when they were allowed.

1.https://en.wikipedia.org/wiki/Japanese
2American_service_in_World_War_II#Servicemen_in_the_Army_Air_Forces

PUERTO RICAN PLATE

Puerto Ricans were treated as two seperates groups during World War II. The white Puerto Ricans were the 65th Infantry a segerated unit for whites only. They were also in the National Guard. The black Puerto Ricans served in black units, including the 99th Fighter Squadron , the Tuskeegee Airman. They served in all branches of the armed forces, including the Harlem Hell Fighters which was formed in New York. [1]The 369th Infantry Regiment, formerly known as the 15th New York National Guard Regiment, was commonly referred to as the Harlem Hellfighters. This was an infantry regiment of the New York Army National Guard during World War I and World War II. The Regiment consisted mainly of African Americans, but also included several Puerto Rican Americans during World War II. With the 370th Infantry Regiment, it was known for being one of the first African American regiments to serve with the American troops.[2]

Hispanic Americans also referred to as Latinos, served in all elements of the American armed forces in the war. They were involved every major American battle in the war. Between 400,000 and 500,000 Hispanic Americans served in the U.S. Armed Forces during World War II, out of a total of 16,000,000, constituting 3.1% to 3.2% of the U.S. Armed Forces.[3]

Over 200 women Puerto Rican women served in nursing and administration in World War II. Carmen Contreras Boaz was the first Hispanic WAC. She served from in the Army from 1941-1945 and formed a chapter of WAC Veterans and the Society of Military Widows.[3]

The military did not keep statistics with regard to the total number of Hispanics who served in the regular units of the Armed Forces, only of those who served in Puerto Rican units; therefore, it is impossible to determine the exact number of Puerto Ricans who served in World War II.

3en.wikipedia.org/wiki/Hispanic_Americans_in...
1.https://www.history.com/this-day-in-history/puerto-ricans-become-u-s-citizens-are-recruited-for-war-effort
2.https://www.liquisearch.com/puerto_ricans_in_world_war_ii

PURPLE HEART & MEDALS

There were multiple black Field Artillery Units in World War II. The 46th Field Artillery Brigade was the largest brigade formed of black troops in 1941. They were battery operators, telegraphy experts, code specialists, had a band, orchestra, and had diverse areas of training. [1]

The 350 Field artillery regiment was a black unit that specialized in the switch boards, trucks, medical and dental sections. [1]

Other notable African American units that served in World War II:

92nd Infantry Division   Marine Units (2)
93rd Infantry Division   Army Nurses
2nd Cavalry Division   WACS Army
Air Corps Unit 332d Fighter Group   WAVES Navy
Field Artillery Units (32)   SPARS Coast Guard
452nd Anti-Aircraft Artillery Battalion   Navy Nurses
555th Parachute Infantry Battalion
US Military Academy Cavalry Squadron
5th Reconnaissance Squadron
Tank Battalions (3)
Tank Destroyer Units (11)

https://digicom.bpl.lib.me.us/cgi/viewcontent.cgi?article=1063&context=ww_reg_his
https://www.liquisearch.com/military_history_of_african_americans/world_war_ii/units
https://guides.loc.gov/african-american-women-military/books

Sabotage overseas primarily involved the Resistance derailing trains. In the United States the fire, destruction, and possible sabotage of the Normandie Ship in New York, led the Navy to address sabotage on the water. They formed a partnership with Charles "Lucky" Luciano to prevent further sabotage on the docks by Germans that had massively infiltrated the country.

Lucky was in jail for Mafia activity but maintained control of the docks. He did not want to live in a country that was ruled by the dictator Mussolini and, instructed his "capos" to act as lookouts for German activities. He also assisted in the United States' and the Allies' invasion of Sicily in 1943. He provided maps and local contacts for aid.[1]

There was not another boat fire during World War II on the docks. Lucky was pardoned after the war in 1946, and then deported.

---

https://www.historynet.com/the-fate-of-the-ss-normandie.htm

SNUFF BOXES

Snuffbox, a small ornamented box for holding snuff (a scented, powdered tobacco) was a way of inhaling tobacco. The practice of sniffing or inhaling a pinch of snuff was common in England around the 17th century; and when, in the 18th century, it became widespread in other countries as well, the demand for decorated snuffboxes, considered valuable gifts, increased.

Snuff boxes were used to house powered tobacco for inhaling. They were more popular than smoking in the 18th and 19th centuries. World War II made it hard to acquire them from overseas. They were replaced with the cigarette which was a more glamorous way to inhale tobacco.[1]

The effects of snuff and smoking were not exposed until cigarette warning labels were placed on packages in 1969.[2]

Vaping is the new glamorous way of processing toxic tobacco through e-cigarettes and e-juice. The vape machine heats up the juice and you inhale it. Vaping is associated with cardiovascular disease, increased bacteria and gum disease, and decreased brain development for those under 25 years of age.[2]

Time studies indicates it will also be associated with cancer like other tobacco products.

1www.britannica.com/art/snuffbox
2 https://blog.vapefuse.com/11-things-you-need-to-know-about-vaping-tobacco/#:~:text=Side%20Effects%20of%20Smoking%20Tobacco%3A%201%20Lung%2C%20Heart,chemica

Classical Entertainment from 1940s and Veterans with Science Fiction Optimism

Playing cards had been introduced to Europe in the 12th century by Arabs. They had been in Asia and Africa in the 9th Century. Some scholars think that playing cards were invented in China during the Tang dynasty around the 9th century AD and that they used woodblock promoting technology.[1]

Dice are the oldest gaming implements known to man. The Greek, Sophocles (496 - 406 BC), a poet claimed that dice were invented by the Greek, Palamedes, during the siege of Troy.[2]

World War II veterans have had a heavy influence in the world of science fiction. Two of the major influences of science fiction in movies, and television, predicted items that would be produced in their futures, and characters that would fight against tyranny. They were Marine Alexander Raymond, and Army Air Force member Gene Roddenberry.

Alexander Gillespie Raymond Jr. was an American cartoonist who was best known for creating the Flash Gordon comic strip in 1934. Flash Gordon was a hero that battled space monsters, power-mad alien dictators and other threats to the stability of the universe.[3]

Raymond joined the War effort first by having Flash Gordon fight dictators in 1941 in the comics. In 1944 he joined the War in earnest in the Marines as a captain. He created a patch for VMT B-143 that dubbed them the "Rocket Raiders". Raymond would continue to support the Marines making his next comic book hero Rib Kirby a Marine reservist that worked as a detective for justice.[3]

Gene Roddenberry, an Army Air Force World War II Veteran and policeman, believed in scientific exploration, military might to protect and serve liberty, and human diversity as an asset and not something to be feared. The commitment to justice and improved racial relations would cost him a television show. When writing the Lieutenant, he was refused support on an episode because he wanted to feature both black and white Marines.[4]

Roddenberry's optimism, and his belief that different nationalities, races and species can happily create a better future, was a basis for Star Trek. The original show had respect for the unknown, and the future could be wonderful, not something gloomy with assets restricted to the powerful few. It was his idealist response to the racial division of the sixties that make him have a Japanese helmsman, combating the racism from World War II. He also installed a beautiful black female scientist and her role was a model to millions for linguistics, cryptography and philology. A half-Vulcan was to symbolize prejudice and the struggle for emotional control.[4]

Roddenberry was to pay a financial price for his convictions. The Star Trek was canceled, and he had difficulty meeting financial obligations. Something unique happened. The Star Trek universe and the concept of racial harmony and a fair and pleasant future refused go away. It became "the show that wouldn't die".[4]

Trekkers and other fans would support him and Star Trek, creating their own movies and books. They believed you should "live long and prosper". The Star Trek universe was promoted through conventions and die-hard support. Multiple Star Trek movies, books, and television shows have been created. There are currently three Star Trek television shows with two others pending.

The casting of Nichols was groundbreaking. It was a rarity to see a black woman on primetime TV, it was even rarer to see a woman cast in a high-powered role. Nichelle Nichols' portrayal of Lieutenant Uhura in the sci-fi series was light years ahead of its time. She had the first interracial kiss in an American TV series, worked with NASA, and civil rights leaders who hailed her as a role model to millions. When she was going to quit, Dr. Martin Luther King asked her to stay and remain a positive example. She did. When Dr. Hankins met her at a Star Trek convention, she thanked Ms. Nichols for remaining to be a light for others to follow. Ms. Nichols said she, "...was proud of her. [5]

1.https://playingcarddecks.com/blogs/all-in/history-playing-cards-modern-deck

2.www.dice-play.com/History.htm

3.https://search.yahoo.com/search?fr=mcafee&type=C211US105D20151123&p=alex+ra
ymond+flash+gordon

4.https://en.wikipedia.org/wiki/Gene_Roddenberry

5.https://www.theguardian.com/tv-and-radio/2016/oct/18/star-trek-nichelle-nichols-
martin-luther-king-trekker

GEORGE AND JANICE TAYLOR

George Taylor was a World War II veteran that served in the Army in World War II and the Air force in Korea.

Janice Taylor was in the 6888. The only black WAC unit to serve overseas in World War II. The 6888th Central Postal Directory Battalion, was nicknamed the " Six Triple Eight ". It was composed of black women, both enlisted and officers. The unit was led by Major Charity Adams Earley.[1]

They were given an impossible task of sorting and delivering 1 million pieces of discarded mail. They completed the task earlier than expected in 1945.

George and Janice Taylor were founding fathers of ACES Museum.

https://en.wikipedia.org/wiki/6888th_Central_Postal_Directory_Battalion

THE FORGOTTEN FIRST: B-1 AND THE
INTEGRATION OF THE MODERN NAVY

This book tells the history of one of the Navy's two all-black pre-flight training school bands. They volunteered and used music to foster integration, build morale, and re-enforce that blacks could function as sailors in full capacity.[1]

The volunteers were representing the reintegration of the Navy. In the nineteenth century the Navy was 20-30 blacks, but this number had fallen to ½ of 1 percent by 1920.[1]

Black leaders called for desegregation and a Double Victory campaign in the United States during World War II. In 1941 President Roosevelt responded by placing 5,000 black bands on battleships to help racial relations. The President also called for 5,000 blacks to be recruited to serve on small harbor craft and at naval shore establishments in the Caribbean.[2]

In 1943 there were 26,909 black sailors.

In 1944, the first commissioned black officers were received in the Navy. They were known as the Golden Thirteen.[3]

1.https://www.questia.com/library/journal/1G1-414272412/the-forgotten-first-b-l-and-the-integration-of-the#:~:text=Alex%20Albright%27s%20The%20Forgotten
2. https://www.history.navy.mil/browse-by-topic/wars-conflicts-and-operations/world-war-ii/1942/manning-the-us-navy/african-americans-in-general-service--1942.html
3. https://www.britannica.com/topic/Golden-Thirteen

THE WHITE ROSE

**The White Rose (weisserose), named after a Spanish
novel (Rosa Blanco)**

The White Rose was a group of students and their professors that
supported Civil Rights and opposed Nazi policies during World war II.
They urged students to think for themselves about the atrocities that were
being carried out in their name.

The group's name and symbol were either named for a book or the white
rose meaning purity. Free thought is pure.

In the summer of 1942, several members that would form the White
Rose, served three months on the Russian front. They saw the horrors of
war and the mistreatment of Jews. They returned home with the thought,
there was a moral obligation to act on one's beliefs. The White Rose
produced literature that challenged State brutality. The goal: excite the
public compassion.

The hopes of the White Rose members that German opposition would be active against the Nazi regime and the war effort did not come true on a mass scale. On the contrary, Nazi propaganda called on the German people to embrace "Total War" and ethnic purity.

Why do you allow these men who are in power to rob you step by step, openly and in secret, of one domain of your rights after another, until one day nothing, nothing at all will be left but a mechanized state system presided over by criminals and drunks? Is your spirit already so crushed by abuse that you forget it is your right—or rather, your moral duty—to eliminate this system? [1]

— *3rd leaflet of the White Rose*

www.thoughtco.com/world-war-ii-the-white-rose-2361252#:~:text=The%20White%20Rose%20

THIS IS THE ENEMY WORLD WAR II

Poster Recreation

World War II propagananda was distributed in a variety of ways. There were leaflets, radio, television, and most important, the poster. Posters were designed to be creative, colorful, eye catching, and to stimulate thought and support.

There were over 200,000 posters designed and printed during World War II. They covered a variety of subject matters. Things related to the war effort included wartime manufacturing, health and safety issues, war bonds, military recruitment, and as noted, racism and its effect on the war's positive production. The posters were created by federal agencies, commissions, and councils, as well as non-federal organizations.

TILTED HAT VETERAN SAM HILL

Sam Hill was part of the black soldiers that served proudly and effectively in the Pacific. The medals testify to his patriotic conduct during a difficult set of circumstances. He still tilted his hat in acknowledging that he was his own man despite Jim Crow laws.

Major Deborah Gary USAF, his daughter, is on the Advisory Board of ACES Veterans Museum.

TOURNIQUET

DR. CHARLES DREW

Dr. Charles Richard Drew was an African American physician who developed ways to process and store blood plasma. He preserved this blood plasma without cells so it would last longer and be reconstituted. He directed the blood banks in United States and Britain but resigned from the United Sates because the Red Cross would only give black blood to blacks denying them access to most of the processed blood.[1]

During World War II most of the blood taken for use was processed into plasma. The plasma was shipped directly to the Army and Navy. This plasma was credited by the surgeons general of the Army and Navy as being the greatest lifesaver of World War II. Plasma was viewed as more important in preventing death during World War II than the new antibiotic penicillin. Plasma allowed more detailed and large scale directed surgeries saving lives and limbs.[2]

Dr. Drew's dried plasma became a vital element in the treatment of wounded soldiers during World War II. The Red Cross ended its World War II blood program for the military in World War II after collecting more than 13 million pints.[3]

1.https://www.biography.com/scientist/charles-drew
2.https://www.britannica.com/science/history-of-medicine/World-War-II-and-after
3.www.britannica.com/.../World-War-II-and-after

Trains were very popular during and after World War II. These can address the effect of war on children both direct, and through their families.

TUSKEGEE AIRPLANE

Official Tuskegee Model Airplane 1940s

Herbert and Mildred Carter were married nearly 70 years and were known as Tuskegee's "First Couple".

Herbert Carter was one of the original Tuskegee Airmen pilots of the nation's first military program for black flyers. He earned his wings as a second lieutenant in 1942. He would earn the rank of lieutenant colonel in a 27-year Air Force career. He also to be ranked as a fighter pilot and squadron maintenance chief.

The Tuskegee airmen would never stray from the bombers they protected and therefore only a handful of the planes they escorted were loss. They painted their planes red tails.

Mildred Hemmons Carter entered college at 15. She learned to fly under C. Alfred "Chief" Anderson, the father of black aviation. She became the first black women in the state to earn her piolet's license while at Tuskegee. The First Lady Ms. Roosevelt visited that day.

In 1941 Mildred became the first female pilot to join the state's Civil Air Patrol Squadron. In 1942 she applied to become a WASP, Women Airforce Service Pilots, but was turned down due to race. Racism may have decreased her dream of flying in the military, but she piloted planes until 1965. After 70 years she received a letter from the government that she had been declared a member of the WASPs and given a medal, "The First Women in History to Fly America."[1]

Together the Carter' home became an aviation museum with multiple awards from several sources. The biggest honor was their enduring love. The "I believe I can Fly" Puppets with History show highlights Tuskegee airmen and women.

www.cnn.com/2012/01/22/us/tuskegee-airmen-first-couple

VICTORY AND PEACE PAMPLET

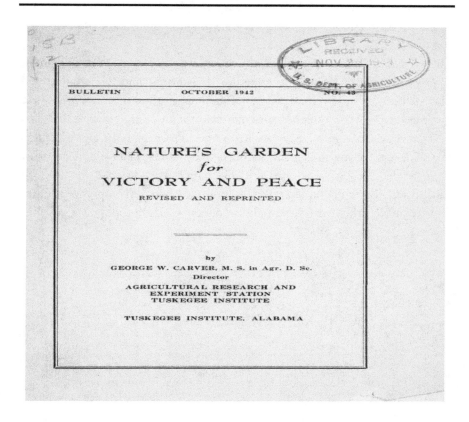

Victory Garden George Washington Carver

Victory gardens were encouraged during World War II. Commercial crops were diverted to the military overseas and the introduction of food rationing in the United States started in 1942. Americans had an incentive to grow their own fruits and vegetables in whichever locations they could find, small flower boxes, apartment rooftops, backyards or deserted lots of any size. Eleanor Roosevelt even planted a victory garden on the White House lawn. The Victory Garden campaign served as a successful means of boosting morale, expressing patriotism, safeguarding against food shortages on the home front, and easing the burden on the commercial farmers. In 1942, roughly 15 million families planted victory gardens; by 1944, an estimated 20 million victory gardens produced roughly 8 million tons of food, more than 40 percent of all the fresh fruits and vegetables consumed in the United States.[1]

The scientist, George Washington Carver was born a slave in Diamond, Missouri. Carver's insatiable appetite for learning and his intellect led him to become one America's most famous agricultural scientists. He invented over 300 products including crop rotation. He became the head of Tuskegee College's Department of Agriculture in 1910 and educated poor farmers through movable schools. He wrote, "Nature's Garden for Victory and Peace", bulletin No. 43, which was printed in 1942. It functioned as a manual helping to promote and develop the Victory Gardens of World War II, and todays concept of fresh foods. [2]

1 https://www.history.com/news/americas-patriotic-victory-gardens
2 https://henderson.ces.ncsu.edu/2020/04/george-washington-carvers-natures-garden-for-victory-and-peace-pamphlet-1942/

WACS WOMEN ARMY CORP

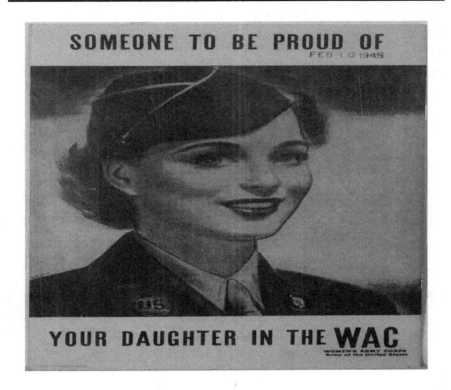

The Army had female support as nurses, and others, but they created a formal unit for women to serve in 1942, first as an auxiliary unit, then in 1943, as an active duty unit. In World War II there were 150,000 women that enlisted. In 1978, women were integrated into the whole Army.[1]

From the beginning black women were admitted to the WACs on a ten percent ratio. Black women were also part of the WACC. From 1942, black women had to follow the percentage recruitment limitations that matched the proportion of the black population.[1]

Unfortunately, black women experienced segregation and discrimination. There was a strike by blacks WACS in World War II, and court martial of four of them: Mary Green, Anna Morrison, Johnnie Murphy and Alice Young.[2]

The strike was a protest of racial and gender discrimination in the Army. They were charged and found guilty of disobeying an order of a superior officer. Thurgood Marshall, Congress, and the community demanded an investigation of their jail sentences. They won the appeal, were reinstated. The Army conceded that had not followed protocol.

1 www.britannica.com/topic/Womens-Army-Corps#:~
2 https://www.womensmemorial.org/history-of-black-women#:~:text=From%20its%20beginning

CELEBRATION GLASSES

Glasses c 1940s

History is important if we want to learn, and honor that knowledge in the future. Thanks to the new way of analyzing items from the past via Harvard University's courses, we can take an object from a specific time, address its social implications, and use that data for current situations.

Museums can be places of fun, learning, community support, jobs, or a Veterans' outreach and morale building service.

We thank the people that were **Acting On Hope** during World War II. They are examples to follow.

ABOUT THE AUTHOR

AV Hankins MD FACP MSEd MPA
seeks to graduate life with honors.

CPSIA information can be obtained
at www.ICGtesting.com
Printed in the USA
BVHW011451110121
597543BV00003B/46

THE BATTLE FOR SKY

THE BATTLE FOR SKY

*The Murdochs, Disney, Comcast, and
the Future of Entertainment*

CHRISTOPHER WILLIAMS

BLOOMSBURY BUSINESS
LONDON · NEW YORK · OXFORD · NEW DELHI · SYDNEY

BLOOMSBURY BUSINESS
Bloomsbury Publishing Plc
50 Bedford Square, London, WC1B 3DP, UK
1385 Broadway, New York, NY 10018, USA

BLOOMSBURY, BLOOMSBURY BUSINESS and the Diana logo are trademarks of
Bloomsbury Publishing Plc

First published in Great Britain 2019

Cover design by Eleanor Rose
Cover photograph © Getty images

Bloomsbury Publishing Plc does not have any control over, or responsibility for, any
third-party websites referred to or in this book. All internet addresses given in this
book were correct at the time of going to press. The author and publisher regret
any inconvenience caused if addresses have changed or sites have ceased to
exist, but can accept no responsibility for any such changes.

A catalogue record for this book is available from the British Library.

A catalog record for this book is available from the Library of Congress.

ISBN: HB: 978-1-4729-6490-8
ePDF: 978-1-4729-6494-6
eBook: 978-1-4729-6495-3

Typeset by RefineCatch Limited, Bungay, Suffolk
Printed and bound in Great Britain

To find out more about our authors and books visit www.bloomsbury.com
and sign up for our newsletters.

CONTENTS

FOREWORD

I walked down a steep flight of steps to the basement. Paul Dacre, the editor of the *Daily Mail*, was waiting for me at the bottom. Apart from the two of us, the restaurant was deserted. We shook hands, found a pair of seats at the nearest table and got down to business.

Under any normal circumstances, if someone had suggested I take a secret meeting with the editor of the *Daily Mail*, I would have laughed in their face. There was no newspaper, magazine or website more relentless or immoderate in its criticism of the BBC – something that tended to get under your skin if, like me, you were the Director-General of the said corporation. And even if one could get over one's suspicion, what purpose could such a meeting serve? It was impossible to imagine any issue on which the *Mail* and the BBC could see eye to eye.

Or at least impossible until Rupert Murdoch supplied one. In June 2010 his company News Corp, already the biggest shareholder in BSkyB, announced its intention of buying the remaining shareholders out and taking full ownership of Sky.

The rest of Fleet Street, and the UK's other major broadcasters – including ITV, Channel Four and Channel 5 – were appalled. In addition to its Sky holding, News Corp owned a set of national newspapers. Its rivals feared that complete control of Sky would allow the company to dominate the market in news, entertainment and advertising. In their view, any other player who relied on any part of this market for revenue would inevitably be squeezed.

At the BBC, we had less to lose commercially. But like many others in the worlds of media and politics, we had profound concerns about the potential loss of plurality and impartiality in British journalism. Over the years, Sky

News had earned a first-class reputation for fairness and accuracy. How could that be guaranteed if the News Corp takeover went ahead? Rupert Murdoch clearly relished the sway he enjoyed in British politics. What would happen to democracy if that influence was extended beyond newspapers to TV?

In August 2010, as this book recounts, I spoke out in the MacTaggart lecture at the Edinburgh TV Festival about the multiple risks of the News Corp bid for Sky. The speech was widely reported, and I assumed it would be the last public statement I would make on the topic. But in early September, we received a confidential phone call from a senior Liberal Democrat figure in Britain's new coalition government.

He and his colleagues were convinced that, in return for the support of his newspapers in the UK's recent election, the Conservative prime minister and chancellor, David Cameron and George Osborne, had reached some kind of understanding with Rupert Murdoch. Lib Dem ministers feared that the Tories would try to force the Sky takeover through without proper scrutiny – and in particular without a referral to the industry regulator, Ofcom.

It was essential, he said, that maximum external pressure be applied to Downing Street. The rest of British media were getting together to write a joint letter to the Business Secretary, which would be simultaneously published in multiple national newspapers. If the BBC was prepared to join this chorus of concerned voices, it could make all the difference.

It was this call that led to the meeting with Paul Dacre in that subterranean West End restaurant. I listened carefully to his arguments and, in subsequent conversations, to those of the other organisers of the letter. They sent us the draft letter. We suggested changes. The adjustments were agreed. And then I signed it.

The case against signing was clear. Although the BBC is not bound to remain impartial in debates about media policy, it generally avoids becoming entangled in arguments between rival commercial interests – let alone rival ministers. *The Times*, one of News Corp's British papers, published a leader calling my "campaign" against the takeover a "serious error". One unnamed Sky executive is quoted in this book as saying that adding my name to the letter was "a stupid mistake".

I suspect that most of the BBC Trust, the Corporation's governing body at the time, concurred with that judgement. They were understandably furious when they discovered that I'd signed the letter without consulting them. I hadn't told them because I knew they'd almost certainly forbid me from signing it. It was a provocative – in some ways rather brutal – way to treat a group of loyal and thoughtful supporters of the BBC, but I'd concluded that to sign was not just in the BBC's own institutional interest, but the wider public interest. Signing might not be politic. It was in my view the right thing to do.

The letter was published on Monday 11th October 2010. Shortly thereafter, the Government referred the takeover to Ofcom, which in due course recommended a full referral to the Competition Commission, a body with the power to block the deal entirely. The bid was far from dead, but official approval was now going to be more protracted and uncertain than its proponents – led by Rupert's son, James Murdoch – could have wished or expected.

Meanwhile, in a bizarre twist, exactly one week after the letter was published, we found ourselves making a desperate phone call *back* to the Liberal Democrats, beseeching them to help us reverse a separate decision by the government to stop compensating the BBC for the free television licences enjoyed by the over-75s. At stake were many hundreds of millions of pounds. Now it was the Lib Dem's turn to stick their necks out – which indeed they did, playing a critical role in helping to get that decision reversed.

I've recounted this episode at some length because it's so characteristic of the broader story of Sky and British political and media establishment which is told so compellingly by Christopher Williams in this book. It's a story of a seemingly unstoppable commercial force colliding with an immovable political and cultural object. Rupert Murdoch had conceived of Sky as a broadcaster that could flourish and grow precisely because it would operate outside the web of subsidy and state interference which he believed spoiled and smothered the rest of British TV. The paradox was that – at least for as long as he, his son James, and their company were involved in it – Sky would remain intensely and unavoidably political. Release from politics, something which many Sky executives would come to yearn for, could be achieved only when the Murdochs themselves relinquished their ownership entirely.

I was an unashamed opponent of the takeover bid. But don't assume from my stance on that topic that I was generally an enemy of BSkyB. On the contrary, I believed that its impact on British television had been almost entirely positive.

Rupert Murdoch was right: the world of broadcasting with which I grew up *needed* disrupting. Viewers lacked choice, lacked significant access to live sport. TV production was almost entirely in the hands of an in-house BBC and ITV oligopoly. The broadcasters held most of the cards, the public almost none. This tightly controlled industry had produced some of the best TV in the world. Rupert Murdoch was not the only person to realise that advances in technology meant that its days were now numbered. But no one was bolder or risked more than he was in turning a theoretical vision of the future of broadcasting into a living, breathing reality.

By the period covered by this book, Sky had grown into a formidable and immensely profitable company. Unlike many successful companies, however, it hadn't allowed incumbency to dull its edge in innovation, nor lost its sense of itself as a disrupter. That was significantly because of the calibre of its management team, and notably a series of outstanding CEOs, all of whom I knew and admired. Jeremy Darroch, its present chief executive, has been both the least visible leader of the company and the most successful. Under his leadership, Sky grew into a multinational, multi-platform pay-TV giant despite facing growing competition for both rights and customers – and the growing disruptive threat to its own distribution model by the new digital TV streaming services.

As several witnesses remark to Chris Williams, if the task of securing regulatory permission for News Corp to take full ownership of Sky had been led by Jeremy, it would have been a carefully planned and undramatic campaign. It might well have succeeded. Instead, leadership of the bid fell to Sky's chairman: James Murdoch.

James had arrived at the company as CEO in 2003. He was made chairman four years later. Both appointments came in for extensive public criticism, the charge being that, despite the supposed protection of a company board, the Murdochs still managed to run Sky as a nepotistical shop. In fact, James soon demonstrated that he was a formidable executive – forceful, well-informed, assiduous, imaginative. Anyone who interacted with him at close quarters was quickly forced to recognise the clarity of his strategic thinking and his restless energy. Those who expected a political 'Mini-Me' of Rupert were also wrong-footed: on many issues, most notably the environment, James was downright progressive – at least compared to most other British leaders of the time.

It was a different matter when it came to public intervention in the TV business, whether in the form of the BBC, the other public broadcasters or Ofcom. In a country that venerated the NHS, and was accustomed to largescale subsidy across the arts, there was nothing either surprising or objectionable to most people about the role that public money and regulation played in British broadcasting. To James, it was not just unnecessary but morally unacceptable. The market was not only a more effective, but a more just way of ensuring quality, creativity and plurality.

James tried to convince me of that in a serious of friendly, combative and entirely futile private conversations. Then in the MacTaggart lecture he gave at Edinburgh in 2009, the year before mine, he tried to convince the whole country. The speech was a full-frontal attack not just on the BBC but the whole notion of public intervention in media. "The only guarantee of independence is profit," was the sound bite he finished on.

In retrospect, that speech represented a high-water mark in the Murdochs' long campaign to persuade the UK to abandon its broadcasting traditions in favour of a radical free market model. The speech was initially well received – the audience being rather taken with its swagger and tell-it-like-it-is clarity. With or without a special understanding with Rupert Murdoch, the election of a Conservative-led coalition the following spring was no doubt received by James and News Corp as further evidence that the public mood was ready for the bid. By the time I and the other opponents of the deal came to sign that letter in the autumn 2010, even we feared that – while James had probably overplayed his hand rhetorically – eventual approval of the bid for full ownership was very likely. Perhaps the best we could hope for was a lengthy delay.

But events took a different turn. In mid-2011, *The Guardian* broke the story that *News of the World* reporters had hacked the phone of the murdered schoolgirl Milly Dowler, and News Corp's phone-hacking scandal exploded into a full-scale crisis. Ministerial approval for the bid went from probable to impossible. On July 13th that year, News Corp withdrew its bid.

Sky continued to thrive and six years later the Murdochs launched a second attempt to achieve 100% ownership of the enterprise. By this time News Corp had split into two different companies. The new News Corp held the global newspaper assets, including the British titles. The stake in BSkyB was held by the other new public company, 21st Century Fox. On the face of it, this new configuration should have made government approval for the second bid somewhat easier to achieve.

But much had changed in the global media industry since that high-water mark of 2010. Legacy entertainment players now faced being overwhelmed by new digital insurgents, most notably Netflix. A new Great Game – or Game of Thrones – had begun and defensive consolidation was the order of the day. The Murdoch empire which had once loomed so large in the British imagination was now at risk of being too small to succeed.

In 2014, an attempt to take over Time Warner had failed. In 2017, the Murdochs decided to sell the majority of their entertainment assets to Disney. A year later, Sky finally came under single ownership, but to a purchaser who clearly had no designs on British politics and posed no threat to journalistic plurality. At last, the attacks and counter-attacks, and the endless jockeying with the BBC and Ofcom and the rest, could cease. The company was finally free to pursue its commercial destiny, albeit as a division of a vast media conglomerate.

Rightly or wrongly, their critics had seen Rupert and James Murdoch as sharks. There's no doubt about the single-mindedness of their ambition or their contempt for the rest of the British media industry. Yet they were also genuine reformers, convinced that they were building a better model for UK broadcasting than what had gone before.

But now the era of sharks had given way to one of leviathans for whom Britain was in the end – despite its wealth in creative talent and production expertise – just one more market in a world of markets. The moments of high drama, the clash of outsized egos and that very British interplay of business and politics would likely never be repeated. It's a story worth capturing for the ages. Thank goodness Chris Williams has done that, and done it so well.

Mark Thompson
CEO of The New York Times Company
BBC Director-General 2004–2012

PROLOGUE

James Murdoch looked out across the conference theatre and saw a sea of enemies.

It was September 2017 and the British television establishment was gathered in Cambridge for its biannual jamboree. The Royal Television Society (RTS) Convention was three days of chin-stroking, back-slapping and heavy drinking in the halls of those ancient colleges that have tended to provide the BBC with an inexhaustible supply of the right sort of young men and women.

This may not have been natural Murdoch territory, but James knew the terrain well. A decade earlier, just 34 years old but already in the final stretch of his reign as chief executive of Sky, he had taken charge of the Convention schedule.

The young outsider delighted in criticising and mocking the likes of Ofcom chief executive Ed Richards and BBC director-general Mark Thompson. On stage, Murdoch compared a speech by the Labour Culture Secretary James Purnell on the balance between open markets and government intervention to the "agonising intellectual contortions" of communist China's modern tilt towards capitalism.

To further signal his contempt for what he viewed as an out-of-touch elite, Murdoch brought in coachloads of ordinary viewers and made delegates meet them. Ever since his father, Rupert, risked everything to invade British television in the late 1980s, Sky had always prided itself on giving the people what they want. In James's three years as chief executive, the 'customer-led' approach became enshrined as both public mantra and management doctrine. Complacent RTS delegates would be given a lesson in listening to audiences, if for only an hour or two.

"When you go into these rooms, there will be people with non-white faces," one Sky executive warned delegates, tongue only half-in-cheek. "Don't be shocked."

The stunt would prove to be a high point of James Murdoch's career in Britain. He stepped down from day-to-day duties at Sky three months later for a move eastwards across London. Murdoch swapped his Sky office on a windswept business park under the Heathrow flight path in Osterley, for one at the similarly gritty Wapping headquarters of News Corp. Confirmed as heir apparent to his father, James would run all of the company's European and Asian interests, including its British newspapers and its 39% stake in Sky.

But scandal awaited him. The extent of phone hacking and other wrongdoing at the Murdoch tabloids would, in coming years, threaten to consume him. His plan to forge the future of global entertainment by taking full control of Sky was foiled by his family's political adversaries, some of them targets of his derision at Cambridge. Murdoch's own reputation would come under heavy bombardment and he would be forced into years of exile.

By 2017, however, that was all history. Alongside his father, and brother Lachlan, Murdoch had reshaped and restored the empire from a new base in the United States. As 21st Century Fox, a thriving entertainment concern divorced from the struggling and noxious business of newspaper publishing, they had come again for full control of Sky.

The usual suspects had rallied against him, but James Murdoch saw the world had changed. The new empires of Facebook, Amazon, Apple, Netflix and Google had bigger audiences, more money and more sway over the media landscape than News Corp could ever have grasped. He was again ready to face the British television establishment and to tell them they were still wrong.

"Tomorrow's commercial media needs to be able to compete globally and at unprecedented scale," Murdoch began.

Tieless and from behind thick-rimmed glasses, he smiled and spoke from an autocue. The aggression and sharp wit of Murdoch's previous appearance at the Convention were neutered, replaced with a script carefully calibrated by a coterie of advisers.

There were certainly glimpses of his earlier disdain, as he noted that since Sky had last chaired the RTS Convention "an appetite for disruption has been the essential ingredient for success in the digital world, a world we all inhabit today, like it or not".

"I think I was actually CEO then," he deadpanned.

Otherwise, James played the statesman. He advocated for the takeover of Sky but did not seek to intimidate. He expounded on Fox's approach to storytelling, investment and technology, casting it as a longstanding friend to British television. It was a performance as slick as his image, tested only when he sat down for questions from Sarah Sands.

The former *Evening Standard* editor had controversially landed a plum job as editor of the BBC's flagship morning radio news programme, *Today*, and she knew that Murdoch had not faced public questions since the Leveson Inquiry hearings of 2012. Sands had spent most of her career in features departments on the softer side of Fleet Street and would not allow the cosy atmosphere of the RTS Convention to ruin a golden opportunity to burnish her hard news credentials.

Sands challenged Murdoch on his handling of sexual harassment at Fox News, then making front page headlines in the United States. He fought to contain his irritation as she repeated claims that he had overseen "rotten" and "toxic" corporate cultures at the British newspapers and in the United States.

When Sands ventured that Murdoch had been line manager to disgraced Fox News chairman Roger Ailes, the one-word rebuttal came before she finished her sentence. "No." Was he wounded by questions over Fox's commitment to broadcasting standards? "You're over-personalising that a little."

Murdoch's eyes showed flashes of anger and frustration as once again his father's political entanglements appeared an obstacle to the takeover of Sky that he had wanted for so long.

"Whether or not 30 years ago someone has a grievance about a political position that a newspaper took that is no longer part of the business is irrelevant to a process that should be transparent and fact-based," Murdoch said, his gestures becoming more forceful.

By the end of the inquisition, he had regained any lost composure. Another question came from the conference floor from Dr Evan Harris, a former hospital medic and Liberal Democrat MP. He had found a third calling as a crusader against the press, under the auspices of the phone hacking campaign group Hacked Off. He asked whether Murdoch would lobby against a second phase of the Leveson Inquiry, envisaged as an examination of the relationship between journalists and the police.

By now Murdoch was fully in control of himself and the situation. He swatted Harris away and raised a laugh by lamenting that "the government won't take a meeting with me".

As delegates filed out of the theatre, most begrudgingly agreed that Murdoch had made a successful return to the front lines of British media. Few minds were changed over whether Fox should be allowed to take full control of Sky, but he had addressed the past and made his case. Perhaps he had even been right all those years ago about some of British television's failings.

Not everyone saw things that way though. Behind the scenes, Murdoch's advisers were furious at Sands' line of questioning. This was the RTS Convention, not the *Today* programme, and their man had been pilloried on stage, by a senior BBC journalist, no less, in a way that no other senior industry executive ever had. A few weeks later, when *The Sun*, a newspaper not usually known for its coverage of Radio 4 programming, ran a story branding the new *Today* programme as "dull", Sands wondered if she wondered privately if she had been the target of tabloid revenge, as unlikely as it seemed.

While recriminations continued in Cambridge, Murdoch himself immediately returned to London as planned and was undaunted. This time his enemies could attack and oppose his plans for Sky as much as they liked.

"We will win," he said back at Fox's base in Soho. "We will win."

It showed Murdoch still had the single-minded determination that had characterised his tenure as Sky chief executive. But it was not to be ... at least not in the way anyone expected.

Introduction

This is the story of how Sky became one of the hottest properties in global media and the subject of the most dramatic takeover battle in British corporate history. It is based on extensive research and more than two dozen interviews with major players.

Most of my sources were unwilling to speak openly, which reflects the fact that they were speaking when the fate of Sky, and therefore the fate of their careers and business relationships, was still unknown.

In general, and perhaps regrettably, business leaders are also less open than they used to be. In the more than 20 years since the publication of Mathew Horsman's book *Sky High*, which gives an excellent account of Sky's early fight for survival under Rupert Murdoch and Sam Chisholm, the rise of the public relations industry has contributed to a decline in accountability. To get to the truth of what has happened since that time, this book has had to rely on many anonymous sources.

Sky's success this century has been astonishing. In 1999 it had less than four million satellite subscribers and a business that appeared to be running out of steam, based almost entirely on Premier League football and Hollywood films. Today it is a pan-European leader and the latest addition to the vast Comcast empire, at the eye-popping price tag of £37bn. Sky has 23 million subscribers, extensive broadband and mobile operations, and the technological agility to play a role in the biggest shift in entertainment since the introduction of television.

The turbulent rise of Sky reveals a company that, for better or worse, has always needed an enemy to spur itself forward. Over the years there has been no shortage of players to assume the role of nemesis. The BBC, ITV, the UK cable industry, regulators and BT have all found themselves on the wrong side of Sky's will to win.

No British company has been at the centre of more controversies. The long battle fought and lost by News Corp, and subsequently by Fox, for control of Sky ranks as the most extraordinary takeover saga in memory, as business, technology and politics clashed dramatically, often with unpredictable results.

The new titans of media come from Silicon Valley and have international reach and financial clout that the Murdoch family and even Comcast cannot hope to match. The likes of Netflix, Amazon, Apple, Google and Facebook threaten Sky on a whole new scale.

Yet history shows that Sky is, above all else, adaptable and ready to fight. And as its opponents have come to realise over the years, it should never be underestimated.

1

It Was War Time

Tony Ball was happy with his new life in America. He had left Britain and Sky behind, and become a valued member of the court to the man they still called the Sun King (if they liked him) and the Dirty Digger (if they didn't): Keith Rupert Murdoch.

Ball's rise had been spectacular. The son of a London bookie, he had started in broadcasting as a 16-year-old trainee engineer in the early 1970s at Thames Television, one of the regional antecedents of ITV. Unapologetically brash and ambitious, Ball quickly joined the executive class and gravitated towards the macho world of sports broadcasting.

In the 1980s, he spotted there was money to be made in the emerging pay-TV market and became a co-founder of Champion TV, owner of Britain's first subscription sport channel. Ball made the defining step in his career in 1993 when he joined the Murdoch empire at Sky Sports.

Within a few years he fell out with Sam Chisholm, Sky's pugnacious and mercurial Kiwi chief executive, and engineered a move to Murdoch's Australian television business. There he won the mogul's trust by helping to uncover fraud in his sports channels. Murdoch marked him for promotion.

By 1999 Ball was in his early forties and president of Fox/Liberty Networks, Murdoch's US sports channel joint venture with fellow billionaire John Malone, known as 'the Cable Cowboy'. Ball enjoyed the trappings of his success in Los Angeles: he rode motorbikes along the Pacific highway and, along with his

Spanish wife Gabriella, was a regular guest at Murdoch's glittering dinner parties.

The Sun King was already in his late sixties but still very much in the prime of his career. He surrounded himself with politicians, economists, business subordinates and family as he continued to build the world's most powerful media company, News Corp. Ball felt like family and Rupert had big plans for him.

Ball had already secretly accepted his next assignment from Murdoch. He and Gabriella were to move to New York, where he would lead Fox Cable Networks, a new unit that was to oversee News Corp's fast-growing pay-TV channels business.

Murdoch planned to put Ball in charge of 22 channels that would be bundled together into a must-have package capable of extracting the maximum possible fees from US cable operators. Ball was revelling in the freewheeling, aggressive deal-making atmosphere of American pay-TV and could not wait to get started; the contract was duly signed. Then Murdoch summoned him for a meeting and tore up the plan.

Murdoch no longer wanted Ball in New York, and Ball feared he would be dispatched to News Corp's Latin American backwaters. Instead, Rupert said he should return to London and to Sky. Mark Booth, the personable American who had replaced Chisholm as chief executive little more than a year earlier, was not working out. Murdoch had dreams of a European, and then a global, pay-TV operator. Sky was doing well and had good foundations, but new threats were emerging.

Ball was initially crestfallen. He had left Sky in difficult circumstances in 1996, walking away from clashes with Chisholm and into an international career. The arrival of Elisabeth Murdoch, Rupert's daughter, had also helped spur his departure. She was made 'general manager, broadcasting', which she and Ball realised happened to be his title too.

Unsurprisingly, he was wary about taking what might look like a backwards step in his career. 'Cool Britannia' may still have been in full swing in London, but the idea of swapping parties in Beverly Hills and Manhattan for a Sky office with views of a Tesco car park just off the A4 arterial route was hard to swallow.

Yet Ball knew he had little choice but to accept Murdoch's invitation. In an attempt to soften the blow, the mogul appealed to Ball's status anxiety, pointing out that as Sky chief executive he would enjoy the services of his own chauffeur, at a time when everyone in Los Angeles still drove their own car. Sky would also pay very well, he was also assured.

Murdoch pointed out that there were big challenges for him to tackle. Sky Digital, a more advanced set-top box that used digital encoding to offer dozens more channels via satellite than the old analogue system, as well as an internet connection to deliver interactivity, was launched in late 1998. It was a crucial part of the vision Murdoch had set out when he risked everything to launch Sky in 1989.

In a speech to appalled BBC and ITV executives, Murdoch had predicted that "the television set of the future will be, in reality, a telecomputer linked by fibre optic cable to a global cornucopia of programming and nearly infinite libraries of data".[1] Sky Digital could be a big step in that direction, but its success was by no means assured.

Britain's regional cable operators were merging and becoming a more credible national threat. Sky believed that NTL, the biggest player, had an eye on bidding for Sky's precious Premier League rights deal, which would be up for renewal in 2001.

Meanwhile ONdigital, a new pay-TV service backed by the commercial terrestrial broadcasters behind ITV, represented brand new competition and, more importantly, it had rights to the Champions League, the biggest competition in European football. ONdigital was selling better than Sky expected and Murdoch doubted that Mark Booth had the stomach for the battle. Sky's chief executive was written up in the press as "fair and polite – the opposite of Chisholm".[2]

"It was war time," recalls one Sky executive close to Ball's appointment. "We needed a war-time management and we didn't have a war-time management."

A contemporary agrees: "Mark was a nice, soft East Coast liberal; Rupert wanted a street fighter. Arguably, Mark was just a CEO too soon. We've always had the right CEO for the right time but Mark was probably the exception."

Murdoch's view was confirmed by Sky's disastrous attempted takeover of Manchester United under Booth. On a visit to Milan in 1998, Murdoch had heard from rival media tycoon Silvio Berlusconi, then briefly out of government, how ownership of AC Milan had massively increased his power in football rights bargaining for his pay-TV operator.

Murdoch wanted the same for Sky and instructed Booth to make a bid for Manchester United. It was established as the Premier League's top club and as a public company was for sale – if a price could be struck.

Booth duly agreed a £623m takeover with Martin Edwards, Manchester United's chief executive and largest shareholder. Within 24 hours, Carlton, an ITV franchisee, scrambled to respond by opening talks to buy Arsenal. NTL quickly decided to get in on the act too and began discussions with Newcastle United.

Booth had not reckoned on the strength of opposition to Murdoch ownership of a football club, however. Manchester United fans, and Greg Dyke, a non-executive director of the club, swiftly organised a campaign against the takeover. Dyke was a well-connected member of Britain's commercial television establishment, and as such a committed enemy of Murdoch and Sky.

He ran rings round Texas-born Booth in the lobbying battle that ensued. After a few months, the New Labour government, which had worked for years to secure the endorsement of *The Sun* newspaper in the 1997 general election, surprised many in the media, not least Murdoch himself, by taking a stand against the deal.

"It is very hard for small shareholders of Sky that we should be punished for the fact that we supported the Government in the last election," he complained at Sky's annual general meeting in October 1998.

The Sun was furious when the bid was blocked the following year, branding the decision 'disgraceful' in an editorial. Trade and industry secretary Stephen Byers said that "under almost all scenarios... the merger would increase the market power which Sky already has as a provider of sports premium channels".

"Mark was just floored by that," recalls a colleague. The decision to block the Manchester United takeover was announced on 10 April and his departure was confirmed 18 days later.

"I think he was relieved," says the colleague. "He was a fish out of water really."

Booth remained in the fold, however. News Corp gave him $100m to establish a venture capital fund to explore the new opportunities on the emerging internet. The fund closed soon after the dotcom bubble burst and Booth handed back most of the money.

Murdoch, Sky's chairman, had lined Ball up to take over at Sky months before his departure was revealed to investors in May. Ball spoke to Booth and pored over Sky's strategy as he prepared to return to Britain. He wondered if he had made a mistake in accepting the job, as the slowdown in growth and rising competitive threats had concerned him.

After an early near-death experience that nearly bankrupted Murdoch, Sky had dominated the first decade of British pay-TV. By the time regulators scrutinised its bid for Manchester United, Sky controlled 63% of the UK market. From the outside, Sky looked like an unstoppable juggernaut. In 1998 turnover rose 15% to £1.4bn. Profits dipped to £271m as Booth invested in the development of Sky Digital and paid more for sports rights, but Sky itself had never been more powerful.

It may have had a difficult birth and a troubled childhood, but Sky had grown up into a strong young company. City investors, who effectively bailed

Sky out when Murdoch was forced to float it on the stock exchange in 1994, were ready to reap their rewards. Sky was paying chunky dividends and its share price was rising steadily. They were confident in Booth's prudent digital plans, which involved a partial subsidy for new set-top boxes, but no dramatic moves.

Ball saw things differently. He believed that without radical action Sky risked losing its grip in the second epoch of pay-TV, when digital broadcasting would allow rivals to offer more of the choice that had been Sky's unique strength. The ITV companies backing ONdigital had plenty of financial muscle and the support of a political and regulatory system that wanted digital terrestrial television to succeed as a pay-TV rival to Sky.

Ball and Murdoch agreed that, in order to tackle ONdigital, they had to start giving away Sky Digital boxes. In the first few months, Sky had been charging £299 to cover most of the cost of the new technology, and the result had been only lukewarm demand. After eight months, Sky Digital had only half a million subscribers.

The investment would completely wipe out profits and mean no dividend for the City, but chairman and number one shareholder, Murdoch himself, would have no problem pushing the decision through the board. Sky was a public company with a majority of independent shareholders (News Corp then owned 35.4%), but despite concerns Murdoch used it for his own ends, they let him take the big decisions largely unopposed.

"Back then people went on the board of Sky for reasons that they worked for News Corp or because they wanted to hang out with Rupert," says a well-placed source. "There were two exceptions, Dennis Stevenson and Philip Bowman, who were really independently minded, but lot of people on the board just went along with it."

As it turned out, City investors were wowed by the audacity of the giveaway and rewarded Sky with an 11% surge in its share price on the day it was announced in May. Analysts nevertheless cautioned that Carlton and Granada had deep pockets and that they represented tougher opponents than Murdoch had faced in British Satellite Broadcasting at the dawn of British pay-TV.

Ball officially took the helm the following month and immediately began installing a tough new regime. He moved his "very dangerous and very red" Ducati motorbike into his office, and told friends that Sky had grown complacent, and that executives were "still in thrall to the cult of Sam".

"I think Tony had decided long before he arrived that Sky needed a massive kick up the backside," says a colleague. "He put a rocket up the arse of the sales and trading organisation. They had started to believe in their own greatness."

Many did not enjoy working under Ball but he showed little sign that he cared. Some were alienated as he focused on tactics more than strategy, and worked through a very small group of senior executives. He swore like a sailor and was prone to fits of temper; on learning in a meeting that one of his team used to work at the BBC he called the individual a "fucking c*nt" to his face.

Ball stamped his authority quickly. David Chance, a former senior executive who was close to Chisholm and had become a non-executive member of the board, was out within weeks. The new chief executive wanted Sky to move faster and more aggressively, and anyone in his way would pay the price.

"Everyone was shit scared of him. Everybody. But for that time I think he was good," says one long-serving Sky executive. "We had a laugh but never in his presence."

A former colleague agrees: "I was not at the level then where I was dealing with Tony Ball every day. It was one of those things where we'd go and see him and it would be a sufficiently terrifying experience that you'd be glad the next one didn't come for a few weeks.

"It slightly worked to our advantage because the rest of the industry were sort of scared of him and we say if you won't agree this we'll need to get Tony involved.

"But you felt you were part of something successful."

Under Ball, Sky was run by his lieutenants as a series of fiefdoms. Each reported to the feared ruler and were often suspicious of each other. Collaboration between different parts of the business was rare. Ball readily admitted he liked it that way.

"I might sometimes nurture an environment of confusion," he said.[3] "I think often you get the best response out of executives when you've got them on the back foot."

One weekend in August, Sky ran out of the digital set-top boxes that it was now scrambling to give away to new and existing subscribers. Ball was apoplectic. On Monday morning he arrived at headquarters, which then amounted to one purpose built office and a collection of converted sheds on a business park in Osterley, West London, and delivered the reprisal.

Ball summarily dismissed Ian West, the man in charge of the rollout, who he also believed wanted the top job. West had been with Sky since its launch. Colleagues arriving at work saw him retreating from Osterley ashen-faced. Ball met him the following day at Blakes, a five-star hotel in Kensington, to agree his exit package.

David Chance and Ian West would later return to haunt Sky, but for now Ball was consolidating his power. He promoted Jon Florsheim to run the marketing of Sky Digital, and Brian Sullivan to run product development and sales. Richard Freudenstein, an affable Australian who Ball had got to know in Sydney, was brought in as general manager, and swiftly promoted to chief operating officer.

Sullivan had been brought over from the United States under Chisholm to sharpen up the way in which Sky managed its subscription business and handled crucial customer retention processes. Chisholm, who was focused on programming, was not interested. Under Ball, such functions would move closer to the centre of Sky's operations and become the foundation of its long-term growth.

Ball otherwise had limited time for the big picture; after all, he had been sent to fight a war. Ball gave scathing assessments of Sky's efforts under Liz Murdoch to make more of its own programmes, and she left Sky within a year to found the independent producer Shine. Ball did not seek to replace her with a powerful programming chief for two years.

Those who wanted Sky to spend more on brand advertising to soften its image were also ignored. Ball thought it was time for the hard sell: a new brand campaign developed by the agency Wolff Olins at a cost of £1m, involving fluffy clouds, was swiftly abandoned.

Ball's generous pay package, at £1.5m a year plus millions more in share options, depended on hitting Sky Digital targets, and little else seemed to matter.

In strictly financial terms, the decision to give away Sky Digital set the company back several years. Between the set-top box, the new smaller satellite dish and the installation, each subscriber cost about £500 up front. It would be years before the investment paid off. As well as scrapping the dividend, it also meant a return to the sort of penny-pinching Sky had not seen since its financially perilous early years.

Ball came to rely heavily on Martin Stewart, his chief financial officer, as Sky diverted all its resources into the digital rollout. Every Friday, Stewart would gather executives in the finance department and divide a pile of invoices into those that had to be paid and those that could wait.

"We were about to go bust but we had to really manage cash flow," one executive recalls.

Ball, with cropped silver hair and a sharp suit, may have appeared confident but told friends that, privately, he was "shitting himself", as Sky once again took serious financial risks in order to buy a stake in the future.

His worries were misplaced. The Sky Digital launch offer of 120 channels, better picture quality and interactive services at no extra cost quickly proved irresistible to households that had rejected analogue satellite television. In the three months after Sky announced the giveaway, it signed up more customers than in the first eight months, to take the total to 1.2 million by the end of July. The majority of subscribers were new to Sky. When it was charging for Sky Digital, existing subscribers dominated.

Sky was forced to borrow heavily to meet the demand from consumers, and in 1999 it issued a total of £1bn in bonds to fund the rollout. Ball took advantage of money markets that were gripped by dotcom fever to attract investment in the digital future.

"Our aim is to bring digital to every home in the country, as quickly as possible because, by increasing the number of digital customers, we increase the value of our company," he said.

Sky was not itself immune to the dotcom madness. In 2000, just weeks before the bubble burst, Ball paid more than £300m for Sports Internet Group, a listed online media company with a turnover of less than £20m and losses of nearly £10m a year. Ball had little insight into the development of online media, but had poached John Swingewood from BT as Sky's internet guru. Swingewood carried the can for the Sports Internet deal and was sacked in 2001. Sky never wrote off the investment, however, and it went on to become the foundation of the massively successful Sky Bet operation.

In any event, online media was something of a sideshow. Ball would update Murdoch on progress as Sky raced to crush its new competition in pay-TV; they had set a target of five million digital subscribers within two years. ONdigital was forced to respond and announced its own giveaway in a costly attempt to keep up in what amounted to a land grab. Its main shareholders, the ITV franchisees Carlton and Granada, doubled their funding to £800m a year.

"The adage that if you take on Rupert Murdoch you need strong nerves and deep pockets was becoming all too obviously true," the head of ONdigital Stuart Prebble later recalled, as he complained of Sky's "predatory" pricing.[4]

Ball used Sky's dominance of sports and Hollywood film rights to further increase the pressure. Sky charged ONdigital more to carry Sky Sports and Sky Movies than it did its own customers at retail. Prebble complained to the Office of Fair Trading, but the gears of regulation could not turn quickly enough to help him. Sky set its legal team, including regulatory affairs chief Michael Rhodes, then regarded by regulators as the shrewdest legal operator in the industry, against the investigation.

"Tony just smelt that we could kill these guys and that we could dominate," says a colleague.

While ONdigital spent heavily on television and outdoor advertising, Ball focused Sky efforts on a determined sales operation on the ground, recruiting electronics retailers to push Sky Digital to consumers buying the new generation of bigger televisions.

He kept adding channels to the service, taking advantage of digital satellite broadcasting's capacity advantage over the terrestrial signals relied upon by ONdigital. Sky trawled the US broadcast market and quickly built up a catalogue of hundreds of channels. Its rival offered a few dozen.

Ball believed the ITV grandees behind ONdigital, Michael Green of Carlton and Granada boss Charles Allen, were arrogant. He had been a shop floor union leader as a broadcast engineer, and though colleagues later saw him – a multimillionaire and committed free marketeer – as an unlikely working-class hero, he retained a disdain for British television's upper ranks.

Carlton in particular was viewed by Sky as a den of entitled and out-of-touch public school boys. Its corporate affairs function was run by a young David Cameron, on a stop-off on his gilded path from the playing fields of Eton to 10 Downing Street.

"They peppered their limited spectrum with their own channels, like Carlton Food Network, instead of signing up channels people wanted to watch," Ball said.

"We had a better product," recalls one executive. "Part of the strategy was instead of getting content, let's just get more channels. There's a lot of data that shows that consumers don't use 500 channels if they have them, or even 50, but they do value them. So the proposition was about choice, even too much choice."

Unable to match Sky's offering, and hobbled by the cost of competing with Sky Sports and Sky Movies, ONdigital decided to go after exclusive sports rights itself. In June 2000 it outbid Ball for rights to live football. The deal would cost £105m a year and covered lower league matches and the League Cup, the English game's secondary tournament. Sky bid aggressively, but it was bluffing. Ball was content for ONdigital to win, but he was determined to make them pay through the nose for the privilege. In the end, the price was four times the value of the Football League's previous deal.

That same month Ball consolidated his advantage with a new deal for the rights that mattered most. Following a fraught bidding process, he paid £1.1bn to renew Sky's deal with the Premier League for three years. Sky came close to losing its dominant position and for the first time clubs sold rights to a minority of matches to rivals, albeit only on a pay-per-view basis, which had proved a successful formula for Sky in boxing but was untested in British football broadcasting.

NTL was forced to pull out, as the burden of the massive debts it had built up building cable networks began to weigh heavy as the dotcom crash made borrowing more expensive. It left ONdigital effectively paying to run an experiment on behalf of the football clubs.

Together it meant ONdigital's peak funding shareholder requirement reached £1.2bn. By the end of 2000, Sky's victory already seemed assured. Ball hit his five million subscriber target six months ahead of schedule; ONdigital scraped over one million.

While the competition to give away set-top boxes was costly, the challenger had also been hampered by the slow introduction of digital terrestrial transmitters. ONdigital anticipated 70% coverage at launch. Instead only around 40% of homes were in range. Prebble said the delay cost ONdigital 750,000 customers in the early days.

"Sky is like any established dominant player who sees a new challenger and plays the regulatory system hard and long enough to see them off," he later said. "Sky is the scorpion: you know what it is capable of when you go near it – you cannot blame the scorpion for stinging."

"Do I blame the regulators? Absolutely. Sky's well-resourced and aggressive stance against regulators, coupled with the political power of its media empire, has effectively neutered the systems that should have prevented it from eliminating competition."

Prebble also claimed that piracy cost ONdigital £100m. In early 2002, by which time it had been rebranded as ITV Digital, about 100,000 counterfeit smart cards were in circulation. They allowed consumers to decode ITV Digital broadcasts without paying and were widely traded in pubs across the UK.

The flawed technology was licensed from Canal+, the French satellite broadcaster. It claimed that its encryption system had failed because NDS, an arm of News Corp, had reverse engineered the technology at its lab in Israel and leaked the results online.

Prebble said that if NDS was behind ITV Digital's piracy problem, the "implications are extraordinary and should be taken extremely seriously by regulators, competition authorities and politicians looking at the increasing dominance of Britain's media by News Corp". There was no such response, although the controversy would resurface a decade later as a sub-plot in the phone hacking scandal that engulfed Murdoch's British newspapers.

Instead the allegations were effectively settled in 2003 when News Corp agreed to acquire Telepiu, a loss-making Italian pay-TV operator, from the parent company of Canal+, Vivendi. This would later become a cornerstone of Sky Italia.

The crushing nature of ITV Digital's defeat suggests Sky's tactics would have been fatal regardless of piracy. Once its bills from the Football League came due at the start of the 2001/2 season, its finances quickly unravelled. ITV faced an advertising recession sparked by the dotcom crash, and the cost of fighting a losing war with Sky was simply unsustainable.

After a failed plea to the Football League for a steep discount on rights costs, on 27 March 2002 Carlton and Granada put the business into administration. No buyer came forward and within a month ITV Digital was in liquidation, leaving behind debts of £1.3bn.

Sky had meanwhile been transformed. Prior to the digital revolution its business had relied almost as much on supplying channels to cable operators as on its own satellite subscribers. Some analysts had forecast that the dawn of the digital era would mean Sky's days as a near-monopoly were coming to an end. Instead it maintained its grip on sport and Hollywood films, and increased its own reach into homes. Its analogue subscriber base had peaked at 3.6 million. The success of Sky Digital meant it could focus more on its own direct relationships with consumers. After it crossed the five million threshold, Ball increased Sky Digital's subscriber target to seven million by the end of 2003.

Sky Digital's growing reach meant that in late 2001 ITV was forced to relent and provide its main channel, even as its own pay-TV service was drawn headlong towards oblivion. Sky was meanwhile ready to turn off its analogue signals.

ITV's senior executives had overestimated the British public's disdain for Rupert Murdoch and underestimated how many people would be willing to fix a satellite dish to the side of their house in exchange for more choice. Ball himself said that a satellite dish had once been a "badge of bad taste" but that now it was "totally normal". ITV Digital had not reckoned on free set-top boxes, Sky's mastery of sports rights or the weakness of its own line-up of channels.

"Of the competitors that were there, ITV Digital over-promised and the cable companies over-borrowed," Ball later said.[5]

Ball revelled in the triumph. As the financial pressure mounted on ITV Digital, he told a parliamentary committee that "all their problems are of their own making".[6] "They couldn't run a bath," he added.

When ITV Digital collapsed, Stuart Prebble, who had become chief executive of ITV, was forced to resign. His complaint to regulators about Sky's dominance of sport was still stuck in the system, and in any case would ultimately be defeated at the end of 2002.

"The problem wasn't running the bath, it was that some bastard kept on pulling the plug out," Prebble said. "Sky will inherit the earth."

2

The Whiff of Nepotism?

Sky's victory in the war with ITV Digital was total. Tony Ball had established his credentials as a ruthless 'bastard' in the Murdoch mould.

In the summer of 2002, *The Guardian*'s weekly media supplement, then the industry's bible, ranked him fourth on its power list, comfortably ahead of Charles Allen and Michael Green, his defeated foes at Granada and Carlton. Rubbing salt into their wounds, in September of that year Ball poached Dawn Airey from Channel 5 to run Sky's programming efforts, on £1m a year; Carlton and Granada had been wooing her for some time for the top job at ITV.

Ball was allegedly more influential than Sir Martin Sorrell, the founder of advertising empire WPP, than the feared *Daily Mail* editor Paul Dacre and than Sir Christopher Bland, the chairman of the national telecoms monopoly BT. *The Guardian* claimed that only Murdoch himself, the Prime Minister, and Greg Dyke, who since the Manchester United takeover row had become director-general of the BBC, held more sway over the British media landscape.

Ball teased ITV further by suggesting that, if it were not for media plurality rules that sought to curb Murdoch influence over Britain's news, he would mount a takeover bid. Indeed, he worked with Airey on a potential bid for her previous employer, Channel 5, prompting serious concern at the BBC that Sky could dominate the television rights market still more.

Ball's position appeared unassailable and once again Sky looked well positioned to reap the spoils of war. By the end of 2002, it had 6.6 million digital subscribers, the debt burden it had taken on to fund free set-top boxes was falling, and average customer bills were rising. It was under pressure to raise prices and cut costs to deliver returns for shareholders, and investors still hoped that Sky would settle into life as an effective pay-TV monopoly.

To his colleagues, Ball seemed keen to indulge them. Sky ended 2002 on an operating profit margin of more than 10%, but Ball said it could hit 30% by squeezing spending on programming and set-top boxes. Although Sky had made a high-profile hire with Dawn Airey, its original commissioning had been pared back since Liz Murdoch's departure.

Customers would soon be paying an average of £400 per year, up from £350, Ball confidently forecast, as he sought to drive the Sky share price, and the value of his own options, even higher. "We're just going to blow right through it," he said.[1]

Sky was seeking higher subscriber fees from services such as its set-top box with a built-in hard-disk recorder, known as Sky+. Named after Canal+ by Ball's wife Gabriella after he had rejected a series of suggestions from Sky's own marketeers, the service had the potential to transform television. Part of a wave of Personal Video Recorder (PVR) technology, Sky+ allowed viewers to schedule recording with the press of a button and fast-forward through advertising.

It was introduced in 2001 alongside the standard free Sky Digital set-top box, but was making a slow start. Sky struggled to communicate its benefits and charged £300 for the equipment, plus £10 a month for the service, on top of a Sky Digital subscription. Ball had high hopes for Sky+, but did not see any need to support its growth with another costly round of subsidies.

The Sky board was in Ball's grip and his decisions were usually final. Ball controlled the flow of information up to the directors and down to his staff more tightly than ever. Murdoch was chairman but less engaged; he had been diagnosed with prostate cancer in 2000 and underwent treatment which left him unable to travel. Ball effectively chaired Sky board meetings throughout the digital television battle and as Murdoch's proxy his decisions were rarely challenged.

Ball may have been in charge, but the seeds of his exit were already being sown. A reckoning was due over Sky's disastrous investment alongside the German media empire Kirch Group in 1999. Murdoch had been seeking a foothold in Germany as part of his plans for a European and then a global pay-TV operator. Ball was dispatched to do a deal with Leo Kirch, the reclusive Bavarian media mogul known for wielding Murdoch-like political influence over German politics.

The tie-up was Plan B after merger talks with Canal+, France's successful pay-TV operator, had collapsed earlier in the year. In February 1999, senior executives were summoned to Osterley on a Sunday and told that Murdoch had been discussing a Sky takeover of Canal+ with Pierre Lescure, its chief executive. It would certainly be a coup; at the time, Canal+ was Europe's most successful and advanced pay-TV operator.

The Sky team flew to Paris and discovered that Lescure was under the impression that he and Murdoch had discussed a French takeover of Sky, rather than the other way around. After an awkward meeting, the talks were quickly scrapped. Later that year Vivendi took a 24.5% stake in Sky and aimed to install two directors. A senior Sky executive recalls that Murdoch "shat himself" over fears that Vivendi's ambitious chief executive, Jean-Marier Messier, was plotting a hostile takeover.

The incursion came to nothing, however, and Vivendi was forced to sell its stake in 2002 as Messier's heavy borrowing threatened to break the company.

Kirch was a different type of opportunity for Sky. It was a massive potential market for pay-TV, with 33 million homes compared to 24 million in the UK, but it was proving hard to crack. German consumers were parsimonious and had plenty of choice, including live top-flight football, on free-to-air television.

Kirch had been borrowing heavily to fund the rollout of Premiere World, its satellite pay-TV brand, but it was still losing money fast. Murdoch and Sky sensed a chance to break into a media and political scene that was generally hostile to foreign ownership, and moved in.

Sky took a 24% stake in KirchPayTV, the holding company for Premiere World, for about £1bn in cash and shares. Premiere never delivered on its promise and struggled to build on the two million subscribers it had when Ball invested. In 2000, Sky's share of the losses was almost £200m.

In the next six months Premier World lost another £74m on behalf of its British shareholder, which was growing increasingly concerned that the Byzantine business assembled over decades by Leo Kirch was teetering towards collapse. In February 2002, even as Sky was triumphant over ITV Digital, Ball was forced to write off the entire value of the investment in KirchPayTV.

Kirch duly went bust weeks later, in what was Germany's biggest post-war bankruptcy. Permira, a private equity firm, bought Premiere. Years later it would become Sky Deutschland, but in 2002 it was nothing more than an embarrassment to Sky and to Ball.

The Kirch debacle was widely viewed as a sideshow in the grand scheme of Sky. But within News Corp, fingers were being pointed. Murdoch was back at the wheel after his illness and questions were being asked. The chairman had pushed Sky to expand into Germany, but Ball's standing at the News Corp court had been damaged when that expansion went wrong.

"There were really two types of News Corp executive," says a former Murdoch associate. "To stay there at the top you can be all in and know that you're only ever going to be there. Then it's a bit cultish and it's all about being close to Rupert.

"Or you can do well and have a good relationship with Rupert for a period but be your own person. And being your own person in the end can cause some difficulty."

Others in the News Corp camp recognised Ball's growing stature as "the big man on campus" as a problem.

He began to butt heads with Murdoch in an effort to maintain a degree of independence. When Murdoch wanted to use the Sky brand for News Corp's new Italian pay-TV assets, Ball insisted on more favourable terms for Sky. Combined with tensions over Kirch, their relationship was gradually transformed.

The two men had been genuine friends. When Murdoch was ill, Ball would regularly fly out to New York or the Murdoch family ranch in Carmel Valley, Northern California, to spend the weekend with him. They drank and gossiped about politics together.

As Ball asserted himself at Sky, relations turned frostier and more business-like, particularly as his three-year fixed-term contract came up for renewal in mid-2002. Convinced of his own value, he negotiated hard for more generous share options and bonuses linked to the strategy he had laid out. While some senior colleagues saw him as greedy, Ball himself believed he deserved more credit for the success of Sky. A two-year extension was agreed, along with another executive bonus scheme on top of the existing remuneration plan.

Murdoch was increasingly irritated by his protégé, but remained an admirer of his talents as an executive. In early 2003, the mogul took what was expected to become a crucial step in the creation of Sky Global when News Corp acquired a controlling stake in the US satellite broadcaster DirecTV. Murdoch aimed to disrupt the US cable industry, which had held a highly lucrative pay-TV monopoly for decades. Ball was perhaps the battlefield campaigner for the job.

Via Chase Carey, a News Corp veteran with a polite, old-fashioned manner and an Old West moustache to match, Murdoch asked Ball to return to the US to run DirecTV. It had been the plan all along as far as the mogul was concerned. He had been in pursuit of DirectTV for years and intended for Ball to be part of an overhaul of the business under News Corp.

Ball decided he was having too much fun at Sky, however, and in another act of rebellion turned down the offer. His days were numbered.

"Once they ask you to do something in America then that's a sign that they don't want you doing what you're doing now," says a former senior News Corp executive.

Alongside the discussions over DirectTV, Murdoch installed his second son, the 30-year-old James, alongside Chase Carey, as non-executive directors on the Sky board. James had a day job in Hong Kong running News Corp's Asian pay-TV operator, Star Television, where he had pleased his father by delivering both a financial turnaround and better relations with the Chinese government.

Ball viewed the new arrivals as a challenge. The reshuffle was prompted in part by new corporate governance rules that said listed companies should have a majority of independent directors. The changes Murdoch made arguably tightened his grip on Sky, however, and sent a strong signal to Ball that he was in fact under closer supervision. Ball began to wonder if he had not been returning Murdoch's calls quickly enough.

James and Carey had replaced Les Hinton, an ultra-loyal executive drawn from the newspaper business, and Martin Pompadour, who was running a collection of profitable but low-profile Murdoch media interests in central and eastern Europe. Ball had felt that neither Hinton nor Pompadour was a threat to his authority. Murdoch's son *and* one of his closest lieutenants at the heart of News Corp, both specialists in the pay-TV business, were a different matter and were unlikely to defer to the chief executive.

That was made clear immediately. Hong Kong was at the centre of a global outbreak of SARS, a potentially deadly viral infection. Ball had issued an edict that nobody from Hong Kong was allowed in Sky headquarters – James ignored it in order to attend his first board meetings.

Ball's final courtly transgression came in August 2003, when he took to the stage at the Edinburgh Television Festival to deliver the prestigious MacTaggart Lecture. He arrived in Scotland having again secured Premier League rights: Sky would be the exclusive broadcaster until 2007, despite the protests of European competition watchdogs in Brussels.

Rupert Murdoch had himself used the MacTaggart lecture as a launchpad for Sky in 1989, and Ball gave a speech that he thought would please the boss. It was an extended attack on the dominance of the BBC, which Ball said should be pruned back to allow commercial rivals to blossom.

He also made specific suggestions for the upcoming review of the BBC's Royal Charter that would have made life much easier for Sky. Ball said that most of all the BBC should be banned from using public money to compete for rights to US programmes. He wanted to dominate the UK market for the new wave of big budget dramas, such as 24. The first two seasons had been a big hit for the BBC, and Ball and Dawn Airey wanted future seasons to run on Sky One, the pay-TV broadcaster's main in-house entertainment channel.

"I really cannot see why public money is being diverted to those poor struggling Hollywood studios in this way," Ball said.[2] "BBC resources should be redeployed to commission more independently-produced UK programming."

It should have been red meat to Rupert Murdoch. He had, after all, defined Sky in opposition to the BBC, its fusty costume dramas and its establishment leadership. Murdoch was always more interested in how Sky was challenging the BBC than any other aspect of its business. In its first decade, the Corporation had played the role of nemesis, and in the founder's political mind it remained the biggest threat to Sky's success.

Yet Ball's MacTaggart Lecture did not go down well at News Corp. Murdoch resented what he saw as a very public attempt to take credit for Sky's success. In the run up to the speech, in a laudatory profile of Ball in *The Observer*, the BBC business editor Jeff Randall said Ball's "genius" at Sky had been "'knowing exactly how far he can go with Rupert Murdoch". Nevertheless, it seemed that this time he had gone too far.

"Success has many fathers and if you have a founding shareholder you can't go around saying how bloody brilliant you are," recalls one contemporary Sky executive.

Ball's departure was announced exactly a month later, on 23 September 2003, eight months before his contract was due to end. His relations with Murdoch were still professional and he had prepared for life after Sky by lining up an even more lucrative career in private equity, but the end came a bit sooner than expected.

"I don't think Tony was in it for anything more than to make as much money as he could in the shortest time possible," says one of his executives.

Ball's last set of annual results underscored the progress that Sky had made in four years. Revenues were £3.2bn, more than double the figure before he arrived, and operating profit was £371m, about £30m higher than it had been before the digital revolution.

Sky was still adding to its subscriber base. Nearly 750,000 more homes signed up for a dish in Ball's final year, to take the total to 6.8 million and bring the target of seven million by the end of 2003 comfortably within reach. Sky had emerged from the dotcom boom and bust largely unscathed, too, although it had spiked and crashed along with every other media and technology stock. On the day that Ball's departure was announced, the shares cost barely more than the day he arrived, but the underlying business was confirmed as Britain's dominant pay-TV operator. As one columnist put it, Sky was no longer a scrappy pirate ship, but Britain's biggest listed media company and the flagship of the Murdoch fleet.

The founder believed Sky had further to go, and should go faster, but Ball was handsomely rewarded. On exit he agreed a deal that swapped share options he not yet exercised for a cash payment of more than £10m and an undertaking not to work for a rival British broadcaster. News Corp also paid him not to work for any American pay-TV operator. Overall Ball made more than £30m from Sky.

His young successor was a billionaire by birthright. James Murdoch had his own reasons to seek the top job at Sky, but also reasons to stay in the Far East. Shortly before he was shipped out to run Star in 2000, he had married Kathryn

Hufschmid, a model from Oregon. By 2003 the couple were preparing for the arrival of their first child, a daughter, and house hunting in Hong Kong; they intended to stay for the long-term. Yet when James learned that his father planned to jettison Ball early, he rushed to his side and asked to be considered for the job.

In broad terms James believed he already knew what to do. He had been on the Sky board for several months and had witnessed, and been part of, the tension between management and the non-executives over the direction of the business.

James thought the plan to expand profit margins and cash in on the digital infrastructure Sky had built at a cost of more than £2bn was premature. In his few months as a non-executive he agreed with his father that the company was at a crossroads and not growing fast enough. The new target of eight million subscribers by the end of 2005 was too conservative for him. He believed the company needed another round of major investment to navigate more technological shifts.

Already a new challenge had emerged from the ashes of ITV Digital. The broadcasting capacity left behind had been reallocated to Freeview, a joint venture between the BBC, Sky and the company that ran Britain's transmission network. ITV and Channel 4 would become shareholders later. Freeview would not compete with Sky's pay-TV service, so it was left to Ball to provide some free channels such as Sky News that would benefit from bigger audiences for advertisers. However, it posed a subtler threat than ITV Digital when it launched in late 2002.

Sky's growth had previously depended on convincing households who were getting five analogue terrestrial channels for free to pay for hundreds of digital satellite channels. The gulf in choice was vast. Freeview offered 30 digital channels for free, including well-funded news services from the BBC. In the long run, it would mean Sky would have to work harder to convert households to paying subscribers.

In Hong Kong, set-top box makers reported to James that the Freeview kit was selling very well in Britain and he was concerned that Sky did not appear to be responding to the risk to its growth with more investment and sophisticated marketing. Instead, Ball planned to reap the rewards of Sky Digital. James thought he was being too smug; he also disliked the culture of distrust that Ball deliberately created among executives. By the time his father decided Sky needed new leadership, James had the sketch of his own plans for the company.

Both Murdochs knew that if James was going to secure the job, the Sky board were likely to demand a full, formal appointment process. Even then the company would struggle to convince investors that it was not a charade. Nevertheless, days before Ball's exit was confirmed, Murdoch-owned newspapers were briefed by Sky insiders that James was expected to take the helm.

Just as it is today, reporting of News Corp manoeuvres by Murdoch-owned newspapers was perceived as highly likely to be at the very least accurate and possibly written under direct instruction from Rupert himself. Journalists at *The Times* have long understood that getting it wrong can limit their career prospects.

News of James's potential appointment did not go down well among other Sky shareholders.[3] Ball had a large fan club in the City, where fund managers prized the degree of independence from News Corp that he had been able to carve out. His exit may have been rumoured (it was widely known that his contract was up for renewal) but the news was still a shock when it came.

James, meanwhile, was an unknown quantity, still just 30 years old and seemingly inexperienced, and the son of the dominant shareholder. When he joined the board as a non-executive director, Sky shareholders expressed concern. When Ball's departure was announced, many believed he had been sacked to make way for the coronation of James. The reality was much more complicated.

"The actual period between James joining the board and becoming CEO was very short and if anything it buggered up any succession plans because why would you go through that pain twice in such short order?" recalls one source involved in the discussions.

As soon as Ball was out, battle lines were officially drawn. Sky's independent directors, mindful of their own reputations in the City, resisted pressure from Rupert Murdoch to rush through the appointment. They called Jan Hall from headhunter firm Spencer Stuart to conduct a full international search and draw up a shortlist of candidates for interview.

The committee of Sky directors handling the process now included Allan Leighton, the chairman of Royal Mail, and Gail Rebuck, the chairman of Random House, the book publisher. Both were respected in the City and viewed as sufficiently independent of Murdoch. Lord Richard Wilson, a retired head of the civil service who joined the Sky board as an independent director in the same reshuffle as James and Carey, was also on the panel.

Investors were also concerned over the involvement of the Tory peer Lord St John of Fawlsey, however. The 74-year-old former Tory arts minister had been on the Sky board since 1991, ostensibly as an independent director but frequently viewed as a Murdoch stooge. The committee was summoned to a meeting with Sky's biggest City shareholders, who warned they would come down hard on any attempt to fix the process in favour of James. As concern mounted, Fawlsey refused to attend a second meeting, compounding investor resentment of him.

The charge of nepotism was inescapable. The journalist Andrew Neil, who had served as Sky's first chairman and was a fixture at the Murdoch court before he was ousted over a *Sunday Times* story that threatened News Corp pay-TV interests in Malaysia, joined a chorus of criticism of the appointment of James.

"It is obviously not his abilities that will take him to the top job at Sky," he said. "It will be his genes. After all, how many other 30-year-old college dropouts get to be chief executive of a £12bn public company."[4]

None of the three other external candidates approached were convinced that they would have a serious chance in what one senior media executive had publicly criticised as a 'predetermined' competition. Instead, Sky senior executives were actively encouraged to put themselves forward. Martin Stewart, the chief financial officer who had been Ball's right-hand, chief operating officer Richard Freudenstein and John Florsheim, the director of sales and marketing, all obliged.

Ball, who had discussed succession with Murdoch and backed James, suggested to the trio that Sky was probably just going through the motions. Freudenstein and Florsheim heeded the warning but Stewart did not.

Stewart suggested to colleagues that he believed he had a real chance in a run off against the chairman's son. After all, under Ball he had been a powerful number two. Sky's finance function controlled the business day to day while the chief executive was doing deals and enjoying the limelight. Stewart's sense that he was owed a shot at the top led him to make a costly mistake.

As the interview process continued through October, Stewart called on the help of Tim Allan, Sky's former communications chief. He had left in 2001 to set up his own public relations and lobbying firm, Portland, but remained close to Ball and Sky. Allan began spinning on Stewart's behalf, putting the word out that James was unqualified and that the finance chief was the safe pair of hands the City required.

The pitch was simple: Stewart was independent. He hit his targets and delivered the numbers investors wanted. James was not only a News Corp man but a Murdoch, a young and untested executive who might threaten the financial progress Sky had made.

"Martin's view was that 'well, everyone on the board is telling me that this is genuinely an open process', and there would have been one or two non-execs that would have told him he should go for it," recalls a colleague.

"He probably thought 'James is ten years younger than me, what's he ever done?' His mistake was hiring Tim Allan to go and do a PR campaign on his behalf to badmouth James."

There was a firm reaction from the Murdoch camp. Peter Chernin, the chief executive of News Corp, publicly endorsed James as "the best person to do this job". He defended News Corp against suspicions that it was acting against the interests of all shareholders in terms that no major media executive would use openly today.

"We have never done anything at BSkyB that isn't in the best interest of that company and I think the results speak for themselves," Chernin said.[5] "I don't think anyone can point to a single instance when News Corp has benefited at the expense of BSkyB shareholders. It's not like we've been raping the company."

Rupert Murdoch himself weighed in days later.

"Nobody is more qualified to take over a multichannel platform than James, with the exception of Charles Ergen of Echostar [a rival to DirecTV]," he said.[6] "But, of course, Charlie isn't available."

James was appointed on 3 November, subject to a vote of shareholders at what was certain to be a stormy Annual General Meeting later that month. The reaction from the City was immediately hostile. Standard Life, the pension fund, said it was "disappointed" by the appointment. Morley, another Sky shareholder, said it opposed James and demanded an overhaul of the board to wrest control away from News Corp. Murdoch responded in kind.

"These so-called investors never put a penny into it [Sky]," he raged in New York. "It was developed entirely by us off our back and other people are now buying shares in it."

Leighton, Rebuck, Wilson and James were desperate to cool the situation. If Sky lost the vote, it would mean humiliation for the board as well as potential chaos.

They embarked on a City charm offensive, taking James around a number of investment houses to disarm them with his polite, professional manner and fluency in the vocabulary of modern management and of pay-TV. Privately, James was irritated; he felt he had proved himself with the turnaround of Star and agreed with his father's assessment that he was one of very few qualified candidates for the job. The whispering campaign criticising him as inexperienced infuriated him.

He nevertheless jumped through the hoops with Sky. Alongside its new chief executive, Sky had named the financier Lord Jacob Rothschild as deputy chairman, a new position designed to strengthen the independent voices on the board. The City grandee came along as James was introduced to rebellious fund managers.

The campaign appeared to win over some critics, but as the vote neared Fawlsey continued to provoke anger. He branded both the protests and calls for him to resign as "absurd".[7]

"If a company is doing well and the results are good and we have good people on the board, what on earth is the point of making that fuss? It is damaging the company," he said.

The AGM, at a packed Queen Elizabeth II Conference Centre on Parliament Square, was a circus. Both Murdochs were there, dozens of press and scores of angry shareholders. Rupert posed as contrite, saying "I can fully understand the suspicion of possible nepotism with my son as a candidate. . . so I refrained from taking any part in the process of selection".[8] James stagily referred to his father as "the chairman".

There were two votes. One on Sky's remuneration report, which was a poll on the £10m payoff agreed with Ball, and one to re-elect Fawlsey as a director, effectively a referendum on the appointment of James as chief executive.

In both about 40% of the shares were voted against. Without the backing of News Corp's 35% stake and some compliant American shareholders, Fawsley would have been ousted. Four out of five independent shareholders opposed him. The peer admitted the credibility of the appointment process he ran had been damaged by public interventions from News Corp, which he branded a "bloody nuisance". Yet James and Fawsley won the day and he stayed on the board for another three years.

It was not the end of Sky's corporate governance problems, but James had successfully run the gauntlet. His first priority was to deal with Martin Stewart. James was well aware of Tim Allan's spin campaign and had resolved to take action as soon as his feet were under his desk at Sky. The finance chief's position was no longer tenable, and he left Sky immediately, pending an exit deal.

"If he had played it straight through the process, he might have survived," says a colleague. "It unquestionably created bad blood from the start because he had used phrases that were derogatory of James rather than positive about his own characteristics."

Sky was on the rocky road to another transformation, with the youngest ever chief executive of a FTSE 100 company now leading the way.

3

Jam Tomorrow

James Murdoch may have been born in London, but he grew up a citizen of the global republic of News Corp. Family life with elder siblings Lachlan and sister Liz was nomadic, and frequently intermingled with family business interests.

As teenagers, both the Murdoch boys were sent on work experience in the Australian newspaper business, where the News Corp empire was founded. Lachlan impressed his father as "most interested" in the trade, working with the printers in the pressroom, "cleaning all the oil and the grease off the press". James fell asleep at a press conference and had his photograph splashed across the front page of a rival title.

James graduated from an exclusive New York private school and then to university at Harvard, but he dropped out and, with friends, set up an independent record label called Rawkus. It released cerebral hip-hop and knowing heavy metal by bands such as Whorgasm (tracks included 'Scream Motherfucker' and 'Michael Jackson's Sex Change'). To the New York social scene it looked as if James was rebelling against his socially conservative father. Lanky and scruffy, he bleached his hair, collected a number of tattoos and got an eyebrow piercing.

"We're doing things that no other company would let us do in a million years," the wannabe music mogul said in a *New Yorker* interview.[1] "This is something I can prove myself with," he told another journalist.

Independence for both Rawkus and James quickly proved difficult to maintain. In 1996, just a year old, the label was struggling to pay its bills. News Corp bought a majority stake and Rupert bought James back into the family business, at age 23, to lead a push into the music industry – one of very few media markets in which News Corp was not a major force. James was then put in charge of getting to grips with the web, first in the United States and then worldwide.

In 2000, when the dotcom crash came, James was dispatched to run the struggling Star pay-TV operation in Hong Kong, where his father had recently found a third wife, Wendi Deng. James continued the work of building relationships with the Chinese government, which viewed the company as a potential threat to its strict control of information.

Communist party officials had good reason. They were enraged in 1993 when Rupert said communications technologies such as satellite broadcasting had "proved an unambiguous threat to totalitarian regimes everywhere".[2] They promptly banned private ownership of satellite dishes and Star had spent subsequent years attempting to gain more access to the vast and untapped Chinese market by bowing to censorship demands.

As chief executive, James went further and publicly attacked Falun Gong, a spiritual movement brutally persecuted by the government, labelling it, in a speech to an audience that included Rupert, an "apocalyptic cult" that "clearly does not have the success of China at heart".[3] By the time he arrived at Sky, James Murdoch had shown his commitment to the pragmatism that had long driven News Corp.

Youthful rebellion had long since been replaced with dedication to his father's cause. In 2000, on his way to Hong Kong, he stopped off at the Edinburgh Television Festival to attack Britain's system of media regulation and the BBC licence fee, branding the former "draconian" and the latter an "evil taxation scheme, subsidising competitors with no accountability".

Within three years, James had turned around Star's finances and was keen to prove himself again, on a bigger stage. Lachlan was heir apparent, running

News Corp's cherished Australian businesses, but to be handed custody of Sky was a major endorsement from his father.

His new staff did not know what to expect. Very few in Osterley had met James as a mere member of the board. They had watched the controversy sparked by his appointment, fascinated by a figure who seemed the young archetype of a modern American media executive: thick, wire-rimmed glasses and open-necked shirts.

Unlike his father, who growled in plain Australian English in both public and in private, James seemed mild-mannered to the point of prissiness. He was fluent in bland management jargon and enjoyed debating business strategy more than gossiping about politics. He peppered conversations with phrases like "game-changing" and "exogenous factors".

Sky executives would soon discover that James's private character was more complex. He was funny, with a dry sense of humour that was more British than American. He smoked and joked, and occasionally drank too much Maker's Mark bourbon. He was polite when sober but could be an obnoxious drunk. He liked pubs better than expensive bars, and was more down to earth than his penchant for corporate lingo might have suggested. James was highly intelligent, but also intense and could easily become frustrated. He wielded power ruthlessly when he thought it was necessary and was mischievous when bored.

"James still likes dropping a rock in a millpond to see the ripples," says a friend.

He had spent plenty of time in Britain growing up, but knew little of the country beyond the London circles in which his father moved. In his early days at Sky he told a journalist:[4] "I must go up to Scotland to see one of those big games they have – what is it, Celtic v Rovers?"

Almost immediately, however, Murdoch brought to Sky something that was, for many, a welcome change from the autocratic style of Tony Ball. He had few close friends, but knew how to fit in with new people.

"We were all older than him," recalls a senior executive. "You have something in your head and you're a little bit nervous and then you actually meet him and he's very disarming. He put everyone at ease and everyone instantly kind of liked him."

"He actually managed to get people like Richard Freudenstein – who might have thought, 'hang on, I should have had that job' – to think I like him as well. Obviously Martin Stewart didn't."

James set about trying to build trust and collaboration in Sky's senior ranks. As well as Stewart, he waved goodbye to Deanna Bates, the long-serving head of legal, and promoted her deputy James Conyers. Bates's departure was sparked by the discovery that her partner David Chance, who had served as Sam Chisholm's number two, was secretly working on a new challenge to Sky in the pay-TV market. He tried to sack Tim Allan and Portland as Sky's public relations adviser, but discovered Ball had tied the company into an almost unbreakable contract. Most people stayed, however.

"It was quite interesting how they had all behaved one way to prosper under Tony and they behaved a different way to prosper under James," says an executive on the lower rungs of the ladder at the time. "Over time he brought in more people but in that first year to 18 months, it was amazing how he changed things without changing the people."

Early on, Murdoch organised Sky's first ever away-day at Wheatley Manor, a spa hotel in the Cotswolds, where mutually suspicious executives were forced to sit in on a circle of stones and discuss themselves and the future of the company.

"It had all been very individualised before, so nobody knew what anyone else was doing and you felt that you couldn't really ask," says one attendee.

"If you were the marketing director and the finance director asked you what your plans were, you'd tell him to fuck off and say it's not any of your business."

"It was clear things were different," says another. "It was clear it was going to be a much more open and collaborative culture."

James set this new caring, sharing Sky to work on developing a new strategy to reignite growth, to be unveiled in summer 2004.

"We had a lot of fun in those days," remembers an executive involved in the overhaul. "Meetings were always a lot of pissing around and laughter before someone said 'no, come on we have got to do some work'. That was the style."

The nexus of power within Sky moved decisively from the finance department to strategy as James attempted to map out the future. Executives who had felt sidelined under Ball and Stewart were suddenly the centre of attention. Led by Mike Darcey, a fearsomely bright economist described by a colleague as "someone you would lock in the basement because he has no emotional intelligence", the strategy team was previously called into action on Premier League rights auctions and little else. Murdoch's arrival promoted strategy above tactics.

He had already seen the pressure Freeview was putting on Sky in internal numbers, and in his first full quarter in charge, it was also apparent to the outside world. Sky added just 66,000 new subscribers, the lowest figure since the launch of its digital service in 1998, to take its total to just shy of 7.3 million.

Disappointed investors who had not yet grasped the challenge faced by the company had expected 90,000 new households to be added. The slowdown raised fears that Sky would struggle to hit Ball's target of eight million by the end of 2005. The three months to the end of June were no better. Sky won 81,000 new subscribers, 40% fewer than in the same period of 2003 and more than 60% down on 2002.

Inside the company, which still had no chief financial officer, plans for radical action were being drawn up. James wanted to abandon Ball's targets, which were the basis of all planning. The first casualty was to be the billing target of £400 per year (per household), which was the basis of City hopes that profits would quickly rise.

It meant that Sky could not create and promote new, cheaper packages to compete more effectively with Freeview for those households which did not want to pay for football and films, but did want some more entertainment options. Four out of five Sky subscribers were paying for the full package and the company could not afford for that proportion to slip if was going to hit its bill target by the end of 2005.

The target of eight million satellite households by the end of 2005 was also to be scrapped. It would be replaced by a more ambitious long-term goal of 10 million by the end of the decade. Ball had predicted Sky would hit the milestone, but never made it a formal part if of the company's financial strategy.

"All the models we had for forecasting, none of our models got to 10 million, none of them," remembers one executive involved in the discussions. "But he said 'I don't care, let's set a bold number'. It was 10 million by 2010, this kind of alliterative target – it was almost as arbitrary as that."

But importantly, it was a shot in the arm, too.

"James decided we would set the ambition and then work out how to get there. By putting it out publicly, you are holding yourself to account and making it something you can't walk away from. He was willing to put his own reputation on the line and I think it was a very galvanising experience."

Murdoch was grasping for levers to pull that would deliver the acceleration in growth required. There would be a "free" version of Sky to compete directly with Freeview. For a one-off cost of £150, households would get a satellite dish, a set-top box and 200 free channels. They would be easier to convert to pay-TV than Freeview viewers, Sky reasoned.

For the top end of the market, there would be high-definition (HD) television. Brian Sullivan had been developing plans for the new technology for some time. It would involve heavy investment in production systems for Sky Sports and other in-house channels, as well as new set-top boxes, and Ball had wanted to wait until there were more televisions capable of displaying better pictures; he thought Sky would waste money if it was too early to market.

Other broadcasters were sceptical that HD would take off in Britain at all. The existing European signal standard, PAL, already provider higher quality pictures than the NTSC standard used in the US and Japan. There was demand for HD there, some said, but British consumers were unlikely to invest in new television sets without there being noticeable improvement.

Murdoch dismissed such concerns and told Sullivan to press ahead. It would be two years before Sky's HD service was ready for launch, but he believed the technical limitations of the Freeview broadcast would give the company a competitive advantage for years to come. The sooner it could get to market, the better; in time for the 2006 football World Cup would be ideal. Television manufacturers such as Sony were gearing up for the shift too, by discontinuing old standard-definition sets and allocating big marketing budgets, and Murdoch wanted Sky to catch the wave.

"James just said 'we're doing it'," a colleague recalls. "Everyone was like 'why?'. He just said let's figure out how we do it and how to make some money from it. It was one of those things where the finance team is following and trying to figure out a plan and retro fit it to give James what he wanted."

"The biggest problem was there was not content available. So we had to work really hard to get it. We had to go to all the providers and get them to make HD channels, which we did.

"That was Sky at its absolute best. Everyone lined up together and made it work over a long period. It was probably the first time we had the whole organisation working together on something really big. There was strategy, technology, product, marketing, and so on."

Sky's move into HD would also set the pattern for its approach to new technologies over the next decade: to be an early adopter in the face of scepticism. The same had been true of Sky+: cable operator rivals did not launch their own PVR set-top boxes until years later.

"That's the story of most of our innovation, in truth," says one Sky executive. "We're quite quick to market. Sometimes because we're creating markets that first wave isn't always a riotous success but it means we are learning faster than others."

Murdoch also decided early on that Sky's brand and marketing needed an overhaul. He wanted to ditch the hard sell favoured by Tony Ball and instead "seduce" new customers. Households that had not been convinced to subscribe by Sky's football and film rights probably never would be, he thought. Murdoch wanted to promote more of Sky's entertainment programming on Sky One, which was due in September to begin broadcasting the acclaimed HBO western series *Deadwood*. He worked with marketing chief Jon Florsheim on shifting the company's focus away from driving sales via promotions and retail partnerships.

Instead, Sky would spend heavily on television and press advertising that would showcase its product and "reintroduce the Sky brand to the nation".[5] At one end of the market, Murdoch wanted to show that Sky could be affordable; at the other, he wanted to demonstrate that it was not hundreds of channels of trash to be sneered at.

"It's the right time to go out and knock some of those misperceptions on the head, and to start really focusing on what are, in many cases really, emotional barriers to purchase, and we don't think they should exist," Murdoch said.[6]

Inside the company they began talking of the need to "release the female handbrake" on the business. Sky believed its focus on marketing its sports coverage had become a barrier to attracting more subscribers. Its research showed that the women in a household would sometimes veto a Sky package in the belief that there was nothing for them on its channels.

By August 2004, James Murdoch was ready to unveil his plan to reinvest in Sky's growth to expectant investors. His 90-minute strategy presentation, along with his Powerpoint slides, was a disaster. The longer he spoke, the further the share price fell; by the time he was finished, Sky had lost nearly 20% of its value, or about £2bn.

Alongside the detailed new strategy, Murdoch reintroduced the shareholder dividend that had been scrapped in 1998 to fund the investment in Sky Digital, but it did not help. Neither did a plan to buy back 5% of the shares. It simply raised fears of creeping News Corp control of the company, as the proportion of Sky that was independently owned would be reduced.

The main problem, however, was that Murdoch planned to spend money that investors thought was coming their way. Sky would instead be boosting advertising spending by 50%. Sky One's programming budget would increase. Capital spending would more than double with a £450m, four-year plan on top of the existing £100m annual budget. Murdoch wanted a new customer database system to replace a botched installation by the US software company EDS, which triggered a lengthy court battle. He planned to call in Dunhumby, the company behind Tesco's successful Clubcard loyalty scheme, to help it zero in on potential new subscribers.

"It sounds creepy but it isn't really," said Murdoch.

Some £300m would be spent over four years to redevelop the chaotic Osterley campus ("he talked about parking and access, for God's sake," one analyst complained).[7] Subscriber growth would not accelerate until 2006 and, rather than expand, as Ball had planned, profit margins would be squeezed.

Colleagues watched in horror as the City punished their young leader for his promises of "jam tomorrow".

"He was talking and as he was talking the share price was just going down," recalls one. "We were just like, 'stop talking'."

Ball tracked the share price fall too, aboard a yacht. He thought he had bequeathed a business on a smooth path to riches and was puzzled by the crisis his young successor had created and rejected the suggestion that Sky's growth had hit a wall.

Some of the company's long-term backers in the City dumped their stakes, as the company's financial future suddenly became less certain. British institutions seeking steady cash returns were largely replaced by American funds more focused on share price growth. Initially seen as a disaster, it would in time give Sky more latitude to make investments and pursue new markets, but it was a brutal early lesson for James. He knew his plans were radical but did not expect the scale of the negative reaction. Afterwards he smoked and cursed outside the venue, but there was no going back. Sky's future, and his own standing within News Corp, depended on proving the critics wrong.

Help was on its way. Once Martin Stewart formally left the business in February 2004, James called in Jan Hall, the recruiter who had helped secure his own position at Sky. She launched a search for a new chief financial officer to work alongside James to deliver the plan he had set out and restore the company's credibility with investors.

The search targeted Jeremy Darroch, the 41-year-old finance chief at the consumer electronics retailer Dixons. He had spent most of his career in the European business of Procter & Gamble, the US maker of Fairy washing-up liquid, before joining Dixons as deputy to finance director Ian Livingston in 2000. When Livingston left for the same role at BT in 2002, Darroch took charge of the Dixons finance department. Soon, the restless grammar school boy was on the lookout for his next step up.

Darroch wanted to be involved with household name brands again and when the Sky job became available in 2004, he leapt at the opportunity. He faced competition from his friend and former boss Livingston, who was also approached by Jan Hall. But James and Darroch quickly clicked, although on the face of it they had little in common.

One was the son of tax accountant, who grew up in Northumberland and married a GP. The other was the son of a billionaire global media mogul, who grew up in New York, London, Sydney and Los Angeles, and married a model. But both were men in a hurry. James valued Darroch's European experience, with international expansion already at the back of his mind. He wanted a right-hand man who could quickly overhaul Sky's finance department to free up resources for the strategic shift he had planned.

Darroch could not join immediately, as Dixons was in the middle of selling off a number of assets, so Sky was forced to wait. Darroch joined on

16 August 2004, little more than a week after Murdoch's disastrous strategy presentation.

"The opportunity at Sky is something I couldn't walk past," he said. "The business is much bigger [than Dixons]."[8]

Almost immediately, however, Darroch walked into another governance row between Sky and its independent shareholders. The share buy-back plan that James had announced alongside his new strategy meant that unless News Corp sold some of its shares back to the company, its stake would increase to 37%. It had no intention of joining in the buy-back, however. Independent investors such as Standard Life complained of Sky's money being used to secure "creeping control" for News Corp.

Under the City's takeover rules, News Corp's stance meant it was obliged to make an offer to buy Sky outright. Murdoch Senior did not want to be forced into such a move, not least because he had his own problems to deal with. John Malone, who had taken a stake in News Corp via the creation of Fox/Liberty Networks in 1999, had shocked his friend and rival by dramatically increasing his shareholding from 9% to 17% overnight.

It represented a serious challenge to Rupert's control of the company he had built, and he was focused on fighting back. A mandatory takeover bid for Sky would be an unacceptable distraction.

Murdoch consolidated his power over News Corp by moving its official headquarters from Australia to the US state of Delaware, where a more elastic corporate governance regime allowed it to set up a "poison pill" to prevent a Malone takeover. Murdoch also sought help from the billionaire Saudi prince Alwaleed bin Talal, who said he would increase his stake to block Malone and that he had "utmost confidence in Mr Murdoch, his management team and his succession planning".[9]

Ultimately, Malone's manoeuvre meant the end of the Sky Global dream. In 2006 Murdoch bought back the Cable Cowboy's News Corp shares with a controlling stake in his US satellite operation DirecTV.

Amid such upheaval, back in 2004 had Sky planned to release News Corp from its obligations to make a takeover offer via a resolution that would be voted on at its shareholder meeting in November. Independent shareholders threatened a revolt, but in the end the resolution was passed by a comfortable margin.

City concerns over "creeping control" were assuaged partly by another boardroom overhaul. Sky appointed two new non-executive directors, so eight out of 15 were now independent of News Corp, and excluded News Corp representatives from the committees scrutinising its accounts and executive pay arrangements. Darroch was awarded a £500,000 starting salary, 28% more than Dixons paid him, plus £1.2m in shares in a three-year incentive scheme.

Worries over James Murdoch's strategy were already beginning to subside as well. Sky added 62,000 new subscribers in the first three months of his plan, compared with City forecasts of 50,000. In the crucial quarter covering the run up to Christmas 2004, Sky blew through a target of 100,000 to add 192,000 new households, roughly the same as in 2003. The longstanding goal of eight million by the end of 2005 once again appeared to be within reach. Existing customers were also responding positively. A marketing push for Sky+, the PVR set-top box that cost an extra £10 per month, which had begun under Ball, was now delivering rapid take-up.

In the background, Sky worked on the overhaul of its pricing structure that Murdoch believed would be crucial if it was to kick on toward 10 million subscribers. In June 2005, it unveiled a new selection of packages that broke up its basic channel package (everything except sport and films) into six 'mixes' based on genres such as 'knowledge' and music. The move actually increased the minimum month spend, but breaking up the cost gave subscribers more control.

In some ways it was a standard marketing approach of the type that Darroch was intimately familiar with from his years at P&G. It sold products that were essentially identical under multiple brands at multiple price points to target different segments and thus create the perception of choice. For the pay-TV industry, however, which had been wedded to bigger and bigger bundles of channels to convince subscribers to accept price rises, it was a revolutionary world-first.

A year after Murdoch's strategy presentation, Sky's subscriber growth had been stabilised and, at 7.8 million households, it still had six months left to hit its immediate target. It passed the milestone on 19 December, with less than two weeks to spare.

The chief executive's mind was on the next big move. Sky had defeated ITV Digital, implemented a radical overhaul of its own business and was ready to take on a new nemesis. Murdoch now wanted to pick a fight with the biggest opponent possible, BT.

4

Every Pepsi Needs a Coke

Despite their massive cultural differences, BT and Sky enjoyed a mutually beneficial relationship. BT was at the heart of the British corporate establishment, still close to its roots as the state telecoms operator and, unfortunately, still known then for its poor levels of service. Regardless of its success, Sky saw itself as the outsider, close to its customers and in conflict with the status quo.

Yet both had a monopoly to defend. Each acted as an agent for the other under a cross-selling deal that dated back to the launch of Sky Digital in 1998. BT sold Sky packages and was a partner with it in Open, an interactive shopping service carried on the new set-top boxes (and, as it turned out, a commercial disaster). Sky also promoted BT telecoms services to its customers.

The deal worked for both sides. They had a mutual enemy in Britain's cable industry, which aimed to take pay-TV customers away from Sky and telecoms customers away from BT. By 2005 the pair were in talks about a deeper relationship that would bundle pay-TV with subscriptions to BT broadband.

"There was a deal where we were going to effectively deepen the cross-selling arrangements," recalls a BT executive. "They were going to cross-sell all of our broadband services, voice services and line services, and we were going to cross-sell satellite. We were doing about 150,000 satellite subscriptions a year at the time, so it was quite decent business."

The consumer market for broadband internet access was taking off and BT also aimed to build on its dominance by creating a pay-TV business of its own. It wanted to secure Sky's collaboration on 'Project Nevis', a television-over-the-internet project that would offer access to households that couldn't or wouldn't install a satellite dish. In return, Sky would supply its sports and film channels, which BT viewed as essential to building a credible pay-TV service.

Sky was privately irked by Project Nevis but talks appeared to be progressing well. Ian Livingston, the high-energy Glaswegian finance director who had recruited Darroch at Dixons, had been promoted to chief executive of BT's vast retail business. Through the summer of 2005, his new deputy, former cable executive Gavin Patterson, who had also been a contemporary of Darroch at P&G, was negotiating the details with Jon Florsheim, Sky's marketing chief.

They agreed terms on a new contract for BT to sell satellite packages. Talks on the parallel contracts under which Sky would sell BT broadband and telephone services were taking more time, but as summer turned into autumn, Florsheim continued to assure his opposite number that there was nothing amiss.

James Murdoch had other ideas, however. After Sky's 2005 annual results announcement, he secretly assembled his strategy team at a hotel in South Kensington and told them of his belief that Sky should get into broadband.

"James had a very clear view that we had to do broadband," recalls a colleague. "He had a sense that broadband and TV had to be sold together."

James Murdoch had also begun thinking in more detail about the future of video distribution over the internet. The BBC was starting to develop what would eventually become the iPlayer catch-up service. Sky, on the other hand, drew much of its power in the market from its satellite distribution system. The internet threatened to curb its power by allowing channel providers to bypass intermediaries such as Sky. The future was unclear, which seemed all the more reason to go after the broadband business and take a degree of control.

"We took an additional view, which was if something like video on demand becomes really important, having access to be able to deliver it actually becomes important as well," says a senior Sky executive. "The customer experience wasn't clear if you were going completely over somebody else's network."

A window of opportunity was opening. The industry regulator Ofcom had become alarmed by BT's growing market dominance. At the end of 2004, it set out new rules that would allow rivals to install their own broadband equipment in BT local exchanges, and then use BT telephone lines – the 'local loop' – to connect to homes at strictly controlled wholesale prices.

The regulator's explicit aim was to deliver competition to reduce prices and reduce prices for consumers. Companies such as Homechoice, which had attempted to challenge BT in the broadband market without their own equipment and regulated prices, had racked up massive losses, but Ofcom planned to intervene and slash costs by 60%.

"We put it on a plate for them," says one former regulator. "We literally said 'here you are, a fat margin'. You just buy it and sell it.

"We had priced local loop unbundling so it was as easy as it could possibly be. As far was we were concerned it was literally a no-brainer. It was designed to bring in two or three or four big players and that is what happened."

Before the change, BT was an exceptionally dominant player. At the end of 2004, there were 6.2 million broadband connections in Britain. BT's retail arm accounted for 25%. Operators who bought BT broadband wholesale and resold it under their own brand took 44% of the market. Cable broadband provided the rest.

Murdoch wanted to be sure, however, that using the BT network was the right move for Sky. He also wanted to consider a takeover of one of the two big cable operators, Telewest, which would have given the company exclusive ownership of a superior broadband network. Sky opened discussions with the Telewest board, with a view to developing what would have been an audacious merger with a FTSE 100 rival. Telewest was also a takeover target for the only other major cable operator, NTL, and Murdoch wondered whether he should block the creation of a stronger rival to Sky's pay-TV business.

The attractive economics of local loop unbundling on the BT network ultimately proved irresistible, however. Sky also worried that competition watchdogs might intervene to stop a takeover of Telewest. The cable operator only covered around five million homes anyway. If Sky wanted to offer broadband to all, or even most, of its pay-TV subscribers, a takeover would prompt an unappealing choice: it would either face a very expensive cable network expansion or have to invest in local loop unbundling as well.

"James knew we probably couldn't do Telewest," recalls a colleague. "But he wanted to make sure we looked at it really hard to make sure we couldn't do it."

"We had serious talks with Telewest, but I think our critique of the cable strategy was that they weren't challengers, they were incumbents," says another.

Telewest was duly snapped up by NTL in early October for $6bn, creating the national cable rival that Sky had long feared. It was clear that the combination of pay-TV and broadband was a growing threat, as well as a major opportunity. In areas where cable was available, it was more popular than satellite, and Murdoch believed the growing popularity of broadband was the reason. Sky surveyed the emerging landscape for other ways to stake its claim. It considered Tiscali, a hastily and messily assembled consumer operator, but while that would bring immediate scale, it would also introduce unacceptably high risks.

A little-known business operator called Easynet was identified as the best option. It had no consumer business, but did have the serious technical expertise that Sky lacked, as well as a nationwide network of fibre-optic cables running alongside canal routes. With its own core network, Sky broadband would be able to rely on BT even less and it would have more control over the quality of its service.

Meanwhile, BT was growing increasingly frustrated. Its talks with Sky over more cross-selling seemed to be going nowhere fast, except in relation to the contract for BT to sell satellite subscriptions, which was ready for approval.

Florsheim, who had been kept in the dark about Murdoch's plans, assured Patterson again that he was negotiating in good faith. Then, a week after the NTL takeover of Telewest was announced, *The Times* ran a two-page article lambasting BT and the state of British broadband. Livingston smelled a rat. Days later, Sky surprised the stock market with a £1bn debt fund-raising for "general corporate purposes".

Suspicion was mounting at BT. Patterson cornered a well-refreshed Allan Leighton, a Sky non-executive director, at a City dinner and was told that Sky was indeed considering a move into broadband. Yet Florsheim again denied it. Unconvinced, Patterson told Ben Verwaayen, BT's genial Dutch chief executive, not to sign the deal with Sky on satellite subscription sales. Verwaayen said it was a matter of trust and pressed ahead. Two days later Sky announced the takeover of Easynet for £211m.

Verwaayen was enraged. Livingston felt he had been personally betrayed by Darroch. Instead of collaborating, Sky had been secretly plotting to attack its broadband business. The surprise takeover of Easynet would poison relations between BT and Sky for the next decade, and would prove to be ground zero for what would become Britain's fiercest corporate rivalry.

"They denied they were buying it," says a BT insider. "They denied there was anything other than basic speculation. They then said there was no deal because they had bought their own broadband provider, so the idea of them selling BT broadband went by the wayside and [so did] the idea of us selling Sky."

"Ian and James really fell out after that," recalls another senior figure close to the situation. "Ian thought James was dishonest. He saw James then as entitled inherited wealth and his father's minion, and saw Jeremy as their lackey."

Murdoch knew he was taking a risk but was surprised by the furious reaction. To him it was just business. He saw BT as slow and greedy, overcharging its customers and providing terrible customer service. Murdoch believed Sky needed to offer broadband both to defend itself against the combination of NTL and Telewest, and to elbow its way into new households on the road to 10 million. Easynet was a public company, so by law Sky's plans had to remain secret from BT, he told Verwaayen.

Murdoch agreed to release BT from its contract to sell satellite subscriptions, but there was no going back. Sky had awoken a sleeping giant, and BT would be an adversary on a scale it had never faced. In 2006, BT reported revenues of almost £20bn and a profit of more than £2bn, and it dwarfed the likes of the BBC and ITV. Sky had less than a quarter of its sales and less than half its profits. Murdoch was nervous about taking on an opponent of a different weight class, but BT represented many of the characteristics he most detested in British business.

"Every Pepsi needs a Coke and vice versa," says a BT source. "They had decided BT was Coke."

As soon as the Easynet takeover was completed, Sky began spending heavily to install its own broadband equipment in BT local exchanges. Easynet had done the work at 232 sites, but there were thousands to go.

Sky executives also debated how to approach the market. Florsheim argued that Sky should make broadband free for its pay-TV subscribers. Murdoch and other senior executives feared that Sky would again face accusations of predatory pricing, as it had in the digital television battle. They were nervous that this time regulators might act.

Weeks before Sky was due to unveil its pricing in the summer of 2006, however, TalkTalk, the telecoms arm of Carphone Warehouse that was controlled by entrepreneur Charles Dunstone, announced that it would launch a 'free' broadband service. Murdoch was convinced to follow suit.

"TalkTalk really laid the ground work for us to be able to drive a truck through this barn door that the local loop unbundling regime had opened for us," says a Sky executive.

Murdoch announced Sky's pricing with an attack on BT.

"A lot of incumbent players have been charging a lot of money for a long time for not a lot," he said.[1]

"It could be uncomfortable for them. We can see huge growth in this market from a revenue perspective and from a customer loyalty perspective. We are a new challenger and we can also grow market share."

Sky hoped that by providing broadband at no charge to its pay-TV customers (they still had to pay line rental) it could make existing customers more loyal and convince newcomers that they were not being ripped off.

"We knew there was no point going in a little bit cheaper than BT," says one executive.

"We had to do something that people took notice of. Because it was only available at that time to Sky TV customers, it was a good way of giving a value. Up to that point we had no real value play. Sky was the premium. With broadband we had a way to give money back to customers. TV started to look less expensive."

In truth, Sky had little idea what it was doing. Running a telecoms infrastructure was fundamentally different to broadcasting, and the customer service demands were much greater. It was the biggest strategic shift the company had made since its foundation, and it showed.

"With broadband we didn't have a clue what we were doing," says a senior executive. "It was seat of the pants; it was proper Sky of old. Literally just no idea. We had four people from Easynet that we had just acquired and we had to figure it out as we went along.

"It turned out much harder than we thought. Customer service was an absolute nightmare. You didn't know what you didn't know. We just thought 'BT are doing it, it can't be that hard'. Over time it was like, 'Jesus!'"

Sky was losing money hand over fist on its broadband offering. Murdoch warned investors that the venture would be a drag on profits until 2010; in the first three years Sky planned to invest £400m. It said it would reach three million subscribers by 2010, but got off to a bumpy start.

The potential prize was worthy of Sky's persistence, however. The entire UK pay-TV market was worth £7bn per year. By attacking the telecoms sector, Sky increased its potential market to £25bn. It persisted and developed a new marketing strategy to promote the benefits of a 'triple-play' bundle of pay-TV, broadband and telephony. The 'see, speak, surf' campaign was unveiled in early 2007 and again the business accelerated. In the second quarter of 2007, it added more than 250,000 broadband subscribers and claimed 40% were poached from either BT or cable.

Murdoch's boldness had also won over the City. Between 2003 and 2006, Sky shares had underperformed the European media sector by 60%. Analysts now lavished Sky with praise as the most impressive converged media and telecoms operator in Europe. Even critics of News Corp's outsized influence over the company were silenced by its new growth spurt. As well as broadband, the bet Murdoch had made on high-definition broadcasting three years earlier was now starting to come through. After little more than a year on air, the service had 292,000 subscribers.

James's rise appeared unstoppable. Lachlan, the assumed successor to Rupert, had unexpectedly quit News Corp in 2005 after clashing with Peter Chernin and Roger Ailes, the head of Fox News. Lachlan felt his father had undermined him by siding against him on key areas of decision-making, and retreated to Australia to found his own business.

With Elisabeth Murdoch also ploughing her own furrow at Shine, the success James was making of Sky put him in the lead to inherit the crown. Yet he was continuing to make more enemies than he may have realised, and many of them were now positioning themselves to confront him.

5

We Are Going to Beat Up Sky

The merger of NTL and Telewest created a single cable operator for the whole UK, but NTL's chairman Jim Mooney had grander ambitions still. As soon as terms were agreed with Telewest in October 2005, he turned his attention to Virgin Mobile, the successful 'virtual' mobile network controlled by Sir Richard Branson. It had no infrastructure of its own, but instead had piggybacked on the T-Mobile network via a wholesale deal.

Virgin Mobile surfed a wave of mass market mobile demand triggered by the creation of cheap pre-pay packages, all with the help of the powerful Virgin brand. By 2005, Virgin Mobile had five million customers and was the country's fifth-largest operator. Mooney wanted to add Virgin Mobile to his empire to create a 'quad play' of pay-TV, broadband, home telephony and mobile. By April 2006, a £962m cash and shares deal was done that would make Branson the biggest shareholder in the combined company.

Mooney was triumphant. The European Commission had ruled that the Premier League could no longer sell its live rights exclusively to Sky. With the Virgin brand plastered across all their services, Mooney and Branson planned to go after Sky's crown.

"We are looking at Premier League football. I think the concept of Virgin Sports is one of the most exciting things we can look forward to. We are going to beat up Sky," he said at the press conference to unveil the Virgin Mobile takeover.

"The Virgin brand will be firmly attached to the door and I hope for decades to come to have personal involvement with the company if I'm asked to help with anything," said Branson.

James Murdoch was unamused. He had passed on the opportunity to buy Telewest in the full knowledge that NTL was likely to swoop and create a stronger cable rival to Sky.

Now the addition of mobile, with the whole operation due to operate under the Virgin Media banner, offered cable a further potential boost. The industry had built up a reputation for poor service; NTL had acquired the nickname NTHell for its approach to customers. A confusing legacy of regional brands had not helped matters either.

Murdoch voiced doubts about the strategic logic of the combination of cable and Virgin Mobile . It sold mostly pre-pay vouchers, not subscriptions, and mobile was typically a personal rather than a household expense.

Nevertheless, in private he was concerned by the strength of the Virgin brand and irritated by the excited reception that Mooney's deal received in the press. Murdoch had spent three years and hundreds of millions of pounds to build up Sky as the industry's number one brand. The suggestion that Branson might threaten that position with his trademark beard and stunts made Murdoch want to vomit.

Yet Branson and Mooney, along with Virgin Media chief executive Steve Burch, wanted more. They hired Malcolm Wall, a veteran ITV franchise executive, to run their in-house programming business. It owned a 50% share of UKTV, a joint venture with the BBC that offered re-runs of popular shows supported by advertising on channels including Dave and Gold. The unit was also 100% owner of the reality channels Bravo and Living. However, it accounted for just 6% of viewing, excluding the main terrestrial channels. Virgin Media's pay-TV subscription business remained highly dependent on its deal with Sky, and Wall had been brought in to redress the balance.

Virgin Media wanted to break into Premier League broadcasting, but it also needed to bulk up its channels business. After the Virgin Mobile deal was completed, Mooney, Burch, Branson and Wall began work on an audacious takeover of ITV, despite the relative financial weakness of the company they had created. NTL had a record-breaking bankruptcy on its CV and the enlarged operation remained saddled with debts of nearly £6bn. Yet the financial markets were buoyant and seemed happy to support such risky deal-making.

A combination with ITV would catapult Virgin Media's share of audience to more than 27% and mean that Murdoch and Sky would be less able to bully it at the negotiating table. Sky could probably live without Bravo and Living, but it would need ITV's channels in order to offer its own customers a complete package.

By then the old ITV franchise system was a memory. After their defeat by Sky in the digital battle, Carlton and Granada had merged in 2003 into create a single national broadcaster and producer. Only Scotland and Northern Ireland retained independent franchises. The merger had brought a degree of strength, but by 2006 ITV was struggling.

The BBC expanded rapidly as digital Freeview took off with new channels and programming that ate into ITV's audience, its advertising business and its share price. Charles Allen, the former Granada boss who had become ITV chief executive, was ousted by the board with no successor lined up. Rudderless and relatively cheap, Britain's biggest commercial broadcaster looked vulnerable to a takeover. Private equity firms, which had raised billions for debt-fuelled buyouts, were starting to circle.

By autumn, Virgin Media (the official rebrand of NTL-Telewest did not take place until February 2007) was ready to make its move. On November 9, it confirmed a report in *The Guardian* that it had "advised ITV of its interest in exploring a possible combination transaction" and had "scheduled an initial conversation with ITV to that end". Branson, who had longstanding designs on media moguldom, immediately threw his weight behind the deal. It was reported that Stephen Carter, a former NTL executive and until recently the leader of the industry regulator, Ofcom, was being lined up to head ITV under Virgin Media.

"So you start looking at it, thinking 'okay, these guys are really getting their act together," recalls a Sky insider. "The whole Branson rebranding wasn't something we were particularly concerned about to begin with but then they put it about that they were going to buy ITV. That made you think 'these guys are serious'. ITV and NTL looked like a serious threat."

James Murdoch was rattled. A combination of Virgin Media and ITV would represent an immediate threat to Sky's dominance of pay-TV. Murdoch had made an enemy of BT, but he knew it was years away from mounting a serious challenge. The Virgin Media problem, on the other hand, was becoming urgent.

Murdoch had also hoped that, one day, Sky might be able to acquire ITV's production business and become a major player in the creation of, as well as the distribution of, entertainment programming. If Virgin Media won control, that opportunity would be foreclosed forever.

Murdoch and Darroch debated how to respond. They knew Sky could not make a rival bid because of its News Corp connection. As part of the Communications Act 2003, the Labour government had introduced new restrictions meant to preserve media plurality. Tony Ball had lobbied hard on News Corp's behalf, but could not prevent a ban on any newspaper owner controlling more than 19.9% of ITV.

The laws ostensibly covered any and all proprietors, but were in reality specifically targeted at Rupert Murdoch. As he controlled News Corp, and since in the eyes of British company law News Corp's stake in Sky gave it control, Sky could not challenge Virgin Media to buy ITV outright.

That did not mean James could not intervene, however. The week after Virgin Media disclosed its interest in ITV, Murdoch and Darroch travelled to the Morgan Stanley Technology, Media and Telecoms conference in Barcelona, an annual showcase where industry executives meet investors for two days of strategising and dealmaking. On the sidelines of the conference, they approached the investment houses Fidelity and Brandes, two of ITV's biggest shareholders, to see if they would be interested in offloading their stakes for a tidy profit.

Holed up in a suite at the five-star Hotel Arts, overlooking the Spanish marina, Murdoch and Darroch, together with Andrew Griffith, the former investment banker who was Sky's head of investor relations, ran the numbers. They realised that they could use the cash and overdraft facilities that Sky already had on hand to do a deal with Fidelity and Brandes within hours. The price of 135p per share, nearly 20p more than the market price, was agreed overnight on Thursday. In the early hours of Friday, the trio slipped away to London by private jet to execute the trade.

At 5.55pm on Friday, Sky announced to the stock market that it had acquired a 17.9% stake in ITV and all hell broke loose. Murdoch had outmanoeuvred Virgin Media to block its takeover plans, and he was having fun. "That has put the cat amongst the pigeons," he remarked as he smoked outside the Sky offices after the announcement.

"It was the two of them, James and Jeremy, winding each other up," says a colleague. "It didn't matter what anyone else thought, it was just sort of done. And when things are done you just have to get behind it.

"Would it have been quite nice to own ITV? Sure. Did we need to do it that day? Not really."

The media lapped it up. The idea of indebted, US-listed Virgin Media buying ITV had been unpopular across the political spectrum anyway, and the high drama of Murdoch's raid made great copy. Sky was galvanised.

"One of the things that was amazing about the ITV stake is what it did to morale," recalls one senior executive.

"People loved it. They loved that we did that. It felt like a winner. We could see what was going to happen and we moved quicker than anyone else and we took it away from them. The organisation lapped it up. That's important sometimes.

"Particularly at that time when we were under pressure from Freeview and we were on the path to 10 million [subscribers]. It was hard. You're going as fast as you possibly can and you have to come up with a new idea every week to keep the train going. It was a period of hard yards. So showing some real ambition was good. Screw 'em."

Branson knew immediately he had indeed been screwed. News of Murdoch's intervention reached his Blackberry as he touched down at Johannesburg airport en route to his daughter's birthday party. On Sunday he mounted a counter-attack in the media, complaining that Sky's move was "reckless and cynical"[1] and branded it "the biggest mistake Sky has made in the history of the company". He threatened complaints to the Office of Fair Trading, to Ofcom and to the European Commission.

"Sky's move is a blatant attempt to distort competition even further by blocking any attempt to create a strong and meaningful competitor," Branson said.

"Sky is positioned to strongly influence ITV's operations in a manner that favors BSkyB's long-term plans rather than the interests of the other 82% of ITV shareholders who weren't offered a sweetheart deal on Friday.

"This move is seriously damaging to the interests of viewers, program makers, artists and shareholders and the time has come for regulators, politicians and consumers to finally show that they're willing to stand up to reckless and cynical attempts to stifle competition and secure creeping control of the British media."[2]

Five days after Sky took its stake, the ITV board had rejected an offer of 122p per share, saying that (in the wake of Sky's 135p deal) it undervalued the broadcaster. It dismissed the proposal as having "little, if any, strategic logic".

Branson and Virgin Media were defeated and furious. The entrepreneur knew that fears of Rupert Murdoch's political power were his best weapon as he lobbied for government intervention to resurrect his ambitions.

"The government are scared stiff of Murdoch," he claimed in an interview as he opened a new Virgin Megastore record shop in Manchester.[3]

"Sky, *The Times* and the *News of the World* and a lot of other organisations are all in favour of a particular party and decide who is likely to win the general election. If you tag ITV to that as well, you have let go of democracy and may as well let Murdoch decide who is going to be Prime Minister."

"I think there comes a time when government needs to draw lines in the sand as Murdoch becomes more involved with British media."

James Murdoch thought Branson's attacks were ridiculous, but he was irritated by the implication that Sky would wield power over ITV's news output. It had undertaken not to seek a seat on the board and could not increase its stake beyond 19.9%. The idea that regulators might interfere in an investment by a private company was anathema to a man who had been brought up to oppose government interference in the family business. Murdoch told an Ofcom conference that regulations always meant a "basic reduction in human freedom".

By this time the BBC was no real threat to Sky's business. In commercial terms it remained an irritant to Murdoch, who saw billions of pounds of taxpayer-funded television as a brake on pay-TV adoption, but he had a cordial relationship with Mark Thompson, its Director-General.

Murdoch was as ideologically opposed to the BBC as he had been as a cadet News Corp executive, and took his opportunities to attack what he viewed as a patrician, wasteful organ of authoritarianism. He delighted in telling Thompson that while he liked the BBC, he just didn't think it had the right to exist. Murdoch bristled at suggestions the government might create a "public service publisher" to match the public service broadcasting regime on the emerging internet.

"The UK's main state broadcaster, the BBC, infamously fantasises about creating a British Google and wants the taxpayer to fund it," he said.[4] "This is not public service, it is megalomania.

"Delusions of grandeur will flourish in the absence of proper accountability."

Murdoch's libertarian views were deeply and genuinely held, to the point they sometimes became a source of frustration for more pragmatic Sky colleagues. To the young chief executive, there was no lower species in British politics than a Tory 'wet', a Conservative ready to compromise with the left on economic policy. That same year Ofcom conducted a pilot for the planned switch-off of analogue television signals, in the Cumbrian town of Whitehaven. Most at Sky viewed the work as a sensible step towards a technological shift that was inevitable.

Murdoch saw it differently. To him it represented an unacceptable threat to Sky's business, as it would accelerate the adoption of Freeview, and a basic reduction in human freedom. He insisted on a leaflet campaign that warned the residents of Whitehaven that an authoritarian Government planned to take away their right to watch television.

"I think what James did particularly with regard to the BBC and Ofcom was to add an ideological spin to Sky that I think was heartfelt and probably what he had been brought up with at the Murdoch breakfast table," says a colleague.

"Some of it was also partly tongue in cheek because he liked stirring things up. By the time we did ITV, he was confident and ready to play the pantomime villain sometimes."

"He revels in playing the outsider," says another Sky executive. "It was a case of 'you don't have to like me, but you will listen to me'. In a sense he is an idealist. That's why it can be inspiring. His political views are very deeply held."

"He was trying to relive the nineties, the start-up years, at a time when he had recognised the company culture and strategy had to change," recalls a third insider.

"Virtually everything else about the company James recognised had to change, but he didn't want to lose that aggressive 'us against the world' attitude of taking on the establishment."

Murdoch himself said[5] of Sky's headquarters on the edge of the capital: "I like it out here. You read about Sky being in a bunch of mud huts out in Osterley – that's what they think in Soho – but we like having all our operations in one place.

"It's better to be a bit separate and it allows us to forge a challenger culture which we nourish. At our worst, we slow down and start to think we're established. That's when we are vulnerable."

The new chief executive of Ofcom provided the opponent, as it started to scrutinise Sky's raid on ITV. Ed Richards was the embodiment of the system that Murdoch saw as his enemy. A grammar school boy from Portsmouth, Richards had worked his way up via the London School of Economics to lead strategy at the BBC. He became media policy adviser to Tony Blair and had been the architect of the Communications Act that had clipped News Corp's wings. Now, Richards was sympathetic to Branson's complaints.

Richards had always worried about the power of Rupert Murdoch. He had witnessed it at close quarters as part of the Blair government, when News Corp executives sometimes seemed able almost to dictate policy to ministers. Within days of Sky's move on ITV, he launched a Whitehall campaign for investigation of its impact on media plurality. Richards had designed the Communications Act with new powers for regulators to intervene to protect the public interest in media plurality, and now he wanted to be the first to use them.

In February 2007, the trade secretary, Alistair Darling, ordered investigations by Ofcom and the Office of Fair Trading (OFT), under pressure from Labour backbenchers and trade unions. Sky raged that it was "inconceivable" that it would seek to influence ITV's news coverage and said it had "fundamentally increased choice for viewers". Yet two months later both regulators found against Sky.

Richards' officials at Ofcom said media plurality would be harmed by the Sky stake in ITV. The OFT warned that Sky's power would increase in the markets for sports rights, advertising, pay-TV and television generally. Darling was obliged to order a full investigation by the Competition Commission, a mightier regulator with powers to force Sky to sell its shares. In January 2008, it duly ordered Sky to offload most of the stake. It was required to hold less than 7.5% of ITV.

"Our only argument was that the law says we are allowed to do it. Therefore we've done it. Now that's fine but nobody is going to get very motivated by it," says a former Sky lobbyist.

Sky battled the decision through for two years but lost in the Court of Appeal in 2010. For a company that had become highly adept at arguing, fighting and filibustering its way to victory, it marked a first major defeat at the hands of regulators. It was also hugely costly. When Murdoch bought the ITV stake, he believed the company was undervalued. Weak management and an aimless strategy had left the broadcaster in a slump that Sky believed could be easily reversed with cost-cutting and a focus on production.

It had not counted on the collapse of the advertising market in the wake of the 2008 financial crisis. By the time Sky complied with the courts and sold 10.4% of ITV, the shares had plummeted to less than 50p. The sale raised less than £200m and crystallised a loss of £350m.

"With hindsight it's not so much we miscalculated as the regulators were fucking wrong," says a Sky executive.

"We didn't think they would say something which isn't really true, which is that someone who has got 18% of a public company and no seats on the board was actually going to be dictating the running order of *News at Ten*."

There was one small bright spot: Sky had succeeded in preventing a Virgin Media takeover of ITV. The cable operator's own financial troubles meant that any ambition to become a programming power in its own right was never realised. It never bid for Premier League rights and in 2009 was forced to raise cash by selling Bravo and Living to the only credible buyer, Sky.

Today Sky executives brand the battle over ITV a "complete sideshow" and suggest that it set back attempts to establish an identity independent of News Corp

"It was very noisy but it was very unhelpful in reinforcing the idea that Sky was a disruptive, parasitical sort of company," says one.

"It was a bit of a distraction. Did it help our reputation corporately? Probably not."

In the process, James Murdoch acquired a dangerous new opponent in Ed Richards, who, in time, would prove more difficult for Sky, and for Murdoch, to vanquish.

6

Throw Rocks at Our House and We'll Napalm Your Village

Branson's attempted takeover of ITV may have failed, but Sky was not yet finished with Virgin Media. Sky's early fight for survival had confirmed a 'kill or be killed' mentality that persisted even as it became the biggest beast in the jungle. It was always more aggressive than any company in British broadcasting, with an attitude that was described by insiders and rivals alike as "throw rocks at our house and we'll napalm your village". Virgin Media had thrown too many rocks.

The cable operator's deal to carry Sky's 'basic' package of channels – including Sky One, Sky News and Sky Sports News – was up for renegotiation in early 2007.

Murdoch had invested heavily in Sky One. Budgets for both original commissions and programme acquisitions were sharply increased, from £155m in 2004 to £200m. Sky poached the hit sci-fi mystery series *Lost* from Channel 4 and produced a lavish Terry Pratchett adaptation, *Hogfather*, for Christmas 2006. It was part of the plan to broaden the appeal of a Sky satellite package beyond films and sport, particularly as it was due to lose exclusivity over the Premier League, but it also demanded higher fees from Virgin Media in return for its investment.

"It was all about growing the pay-TV market versus Freeview," says a Sky executive. "They should have understood that but they never did. What we asked Virgin to pay was only proportionate to the investment we were making."

Frustrated by his defeat over ITV, Steve Burch, Virgin Media's chief executive, was in no mood to bow to Sky's demands, which at nearly £50m a year, were double what he had been paying under the old contract. At midnight on 1 March, Murdoch pulled the plug and 3.3 million cable households were cut off from the basic package of Sky channels.

Burch, a Vietnam War veteran, retaliated by replacing the channel names in Virgin Media's screen menus with insults. Sky News was labelled 'Sky Snooze' and viewers were told that Sky was "picking up their ball and going home". Burch declined to cut prices for subscribers and instead pledged to reinvest the money saved in alternative programming.

It was a risky strategy but Virgin Media felt it had little choice. Sky was both its dominant competitor and dominant supplier, and had crushed its hopes of buying ITV. Burch wanted to take a stand against an organisation he could only bring himself to call "the dish company". Virgin Media was already financially stretched, however, and could scarcely afford to lose many customers.

Virgin Media launched a public relations offensive. In a war of financial attrition, it would have no hope against Sky; if it could cast its rival as an oppressive, Murdoch-controlled monopoly, however, then it might be able to force a deal. Branson was deployed to accuse Sky of "acting like bully-boys".

Sky had to respond, but it was short of sympathetic voices to make its case to the public. James Murdoch carried too much political baggage by dint of his family name; Mike Darcey, promoted to chief operating officer, was Australian, and often seen as cold. The task of arguing Sky's case fell to Jeremy Darroch, who for the first time became the company's public face and excelled at it. His down-to-earth style was a perfect foil to the American hyperbole of Burch.

"He sounds very reasonable and what that probably did was cement him as a future CEO, as people saw him in a different way," recalls a Sky insider.

"If you take away some important channels and don't give your customers a discount, they think they are being ripped off."

Soon it became clear that, while the dispute hurt both sides financially, Virgin Media was suffering the most pain. Research by the investment bank UBS found that 45% of cable households would dump their contract if they could and that 10% planned to abandon Virgin Media as a direct result of losing the basic Sky channels. In the first full quarter following the blackout, Virgin media lost 70,000 customers.

Damaged by his miscalculation, Burch was forced to quit after a turbulent 19 months in charge. By the end, the private equity giant Carlyle Group was plotting an opportunistic buyout of Virgin Media that was only halted by the credit crunch that heralded the start of the financial crisis.

Sky was again victorious. The dispute went to court and was eventually resolved amicably more than a year later. Nevertheless, some inside Sky thought Murdoch's roughhouse tactics, delivered by public relations chief Matthew Anderson, were not smart.

"It became very public and nasty," says one executive. "We came out looking really bad. If you look how much we get paid for those channels now, James was absolutely right. But was there a way to deal with it where we didn't come out publicly like that. Our reputation took a kicking. I think people underestimated how badly we would come out of it."

Ed Richards watched from the sidelines as Murdoch beat up Virgin Media once again. He was increasingly convinced that Sky was abusing its dominance in the pay-TV market.

Evidence was mounting. To Ofcom eyes, the raid on ITV and a rumbling row with BT over wholesale supply of the Sky Sports channels to its new broadband-based pay-TV service, BT Vision, were concerning. The recent blackout of Sky channels on Virgin Media confirmed Richards' impression that Sky was too mighty and needed to be brought under control.

A confrontation was inevitable. Murdoch remained implacably opposed to any regulatory intervention in Sky's affairs. He believed in competition and the free market as the best way to ensure consumer choice, and that the history of Sky proved him right. Murdoch told Ofcom officials that they should get out of the way, operate on the assumption that they should not become involved in commercial matters, and exercise "deliberation, discipline and restraint" generally. He dreamt of a day when Ofcom might shut up shop and let market forces take care of the consumer interest.

Murdoch had few allies in the sector, however; unfortunately, there were plenty of enemies.

By the beginning of 2007, BT and Virgin Media both believed they had been wronged by Sky. BT was still angry about Sky's stealthy move into broadband and had been unable to do a deal to bring the Sky Sports channels to BT Vision. Virgin Media was bruised by its defeat in the ITV battle and felt under pressure in talks over the basic Sky channels. The cable operator carried Sky Sports, but believed it was over-charged to give satellite packages an advantage.

There were new opponents too. Setanta, the Irish challenger in Premier League broadcasting headed by former Sky Sports executive Trevor East, was also unhappy. It was due to pay £131m per season to play second fiddle to Sky Sports, with 46 live matches versus 92. Setanta was competing with Sky to buy sports rights, but also reliant on its rival for distribution to the majority of pay-TV households.

The final member of what became known as 'the Gang of Four' enemies of Sky was Top Up TV, a small pay-TV operator founded by David Chance, the former deputy to Sam Chisholm, and Ian West, the man cut loose by Tony Ball for running out of set-top boxes.

Top Up TV allowed Freeview households to receive a selection of pay channels via a standard digital terrestrial aerial. Along with Setanta, a close partner that aimed to offer live sport at relatively low cost to Freeview households, it worried that Sky was plotting to launch a directly competing service. It planned to repurpose its slots on the Freeview platform, hitherto occupied by the free services of Sky News, Sky Three and Sky Sports News, as pay-TV channels channels for Sky Sports.

The Gang of Four knew they had a common foe and were advised by an expert in Sky's regulatory soft spots. Michael Rhodes, Sky's former head of regulatory affairs, had clashed with James Murdoch and left abruptly in 2005 , after it was discovered he was in talks to join Top-Up TV. Nicknamed the Grim Reaper for his 6ft 4in frame and imposing manner, Rhodes had angered his former colleagues by advising Setanta on its bidding strategy in the Premier League auction. As regulatory adviser to the Gang of Four, he would mount a direct attack on the heart of Sky's business.

"This guy was the best," recalls an industry figure. "He had given his life to Sky. He flipped cases for them. But there was a massive showdown with James and he left."

In January 2007, the Gang of Four sent a joint complaint to Ofcom demanding an investigation of the pay-TV market. They alleged that Sky was abusing its dominance of the market it had pioneered, and called on Richards to intervene. They wanted Sky to be forced to supply Sky Sports and Sky Movies to rival operators. It owned the television contract for new films with all the major Hollywood studios.

Richards needed little convincing that an investigation was warranted. Weeks later, and with the Virgin Media blackout as a topical hook, Ofcom announced a full investigation of the pay-TV market and sent Sky's shares tumbling.

"We reached a point when they put a lot of effort into it, they brought the case and we had to respond to it," says an Ofcom insider. "I think Sky thought we should have just said we weren't interested. But there was a case to be examined, no question. The responsible thing to do was examine it."

Murdoch was furious. Sky was now fighting Ofcom over both its investment in ITV and its dominance of the pay-TV market. Next, Richards delayed the review of Sky's digital terrestrial plans.

Murdoch was in a war with Ofcom on three fronts, and the relationship between Sky and its regulator hit a new low. Meetings became increasingly testy as Sky executives sought to defend the company by going on the offensive. It mounted a speculative complaint that the Virgin Media cable network was not open to competition.

Mike Darcey claimed publicly that Ofcom had been "duped into playing along" with "a gang of four united by their aversion to competition",[1] comments that reflected Murdoch's own views. To the chief executive, the Gang of Four were seeking to manipulate the regulator because they were being out-competed. He flatly rejected the idea that Sky's dominance might harm consumers with higher prices. Ofcom did not back down, though it viewed Murdoch's approach as uniquely aggressive in the industry.

"It was straight regulatory stuff," says a senior Ofcom executive of the time. "When companies become very successful, they quite often become dominant and then there are questions, [but] there is no presumption about whether that dominance is being abused.

"One off the difficult things with Sky is that they couldn't possibly believe it. They feigned to find it extraordinary. 'How could it possibly be?' The fact was they were very clearly dominant in premium sports and premium movies. We had to demonstrate that with a proper rigorous economic analysis, but that's what we did."

Both sides believed the other was making political decisions, however. A Sky executive calls: "Our relations with Ofcom were awful. Nobody was speaking to anybody.

"Ed was taking pride in having pissed Sky off. The trouble with Ed was he was never able to leave politics behind. He saw it all as a political fight. There was shouting and confrontation. I imagine that James would have relished it and Ed hated it, because he not a confrontational individual."

In fact, Ofcom's pay-TV market investigation was the start of a long and costly legal battle. Eventually, in 2010, it imposed a 'must offer' obligation that required Sky to offer Sky Sports to rivals at a lower wholesale price. Sky fought every step, all the way to the Supreme Court, at one stage chalking up an embarrassing defeat of Ofcom at the High Court, only for the decision to be overturned later in favour of the regulator on appeal.

Over subsequent years, the Gang of Four was gradually whittled down to one; Setanta quickly went bust, Virgin Media came under conciliatory new ownership, and Top Up TV eventually gave up the fight. But tensions between Sky and BT, the biggest and most dangerous of the group, would only escalate.

Sky's business continued to thrive as Ofcom increased the pressure. Broadband had a difficult start, but Sky soon honed its pricing under Steven Van Rooyen, a former News Corp executive poached from Virgin Media, and began to make a meaningful contribution to finances. Within a year of launch, 70% of subscribers were choosing to pay for a better service rather than take the basic free package.

In the meantime, other products sustained Sky's momentum. In summer of 2007, Murdoch decided to drop the monthly charge for Sky+, in a bid to accelerate the adoption of high-definition services. It would mean another round of investment in millions of new set-top boxes, but Sky's analysis showed households with the PVR service were more satisfied and more loyal.

Murdoch again had an eye on the future. Sky+ HD set-top boxes contained a hard drive. The BT broadband infrastructure was not yet capable of delivering reliable streaming at large scale, but with millions of hard drives in homes, Sky could steal a march by downloading programmes for viewing on demand. The technology offered more of the freedom that Murdoch craved. On the traditional broadcast channel menu, Sky was obliged to give the BBC, ITV and Channel 4 top billing. In the emerging world of on-demand programming, there was no such restriction. Sky could one day prioritise its own programming or strike deals with third parties to promote their material to viewers, beyond the reach of Ofcom.

The free Sky+ offer was an instant hit, and attracted 323,000 households in the first three months, and Sky's overall subscriber base was now close to

8.7 million. Overall product sales hit a new record of 1.2 million, almost double the prior year, as Murdoch's plan to broaden the business accelerated. It would be his last update as chief executive.

Finally, News Corp was empire building again. Rupert Murdoch, 76, had triumphed in a long pursuit of Dow Jones, the owner of *The Wall Street Journal*. The $5bn deal secured control of one of America's great newspapers, and Rupert wanted to bring in his trusted newsroom lieutenants to deliver an overhaul of the stuffy title. Robert Thomson, editor of *The Times*, would become editor of *The Wall Street Journal*, and Les Hinton, chief executive of News International, would take charge of Dow Jones.

The shake-up meant an opportunity for James, too. Rupert was impressed by his stewardship of Sky and created a new role for him at News Corp as chairman and chief executive for Europe and Asia. It was a mini-empire of his own, in charge of Star TV, *The Sun*, *The Times*, *The News of the World* and Sky Italia. James would remain based in London, where his growing family were settled, but travel to New York to attend the main News Corp board meetings.

There, Murdoch Senior was looking towards the future. Peter Chernin, his chief operating officer at News Corp, was becoming a problem. Like Sam Chisholm and Tony Ball, he had begun to overshadow the mogul, and investors were concerned about what would happen when Chernin's contract expired in 2009. Rupert Murdoch aimed to bring his son closer to the centre of the business to show the family was still in charge, and to show Wall Street that News Corp had a strong executive ready to succeed Chernin.

It was an offer James could not refuse, but he was not ready to leave Sky behind. Despite the mounting regulatory challenges, his four years in charge had been a great success and he had formed a strong partnership with Darroch. The Sky board were disappointed to learn he planned to step down as chief executive, but immediately agreed to a plan in which James would succeed Rupert as chairman, and Darroch would become chief executive.

The handover was announced to the stock market on 7 December 2007. *The Times* reported that the move "clearly positions the 34-year-old [James] as the most likely successor to his father, Rupert Murdoch, as chairman and chief executive of News Corp".

Corporate governance campaigners grumbled that it was bad form for a chief executive to become chairman, but such was the turnaround in the City's view of Murdoch that most investors were happy that he would remain on board. When the shareholder vote came around, just 6% opposed his appointment as chairman.

Inside the company it meant there was no change in strategy, with Murdoch remaining closely involved, but Darroch brought a new style of leadership to the operation.

"James has a confidence and impetuousness," says a colleague. "He will chew stuff out in the room and then be like 'okay, decision made, let's do it'. Jeremy would not be that, it would be 'I've heard your views, let me take it back'.

"There is a non-confrontational aspect to Jeremy, in a good way. James was not aggressive to us but he would, some would say, fuck you if you asked him a silly question. Jeremy would never do that. He's more buttoned up. James is more heart on his sleeve."

While James Murdoch was most engaged by bold strategy, Darroch brought a gift for analysis of Sky's day-to-day operations to the chief executive's office.

"You can put a series of spreadsheets in front of Jeremy and it is astonishing," says a Sky insider. "I have never seen it before. He can look at a spreadsheet that finance have been poring over for weeks and weeks and weeks. He will look at that spreadsheet and he'll immediately, literally within seconds, go 'why is that number there, what's happening with that number?'"

"He picks up the pattern immediately. And he's always right. Always. Graphs, numbers, spreadsheets or the trends, it is incredible. He's absolutely a data analyst."

Darroch also made it clear early on that decision-making within Sky would be decentralised.

"James is a super-brain who thinks about every bit of the strategy and is quite comfortable making every decision if he has to," says a colleague. "He wouldn't have felt incapable because he is not close enough to things. I cannot imagine James saying that. It would probably also make quite a good decision most of the time and while other people were thinking he would have been five steps ahead of them.

"Sky was smaller and it was possible to run the company like that. He was just so fast it was hard for everyone to keep up. And he had strong views on a lot of stuff. He is a visionary, no question.

"Jeremy's style is quite different. He has done an amazing job of turning the business round from one that looked up for direction quite often to one where people go 'no, I am going to decide'. I think that was necessary as Sky was getting bigger but it did take a little bit of time for people to adjust to."

With hindsight the timing was perfect. Sky had made a series of big bets and was shifting emphasis to executing on Murdoch's plans just as the global economy threatened to go into meltdown. At the same time, Darroch was a reassuring presence for investors as share prices tumbled. From a high of nearly £8 per star in summer 2007, Sky slid with the market to less than £3.80 as the financial crisis unfolded over the next year.

7

The Rise of the Bike

Almost as soon as Jeremy Darroch got the top job, he set about what would become a never-ending quest: he wanted people to like Sky.

Ever the numbers man, survey data showed that Sky was not widely liked, and Darroch resented it. The customers appreciated and valued its services, but non-customers did not see the company as a good corporate citizen. Many politicians and journalists felt the same. "They thought we were aggressive, self-interested and not very nice," recalls one executive who studied the feedback.

People respected Sky and its success, but still viewed it as a somehow foreign and parasitical force, rather than an asset to the country. Rupert Murdoch's political baggage was partly to blame, and there was nothing Darroch could do about that.

However, by the time he took the reins at the end of 2007 Sky employed more than 14,000 people, contributed hundreds of millions of pounds in tax to fund public services and was beginning to invest more in homegrown programming. Darroch thought it deserved to be liked and that there were good business reasons for a charm offensive. Regulatory threats were mounting and a few more friends might help.

Sky Sports seemed a good place to start. It was the foundation stone of the business and had transformed football by funnelling pay-TV cash into clubs, turning the national sport into a slick product fit for global export. Sky Sports was at the root of how Sky itself was perceived: successful, aggressive and with seemingly little regard for its impact on culture or wider society.

Alongside lieutenants including Graham McWilliam, his new corporate affairs chief, who had previously worked in the Sky strategy department under Murdoch, Darroch decided that Sky Sports needed to demonstrate its commitment to the grassroots of sport. If the public could see that Sky cared about more than the millionaires it had created in the Premier League, perhaps perceptions would begin to shift.

Sky needed to find a sport where it could make an impact and increase participation. It commissioned research into smaller sports in which the public wanted to be more involved but felt let down by lack of facilities or coaching. Top of the list was swimming, which Sky quickly rejected; it was hardly likely to start paying for more municipal pools.

An advertising agency made a suggestion to Robert Tansey, Sky's brand marketing chief, that it should sponsor British basketball. London was due to host the next Olympics in 2012 and Sky had already decided it would not pay the pricey International Olympic Commission (IOC) fees to be an official partner. If it sponsored a minor sport such as basketball for the next few years, it could perhaps join the party through the back door.

The pitch was rejected, in part because it was forecast, correctly as it turned out, that the British basketball team had no prospect of medal success. However, the idea helped to narrow Sky's focus on sports that might bring reflected Olympic glory.

Darroch was also interested in the use of sports coaching ideas in corporate leadership, and vice versa, which was becoming increasingly fashionable. He found common ground with Arsene Wenger, the studious manager of Arsenal Football Club known as 'Le Professor'. It was Wenger who suggested that Sky should talk to Dave Brailsford, the then little-known coach of British Cycling.

Tansey was dispatched to the British cycling team's training camp in South Wales in the run up to the 2008 Beijing Olympics. He excitedly reported back that "the whole culture is similar, they sound like business people". To Sky ears, Brailford's 'marginal gains' theory of sporting success sounded much like their own 'believe in better' mantra, adopted months earlier.

It appealed to Darroch that British Cycling claimed a relentless focus on even the tiniest potential improvement to beat the competition, with riders even travelling with their own pillows to improve sleep. He is not particularly interested in cycling, however; friends say that, to this day, Darroch does not own a bike.

Sky Sports, a quasi-independent organisation within Sky with a culture of its own, had little time either for cycling or for Brailsford and his marginal gains. Brailsford and British Cycling chief executive Ian Drake travelled to Sky headquarters to meet Darroch and Vic Wakeling, the managing director of Sky Sports and architect of its success over 25 years. Wakeling was not interested in Brailsford's academic approach.

"He was about as old school as you get and the only sport he was interested in was football," says a colleague. "He thought cycling was some sort of namby-pamby thing and he had no interest in it. Sky Sports just thought cycling was not a proper sport. It was decided to make the sponsorship a Sky thing rather than Sky Sports."

The goals of the project became broader. In late July 2008, Sky did a quick five-year sponsorship deal with British Cycling before the team flew to Beijing. The IOC's strict rules meant Sky branding could not appear at the games, but Darroch bet that the team's performance would draw attention afterwards and in the run up to the London games.

And so it proved. A month later Brailsford returned triumphant, with eight gold medals and a clutch of newly-minted celebrity sportsmen and women including Chris Hoy, Victoria Pendleton and Bradley Wiggins. But Brailsford wanted more. By the start of 2009, Sky and the star coach were deep in discussions to form a professional road racing team and go after the biggest prize in the world of cycling, the Tour de France. Participation in cycling was now on the rise, as Sky had hoped, and it became clear that a more ambitious partnership could put the Sky brand at the centre of a renaissance in the sport.

Team Sky was going to cost. It would not be a mere sponsorship, but a subsidiary of Sky costing about £30m a year to run. Darroch was keen, but not so much as to want to carry the full cost. Other corporate partners would be needed to share the burden. Yet Sky was determined to keep other brands off the Team Sky shirt as much as possible. There was an obvious solution. Sky Deutschland and Sky Italia, which shared the logo, and News Corp as a shareholder, were asked to chip in.

"They had no money and no interest," says one executive involved in the discussions.

It appeared, for a time, that Team Sky might be stuck on the starting line. Without the support of Sky Deutschland and Sky Italia, the costs were simply unsustainable. Unlike football clubs, cycling teams could not count on income from broadcasting rights.

Team Sky was saved by James Murdoch. As Sky chairman he had paid little attention to the sponsorship of British Cycling, and track racing simply did not interest him. But when Darroch told him that Sky Deutschland and Sky Italia had declined to collaborate on the road, James "thought they were nuts".

"We didn't realise James was actually a massive cycling geek," recalls one Sky executive. "Lo and behold, the purse strings at Deutschland and Italia were opened. Sky Italia ponied up their share. News Corp put in for Sky Deutschland because they were listed and had independent shareholders. James basically forced those guys to cough up several million."

Funding was secured. Sky put up 60% of the cash, with the rest of the burden shared by its German and Italian sister companies.

After a tricky first two years in which a steep learning curve was made more difficult by injuries, Team Sky started winning. In 2012, Bradley Wiggins became the first British cyclist to triumph in the Tour de France, quickly followed by another gilded Olympics for British Cycling during the London games. Darroch formed a strong bond with Brailsford and sought to introduce more of his brand of coaching to the management of Sky.

"Dave reads the *Harvard Business Review* for fun," says a colleague. "We integrated Team Sky into our leadership development programmes.

"Dave would come and talk to the team. We used the Team Sky nutritionist to come and talk about how performance can be affected by what you eat. Dave was really into that in a way most sports people aren't."

Colleagues remember that Darroch began talking like a sports coach as his 'bromance' with Brailsford developed. They gave a joint interview to the *Financial Times* in which they lavished each other with praise.[1] On the day in 2014 when Sky agreed twin takeover bids for Sky Deutschland and Sky Italia, he raised eyebrows with an email to executives who were due to unveil the deal to investors and staff.

"First of all I want you to back yourselves," Darroch wrote. "You are all at the top of your game. Trust your judgement and your instinct. You'll do a great job today, I have no doubt of that.

"Second, we're a team. So let's stay together. Today is just the start, the chance for us to put our best foot forward. But it doesn't end here; this is just the first step in our next chapter.

"Finally I just wanted to say that I couldn't think of a better group of people to be part of today. Enjoy the ride. Let's go."

By contrast, James Murdoch was not interested in whether Team Sky had anything to teach Sky. He was a fan and a patron. In his discussions with Brailsford and other members of Team Sky management he would ask detailed questions about pedal suppliers, bike set-ups and whether the race mechanic could set up his own carbon-fibre Pinarello. During the Tour de France, Murdoch would be in daily contact with Brailsford by text to talk tactics.

As Team Sky was drawn into more scandal in recent years, Murdoch's support proved vital to its the survival. In 2017, a damning report by MPs in the UK found that Team Sky, and Bradley Wiggins, had used performance-enhancing drugs under the guise of treatment for a legitimate medical condition as part of the Tour de France win in 2012.[2]

The allegations were especially damaging for Team Sky, after Brailsford had for years courted the media with claims that he and the team were "winning clean". The sports pages of British newspapers wondered aloud if it signalled the death knell for the venture.

That same week in March, Murdoch was making his first public appearance in Britain for several years, having exiled himself in the wake of the phone hacking scandal. He backed Brailsford, saying "we're looking forward to a great season and the team looks really strong".

Doping allegations have continued to pile up against Team Sky, which the team, and Wiggins, continue to deny. Darroch, however, always remained loyal to the team. According to insiders, that was partly because he believed his friend Brailsford's denials, and partly because Sky did not believe that it was being damaged by association. Despite its heavy investment, research showed there were few links in the public mind between Sky and Team Sky. Given the original goals of the project, under normal circumstances that would probably be seen as a failure, but many inside Sky were relieved.

"People imagine Sky was more worried than it had been," says one executive.

"People just didn't seem to associate the two things. Team Sky was almost its own brand. There was little read-across."

Doubts emerged, too, about the usefulness of Brailsford's methods in a large business, which further eroded some of the links between Sky and Team Sky. Brailsford's total focus on winning was viewed as too simplistic for a complex organisation with long-term concerns such as Sky.

"At Sky you often don't do things that maximise short-term profit," says a Sky insider. "Team Sky doesn't really get that mentality at all. They want a set of rules and then to do everything you can within them to win. When you say to them 'maybe we shouldn't do this because it wouldn't look good', they just don't compute it. They don't understand why you would not do something that is allowed under the rules."

Soon after Sky's fate was sealed, Team Sky – a venture that had always been closely associated with James Murdoch – became surplus to requirements. A new era beckoned for the team, still battling doping allegations, and for Sky.

A new owner was quickly found in the shape of the petrochemicals giant Ineos, controlled by the billionaire Sir Jim Ratcliffe.

8

The Guarantor of Independence Is Profit

The Wapping base of News International, the newspaper business on which Rupert Murdoch built a global media empire, was in some ways a template for Sky's Osterley campus. It too was off the beaten track, not much to look at and a perfect place from which to challenge the British establishment. Sky had a siege mentality, which was somewhat ironic given that News International had once literally been under siege in Wapping, when Rupert took on and eventually broke the Fleet Street print unions in 1986.

James Murdoch should have felt right at home when he arrived at the end of 2007, as newly-crowned chairman and chief executive of all of News Corp across Europe, Asia and the Middle East. In truth, he was a long way outside his comfort zone. Still just turning 35, he had spent almost all of his professional life in pay-TV. He was steeped in a culture of growth, sophisticated marketing and subscriber metrics, big money contracts and investments in technology. In Wapping, he found an atmosphere that was little changed from the 1980s. To James's eyes, the newspaper business was shrinking, sexist, technologically primitive and resistant to change.

'I don't think he really understood what he was walking into," says a Sky colleague. "When he got there he understood that there was just no capability there whatsoever; he then tried to get some Sky people to go with him. The contrast with Sky in the ability to actually come up with something and then just do it was massive."

Murdoch was not particularly interested in newspapers, which, in itself, might not have mattered. His father remained deeply engaged in both British politics and the newspaper business, especially *The Sun*, where his favourite editor Rebekah Wade was already marked for promotion.

The plan was that, after a year or so, once she had completed a part-time course in business management at the London School of Economics, Wade would become chief executive of News International. In the meantime, James could keep the commercial side of the newspaper business ticking over and his father would maintain authority over the newsrooms. Although she was officially under James's management, Wade reported directly to Rupert, and that was how it was going to stay.

"James let that happen," says a News International colleague. "It was easier to let it happen, because of all the other characters involved. And because he wanted to be nice to Rebekah."

"James decided, 'newspapers are not my bag, dad's running that'. The degree to which Rupert was involved was astonishing."

James Murdoch's decision to look the other way in those early months at News Corp would ultimately prove to be a disastrous error, but there were, to him, more interesting matters to attend to than newsroom culture. His top priority was a major overhaul of News Corp's disparate collection of assets across Europe and Asia, which dwarfed the British newspaper business.

The financial crisis was under way, and investors wanted to see the company sharpen up to face the downturn. Its European business was a mess of free-to-air television channels in Bulgaria, Romania and Serbia, and a billboard provider in Russia. Further east, Star was struggling to capitalise on its vast opportunities in mainland China, and in India. There was plenty for James to tackle across his new domain without getting into a turf war over a few struggling newspapers in Britain.

At first, however, his mind was still on Sky. The idea of an intercontinental satellite broadcaster had fallen by the wayside when DirecTV was handed over to John Malone, but the pan-European dream itself had never died. Within a month of his return to News Corp, and in consultation with Sky executives, Murdoch acquired a 14.6% stake in the German pay-TV operator Premiere from the private equity firm Apollo for £214m.

This was the same business on which Sky had lost £1bn in its calamitous dotcom-era deal with Leo Kirch, now available at less than a quarter of the price. It had made little progress in building a German pay-TV market, lost control of top-flight football rights and was creaking under the heavy burden of its debts. Yet as dominant shareholder in Sky and whole owner of Sky Italia, News Corp saw an opportunity to stake a new claim in Europe's biggest economy.

Premiere was soon rebranded as Sky Deutschland. Murdoch sent Brian Sullivan, a trusted friend who ran Sky's crucial customer relationships, as chief executive, with a remit to deliver a radical overhaul. Premiere had mortgaged everything except the furniture to stay afloat, and Sullivan faced a tough task to bring it up to speed with Sky and Sky Italia.

With his customary speed, Murdoch also set about reshaping other News Corp outposts. He sold off the company's stake in the Polish broadcaster, Puls. In the summer of 2008, he hired Lehman Brothers to explore a sale of television stations in Latvia, Serbia and Bulgaria. Within a matter of weeks, that work came to an abrupt halt when the investment bank collapsed in September, but Murdoch shifted focus and worked on splitting Star into separate Indian and Chinese businesses.

Meanwhile, Sky sought to establish an image of itself that was more independent of News Corp and the Murdoch family.

From the start of his reign, Darroch aimed to buff away the ideological edge that James had given the company. Ofcom was still a problem, but any new approach would be more pragmatic. Darroch analysed risks and took time over decisions that to colleagues sometimes seemed trivial. He demanded more than a dozen drafts of a presentation, only to end up deciding that the first version was the best. Darroch studiously avoided making political remarks and did not suggest that regulation should be scrapped, although he certainly believed there was too much of it.

"James had done a lot of changing things internally, but had almost exacerbated things externally," says an insider. "Jeremy believed quite strongly that wasn't the right thing to do. It wasn't his personality either. We started trying to change that without creating tension with James and News Corp."

Yet James Murdoch was still chairman of Sky and remained close to his former colleagues, who were largely implementing the strategy he had set in a culture he had played a central role in creating. After little over a year of rapid-fire dealmaking across Europe and Asia, James saw an opportunity to bring more of Sky's approach to the newspaper business.

His father had become increasingly suspicious that giving readers free access to his newspapers' online editions served only the interests of Google. News Corp's purchase of *The Wall Street Journal*, which successfully charged its digital readers, convinced Rupert that all his papers should have a paywall. It meant that News International would have to become a technologically sophisticated operator of subscription businesses, just like Sky. It was a newspaper project that James could get behind, even if he had to drag *The Sun* along with him.

The early meetings were difficult. Newspapers dealt in simple circulation figures and, at a push, digital traffic. A subscription business, on the other hand, needs to deal in ongoing customer acquisition costs, loyalty and average revenue per user (ARPU).

"It was excruciating," a colleague recalls of Murdoch's attempts to teach News International executives the basics of the business model.

"James started going into the business model, churn and ARPU. It was all very him. But Rebecca could not follow it, and why should she be able to?

"She was an editor, she could not follow it, and every now and again as she was sitting at the side of the this long table, she'd say something and, honestly, you'd go 'what?' It would be total non-sequitur, it was clear, it was like she was in a completely different meeting. James stood up and totally lost it with her. It was so embarrassing."

Murdoch also tried to show enthusiasm for the tabloid hijinks at which *The Sun* excelled. One day in April he was having an off-the-record lunch with journalists from *The Times* and the leadership of Channel 4, when Tom Newton Dunn, the political editor of The Sun, burst in dressed as a chicken. He demanded that the executives join him, Rebekah Wade and the actor Hugh Jackman in a stunt abseiling from the roof of Wapping in aid of Help for Heroes, the military charity. Murdoch accepted the challenge and bounded down the side of the building "Tom Cruise style", according to a colleague, before returning to the meeting for dessert.

James was now making progress at News Corp. By the late summer of 2009, he began plotting a bid for full control of Sky. He wanted to mount a takeover that would allow News Corp to merge and simplify its European pay-TV businesses, and create a stronger competitor to internet giants such as Google, which had laid waste to the newspaper business and already had its eye on television.

"I am aware that some people in the UK thought that Sky was too big, but we felt that it would be helpful to be bigger in order to compete with other international companies such as Google, Apple and large telecoms companies, all of whom are much larger than Sky and have been investing in the audio-visual business heavily on a global rather than national basis," Murdoch later told the Leveson Inquiry.

First though, he had a big speech to give. Murdoch had been invited to give the MacTaggart Lecture at the Edinburgh International Television Festival. It was a big moment for him on the same stage that his father had used to launch Sky in 1989 and Tony Ball had effectively bowed out in 2003. Colleagues believed Murdoch had missed the limelight that he had enjoyed as chief executive of Sky. As chairman, he let Darroch act as the public face. This was his chance to settle a few scores, with the whole of the British media and political establishment as his audience.

By the end of his tenure in charge of Sky, Murdoch was regularly called on to give keynote speeches. He enjoyed his incursions at Ofcom and the BBC, where he was invited by Director-General Mark Thompson to speak to executives at an away day. Murdoch duly explained that the BBC was a cumbersome institution and an unjustified government intervention in the free market. His speechwriter at Sky was public affairs chief Martin Le Jeune, and Murdoch called on him once again to help craft his MacTaggart Lecture.

After months of discussion and little progress, Murdoch summoned Le Jeune to his house in Notting Hill one evening. Together, according to a colleague, "they cooked this thing up using Wikipedia and Google" and sent it around News Corp and Sky executives.

"I was like, 'for fuck's sake'," one of those executives recalls. The speech was textbook James Murdoch. It attacked the BBC, the licence fee and Ofcom, railed against government intervention in the media and mounted a passionate defence of independent, commercial outlets. It reached for Orwell and Darwin for its intellectual foundations and compared the British media industry to the Addams family. Murdoch demanded curbs on the BBC's burgeoning online output and an end to broadcasting impartiality regulation.

It was the payoff line, however, that immediately raised concerns for those who read the speech. Murdoch planned to end on the line "the only reliable, durable, and perpetual guarantor of independence is profit".

"Jeremy got a copy and said 'we have got to get him to change this, it's going to be an absolute disaster'. But he was having none of it," recalls a Sky executive.

"Someone had sent the thing to Rupert. Rupert saw it and said 'fuck, you can't say that, it's too extreme'. So Rupert called Rebekah and said you've got to stop him saying it."

Even Elisabeth Murdoch, who at Shine had proved adept at building bridges with the rest of the British television industry, was against it. Robert Fraser, Sky's external communications chief, wrote an alternative ending that said much the same thing but in a less confrontational style. It was presented to James on the private jet up to Edinburgh. He said he would think about it.

That evening, the combined team of Sky and News Corp executives brought together for the MacTaggart Lecture went for dinner at Martin Wishart, a Michelin-starred restaurant in the Edinburgh port district of Leith.

"James came down and says thank you all for your hard work," recalls one attendee. "He said, 'I know you don't like what I've done and you've even tried to get my dad involved, thank you very much. You've given me this alternative ending and I've considered it very carefully and you know what? Fuck the lot of you and fuck my dad, I'm doing it my way.' And that's what he did."

The reaction was immediate and fierce. BBC executives hit back with attacks on Fox News and the highly partisan style of coverage that News Corp pioneered in the United States. The chairman of the BBC Trust, Michael Lyons, warned that "we have to be careful not to reduce the whole of broadcasting to some simple economic transactions". Even Dawn Airey, a former Sky executive, criticised Murdoch's call to reduce the scope of BBC Online as "self-serving". Over at Ofcom, Ed Richards witheringly described the speech as "a very interesting polemic . . . much of it didn't surprise me".[1]

As it turned out, Murdoch's controversial MacTaggart Lecture would drive debate in British media for years to come. Subsequent speakers, including Mark Thompson and James's own sister Liz, would line up to rebuke him. As recently as 2018, the payoff line was cited by Paul Dacre, the retiring editor of *The Daily Mail*, as he discussed how, for newspapers, the profit motive "sharpens their understanding of their readers' anxieties and aspirations".[2] He said Murdoch had gone too far, however.

But back in 2009, there was rising frustration at Sky.

"It was a good speech," says one senior executive. "If you allowed the last line to be interpreted in a generous way then it wasn't unfair, but James deliberately meant to goad the BBC."

Another recalls: "At that time we were trying to not define ourselves as against the BBC. You can't win. It wasn't helping. The speech set that back."

For Murdoch, there was more newspaper business to attend to before News Corp would be ready to make a takeover bid for Sky. Despite her limited business experience, Rebekah was, as planned, promoted to chief executive of News International in September. Next, News Corp took a decision that would draw Sky further into politics.

The Sun had backed New Labour since shortly before the 1997 General Election. It stayed loyal through two more Tony Blair victories and the Iraq War. Blair had become a close friend to both Rupert and Wendi Deng, but his successor in 10 Downing Street, Gordon Brown, was not to News Corp tastes. He had battled to manage the financial crisis and, by autumn 2009, Britain was nine months into recession. *The Sun* had become a frequent critic of Britain's military involvement in Afghanistan, and of Gordon Brown in particular.

Meanwhile David Cameron, leader of the Conservative Party since 2005, appeared ready to take on Blair's mantle.

Rupert Murdoch later told the Leveson Inquiry: "I supported a shift to Labour by News International's titles when I thought the Conservative Party had run out of ideas, and I supported a shift to the Conservative Party after 13 years of Labour rule for the same reason."

Cameron set out a policy programme that appealed to the Murdoch view of the universe, including a suggestion that Ofcom and many of its powers could be scrapped.

"Give Ofcom, or give a new body, the technical function of handing out the licences and regulating lightly the content that is on the screens," Cameron said in a radio interview in mid-2009, as he courted the endorsement of Murdoch newspapers.[3]

"But it shouldn't be making policy, it shouldn't have its own communications department, the head of Ofcom is paid almost half a million pounds. We could slim this body down a huge amount and save a lot of money for the taxpayer."

With a new editor in place at *The Sun* following the promotion of Rebekah, who was now married to the race horse trainer Charlie Brooks, and an election due within a year, the time was right to switch sides. On 10 September, James Murdoch met Cameron for drinks at George, a private members club in Mayfair, to deliver the good news.

"It was a drink and a catch-up, but . . . he wanted to tell me that *The Sun* was going to support the Conservatives and he told me, I think, from my memory, that it was going to happen around the time of the Labour conference, and I remember obviously being pleased that the Conservative Party was going to get *The Sun*'s support, and I think we had a conversation about other policy issues at the time," Cameron later told the Leveson Inquiry.

The task of delivering the bad news fell to Rebekah Brooks. On 29 September 2009, Gordon Brown delivered his speech to the Labour Party Conference in Brighton. It was an attempt to rally the faithful to "fight, not bow out, fight to win" in the coming election and highlight his own efforts in steering the financial system through crisis.

The Sun had other ideas. It lined up a front-page splash for the following day declaring "Labour's lost it" and pledging allegiance to Cameron. The switch was designed to inflict maximum damage and overshadow Brown's messages to voters. As the presses rolled, Brooks planned to deliver the *coup de grace* at the annual News International party, a boozy, oversubscribed affair, at which it was traditional for the leader to attend and schmooze with executives. Rumours of what appeared to be an ambush had reached Labour high command, however, and a furious Brown did not show.

It was left to Lord Mandelson, an architect of the Blair-era alliance between Labour and News International, to speak to Brooks over the phone. Even the famously unflappable peer lost his cool, telling her that "you have made total c*nts of yourselves", though he later said he had used the word "chumps". The drama created lasting bad blood. Brown spoke to Brooks days later and was "incredibly aggressive and very angry", she said.

Sky felt swift retribution from the Brown government. The Department of Culture was conducting a review of Britain's sporting 'crown jewels', a list of events of 'national resonance' that must be broadcast on free-to-air television. The FA Cup final, the World Cup and the Olympics were already out of Sky's reach.

David Davies, a former BBC presenter and chairman of the Football Association, was appointed at the end of 2008 to conduct an independent examination of the rules. By November 2009, with relations between Labour and the Murdoch empire at a new low after *The Sun* had attacked Brown over a misspelled letter to the family of a dead soldier, Davies was ready to deliver his verdict.

"Brown has revenge as Murdoch's Sky loses Ashes," the *Evening Standard* front page revealed.

International cricket was second only to Premier League football in its value to Sky Sports. Fans were committed and many would pay for a Sky package just to watch test matches. The Ashes, England's historic rival match with Australia, was most valuable of all, particularly after the classic summer series of 2005. Sky had swooped in 2006 to sign a major deal with cricket's governing body, and renewed it in 2008 for five years at a cost of £300m. Now the government planned to outlaw that deal by adding the Ashes to the crown jewels.

Earlier in the year it had looked as though Davies did not intend to take the Ashes away from Sky. The BBC signalled to his review that it did not particularly want them back. Davies's change of heart came after *The Sun* abandoned Brown, though he insisted claims that political pressure on his review were "utter nonsense".[4] Nobody at Sky believed it for a second.

"Davies was a sap," says a Sky insider close to the row. "The only way Brown could really attack the Murdochs was via Sky and the only thing he could really do quickly was reopen the debate over ownership of the Ashes. Davies came up with the report he wanted."

Cricket authorities were furious. They faced a ban on selling their most valuable rights to the highest bidder. With Sky helping behind the scenes, the England and Wales Cricket mounted a determined lobbying campaign against the restriction, claiming that a reduction in television income would harm the grassroots of the sport. The battle ran into the new year and, as it turned out, was unnecessary: in early April 2010, the government triggered a General Election before the rules could be changed.

Brown was defeated, although Cameron was denied an outright victory. Over a few extraordinary days in May, the Conservatives and the Liberal Democrats formed Britain's first coalition government since the Second World War.

Sky was still battling Ofcom and its rivals over competition in the pay-TV market, and it was now in a fight to retain access to cricket rights. James Murdoch had renewed his hostilities with the BBC and the regulator. Yet he was not thinking about politics anymore. Murdoch wanted to make his mark with a takeover of Europe's most successful pay-TV operator that would bring it under full News Corp control.

In Osterley, Sky was focused on the day job. Its shares were heavily sold off as the recession triggered by the financial crisis deepened, and investors feared that consumers would cancel their expensive pay-TV packages as part of belt tightening. One consumer survey found that 10% planned to cancel their Sky subscription, prompting analysts to say that "clearly this is ugly stuff if this turns out to be the case, and surely sentiment will worsen as consumers come under pressure on income".[5] It would be a major test of strength for the subscriber base that Sky had built up since the dawn of the digital era.

It was a challenge that suited Jeremy Darroch's style of management, which was more calculated and tactical than Sky had experienced before. James Murdoch had focused on big, risky projects and strategy. Sky now needed to show investors that it could trade its way, quarter by quarter, through the recession.

"Jeremy, ultimately, is a CFO, " says a colleague. "So, he's much more about weighing up risk."

Darroch's promotion meant his former role in charge of Sky's finances was vacant. The obvious internal candidate was Andrew Griffith, the head of investor relations and M&A. A former Rothschild banker, Griffith had joined Sky in 1999, on the same day as Tony Ball, and gradually built up a powerful position.

He was close to Murdoch, working with him on deals such as the takeovers of Easynet and Amstrad, the set-top box maker owned by Alan Sugar. Griffith and Murdoch remained close after Darroch became chief executive, providing a bridge between Sky and its biggest shareholder.

Griffith had not always been completely committed. In 2001, and again in 2005, he took leave to stand as the Conservative parliamentary candidate for Corby, losing to Labour on the second occasion by just over 1,500 votes. With his political ambitions frustrated, Griffith turned his attention back to Sky and took his chance to launch another campaign when Darroch's old job became available.

"That was open for several months," remembers a colleague. "Although Andrew was the most obvious candidate he wasn't universally appreciated within the business. He could rub people up the wrong way. But for that three or four months he was the most polite person you could imagine.

"Ordinarily he is just very blunt. People can find that quite hard to cope with. But he was sweetness and light for months."

Eventually, an appointment panel led by Allan Leighton and Lord Wilson were convinced that Griffith's strengths outweighed any faults. He was a tough negotiator, understood Sky's business and knew his way around the City. Griffith was appointed chief financial officer in April 2008 and quickly formed a formidable double act with Darroch. Darroch was a commercial finance operator, expert in running consumer businesses on the ground; Griffith was immersed in the City relationships and dealmaking of the corporate world. It also meant that for the first time in Sky's history its ruling duo were both accountants.

"Andrew and Jeremy both know power comes from money," says a Sky insider. "They make sure that no matter what changes, they hold onto the purse strings."

Griffith's bluntness allowed the non-confrontational Darroch to play good cop when tough decisions had to be delivered to staff. His links with Murdoch would allow Darroch to maintain a degree of distance that became crucial when Sky faced crisis and pressure from its other shareholders.

Alongside Brian Sullivan, head of Sky's customer unit, they traded through the recession. By late 2009, it was clear that while some consumer and media businesses were derailed by the financial crisis – Woolworths went bust after 100 years on the high street and ITV almost followed – the Sky juggernaut kept rolling. At its full year results in July 2009, the operator revealed it had added 124,000 satellite subscribers in the past three months, the best figure in five years.

The acceleration was driven by the decision earlier in the year to slash the cost of an HD set-top box by two-thirds to £49, Darroch's calculation being that consumers would still be willing to upgrade their home entertainment even if they cut spending on meals and nights out.

Meanwhile, losses on Sky's push into broadband were being quickly pegged back by smarter pricing and marketing under Steven Van Rooyen. In the last three months of the year the unit lost just £22m, the lowest since launch. The full-year broadband loss of £129m put Sky's telecoms business comfortably on track to reach profitability within two years.

Overall operating profit was up 4%, the share price was recovering from its financial crisis slump and Darroch was making his mark. Wary of complacency, he resisted suggestions that the company had proved "recession-proof", but the evidence seemed to show that it was. As well as Team Sky, he invested more in arts programmes in an attempt to lay to rest the idea that Sky was what he called "council house TV". At the end of 2009, Sky was named Britain's most admired company by a panel of senior business figures for *Management Today*.

It seemed an establishment endorsement of efforts by Murdoch and Darroch to shift the company's image away from that of piratical media outsider. Sky's brilliance was now undeniable, even for those who had once opposed it.

Ofcom nevertheless remained a blot on the landscape. Richards remained determined to increase competition in the pay-TV market and was approaching the end of the investigation he had launched in 2007 in response to the Gang of Four complaint. In March 2010, Ofcom made its decision. Sky would be forced to wholesale Sky Sports to BT Vision and other rivals at a price set by the regulator.

It was a defeat for Murdoch, who had spent considerable time and energy battling Richards in public and behind the scenes in Whitehall, but set against his grand vision to bring Sky into News Corp, it was now a minor irritation. The time had come.

2009 Edinburgh International Television Festival MacTaggart Lecture James Murdoch – 28 August

THE ABSENCE OF TRUST

I

Good evening and thank you for having me here tonight. Thanks also to Tim for those kind words of welcome.

I think this is the first time that someone who has delivered the alternative MacTaggart has graduated – if that's the right word – to the real thing.

So I am both proud and honoured to be paving the way for Ant and Dec, who should be standing here tonight in 2018 if this trend continues.

Of course I'm flattered to be asked, but I am also a little worried. Does this finally mark my invitation to join the British broadcasting establishment? While that thought does terrify me, I am comforted in the knowledge that after my remarks my membership will have been a brief one. . .

And it also occurred to me that I qualified for the invitation only after I gave up my executive role at Sky. I now spend most of my time engaged in other parts of the world and other parts of the media industry. Perhaps that means I am regarded as being safely at a bit of a distance.

But I do welcome the opportunity to talk to you all about the media in the UK – and a slight distancing might help.

You can be the judges of that.

II

When we gather as an industry, it's natural for us to talk about the future. I'd like to do something different tonight: to turn our focus firmly to the present. Because the path we are already on is a dangerous one.

In particular, what I want to discuss is our digital present that is right here – it has been here for a while, in fact. A digital present that ought to compel us to make some urgent choices about where we want to go as an industry and as a society: choices which, I will argue tonight, we are currently either avoiding or mishandling.

It's easy to lose sight of how digital we already are.

The inescapable thing about the present is that everything in it is already digital. Even if part of the consumption of media remains in the analogue world – opening a newspaper or a book, going to see a film in a cinema – the production of those creative works is already wholly digital, and the proportion that is consumed by digital means is growing all the time.

So talking about a coming digital future, or a digital transformation, is to ignore the evidence that it has already happened.

Why do I think we are getting this wrong? Why do I believe we need to change direction as a matter of urgency? It's quite simple.

Because we have analogue attitudes in a digital age.

We have business models and a policy framework based on spectrum scarcity.

We have limited choice, and we have central planning.

The result is lost opportunities for enterprise, free choice and commercial investment.

If we recognise that truth and change in the right way, the opportunities and benefits for all of us and – more importantly – for consumers and society are powerful and attractive.

We know we have to change: the digital present is forcing us to make urgent choices.

First, the velocity of the transformation of our industry has radically increased. You know this and I don't need to dwell on it.

Second, in this rapidly changing world the boundaries between media have broken down.

People consume content in a very fluid way, and that is reflected in the way we provide it. What were once separate forms of communication, or separate media, are now increasingly interconnected and exchangeable. So we no longer have a TV market, a newspaper market, a publishing market. We have, indisputably, an all-media market.

Third, the boundaries of what we mean by media are themselves expanding. In Japan, you can now buy your granny a mobile phone called a 'raku raku' – which means 'easy easy' – designed specifically for the elderly. It has a built-in pedometer to track how many steps she is taking each day. And you can set that so that it sends a daily e-mail to your inbox, letting you know your granny is still up and about and getting the right amount of exercise. There might be an advertisement attached. Is that media? Or health-care provision? Or is it both?

This all sounds like a dynamic, exciting, thriving sector to be part of. Moving faster, being more interconnected, expanding its scope. And in some ways it is.

But the present is not as great as we tell ourselves.

You don't need to scratch the surface very hard to see that opportunities for media businesses are limited, investment and innovation are constrained, and creativity is reduced.

This is bad for customers and society.

This year is the 150th anniversary of Darwin's *The Origin of Species*.

It argued that the most dramatic evolutionary changes can occur through an entirely natural process. Darwin proved that evolution is unmanaged.

These views were an enormous challenge to Victorian religious orthodoxy. They remain a provocation to many people today. The number who reject Darwin and cling to the concept of creationism is substantial. And it crops up in some surprising places.

For example, right here in the broadcasting sector in the UK.

The consensus appears to be that creationism – the belief in a managed process with an omniscient authority – is the only way to achieve successful outcomes. There is general agreement that the natural operation of the market is inadequate, and that a better outcome can be achieved through the wisdom and activity of governments and regulators.

This creationist approach is similar to the industrial planning which went out of fashion in other sectors in the 1970s. It failed then. It's failing now.

When I say this I feel like a crazy relative who everyone is a little embarrassed by and for sure is not to be taken too seriously. But tonight you have invited me to join the party and I am going to have a crack at persuading you that we can't go on like this.

Tonight I will argue that while creationism may provide a comfortable illusion of certainty in the short-term, its harmful effects are real and they are significant.

Creationism penalises the poorest in our society with regressive taxes and policies – like the licence fee and digital switchover;

It promotes inefficient infrastructure in the shape of digital terrestrial television;

It creates unaccountable institutions – like the BBC Trust, Channel 4 and Ofcom;

And now, in the all-media marketplace, it threatens significant damage to important spheres of human enterprise and endeavour – the provision of independent news, investment in professional journalism, and the innovation and growth of the creative industries.

We are on the wrong path – but we can find the right one.

The right path is all about trusting and empowering consumers. It is about embracing private enterprise and profit as a driver of investment, innovation and independence. And the dramatic reduction of the activities of the state in our sector.

If we do take that better way, then we – all of us in this room and in our wider industry – will make a genuine contribution to a better-informed society; one in which trust in people and their freedom to choose is central to the way we behave.

Often the unique position that the business of ideas enjoys in a free society is used as a justification for greater intrusion and control. On the contrary, its very specialness demands an unusual and vigorous ... stillness.

III

Let's explore the role of creationism in our sector by asking a few basic questions.

First question. How do the authorities currently approach intervening in and regulating the media industries?

With relish, is the answer.

In the past five years Ofcom launched nearly 450 consultations – nearly two every week. It has produced three Public Service Broadcasting annual reports, and two Public Service Broadcasting reviews in five phases. These alone have in total – including appendices, special reports and other related material – amounted to over five thousand pages and spawned another 18,000 pages of responses. And those reports have been only a small proportion of the total activity by the regulator. For any of you who missed them this has included science fiction – a report on 'Entertainment in the UK in 2028', and the no doubt vital guide on 'How to Download', which teenagers across the land could barely have survived without.

Second question. Is it rational for the authorities to try to manage the media industry in this way? Not at all.

The study of evolution reminds us that it is very difficult to predict the outcomes of events. Interventions can have unforeseen consequences, even when dealing with organisations or marketplaces which seem very easy to understand.

Witness the international banana market. In the 1950s the banana export industry faced a problem: the then dominant Gros Michel – or 'Big Mike' – variety was being wiped out by a fungus called Panama Disease. The industry took the decision to replace the entire world export crop with a supposedly disease-resistant variety called the Cavendish banana – the one we eat today. Unfortunately it now appears that these bananas may themselves be vulnerable to a different kind of Panama Disease. Since Cavendish bananas are genetically identical sterile clones, they cannot build up any resistance.

There are important lessons here: attempts to manage natural diversity have unpredictable consequences and are more likely than not to fail over the long-term.

Talking of bananas brings me neatly to our own authorities and their interventions in the all-media marketplace. Some of these looked, even without the benefit of hindsight, pretty difficult to justify at the time.

To use an example I am familiar with, take the decision of the European Commission to require the broadcasting rights to Premier League football to be divided up so that no one company could buy all the rights. The consequences of that move were predictable enough: customers having to pay more for the same thing because they'd need two subscriptions. However, in defiance of common sense, the Commission apparently believed that prices would instead fall.

Here, the repeated assertion by Ofcom of its bias against intervention is becoming impossible to believe in the face of so much evidence of the exact opposite.

A radical reorientation of the regulatory approach is necessary if dynamism and innovation is going to be central to the UK media industry.

The discipline required is to contemplate intervention only on the evidence of actual and serious harm to the interests of consumers: not merely because a regulator armed with a set of prejudices and a spreadsheet believes that a bit of tinkering here and there could make the world a better place.

Third question. What do the results of these interventions actually look like? Let's judge by results.

According to the authorities – and I paraphrase – we should have a diverse broadcasting ecology with many PSB providers; a BBC that is not too dominant; growing investment in content of high quality; and high levels of UK production.

Now I invite you to take a look around you. Decades of ever-increasing planning and intervention have produced very different outcomes.

The BBC is dominant. Other organisations might rise and fall but the BBC's income is guaranteed and growing.

In stark contrast, the other terrestrial networks are struggling.

Channel 4 has cut its programme budget by 10%, Five by 25%. Spending on original British children's programming has fallen by nearly 40% since 2004, including, inexplicably, a 21% fall at the BBC at a time when the Corporation has been able to spend £100m a year out-bidding commercial channels for US programming – a figure which has increased by a quarter in the past two years.

The problems of the terrestrial broadcasters are not about the economic downturn, although it has thrown the issue into sharp relief.

It is not a coincidence that Google has a higher percentage of advertising spending in the UK than anywhere else in the world: it is a consequence of a tightly restricted commercial television sector.

That money will not come back. It is not that ad-funded television is dead: it is just a permanently smaller fish in a bigger pond.

Fourth question. Is this creationism good for investment? No. A heavily regulated environment with a large public sector crowds out the opportunity for profit, hinders the creation of new jobs, and dampens innovation in our sector.

We don't even have the basics in place to protect creative work. Whether it's shoplifting at HMV or pirating the same movie online, theft is theft. They are both crimes and should be treated accordingly. The government dithers – dimly aware of what it has to do but afraid to do it.

The investment climate in media in the UK reminds me of Tolstoy's dictum that all happy families resemble one another, while each unhappy family is unhappy in its own way. True, none of the markets I have experience of is completely happy, but there are things to welcome – the regulatory professionalism of Germany, the growth opportunities of India – even France outdoes us in its robust defence of intellectual property. The problem with the UK is that it is unhappy in every way: it's the Addams family of world media.

IV

If such determined efforts to manage the marketplace are failing, it might be useful to look at alternative approaches.

One such approach might be to trust people.

Consider Dutch traffic engineer Hans Monderman – who discovered that reducing the amount of signs and traffic markings in towns and villages does not make roads more dangerous, as you might imagine. On the contrary, people drive more safely and there are fewer accidents. As Monderman said: "If you treat drivers like idiots, they act as idiots. Never treat anyone in the public realm as an idiot, always assume they have intelligence."

In contrast, the authorities in the UK and their clients: those dependent agencies, entities and enterprises, which one way or the other have been made to rely on the largesse of the state – have refused to trust the people who matter – the people who pay the bills as customers and as tax-payers.

Indeed, the defining characteristic of the UK broadcasting consensus is the absence of trust.

Yet there is an example right on our doorstep of the positive developments that come about when we encourage a world of trust and free choice.

Within the next few months, the number of homes in the UK that enjoy some form of television that they freely choose to pay for will top fifty percent. This steady growth of choice-driven television has nothing to do with public policy. In fact, the authorities have consistently favoured so called free-to-air broadcasting. Yet, as you might expect, people who are used to paying for films, books, internet access and other quality content, do not see anything strange in paying for quality television too.

When pay-television began in this country, it did so largely by providing programmes in genres which public service broadcasting served inadequately: such as 24-hour news, and a broad choice of sport and the latest films.

As originally with news and sport, so now with the arts and drama. Sky now offers four dedicated arts channels. Original commissioning by channels that customers choose to pay for is expanding and will continue to do so, not just from Sky but from the likes of National Geographic, History, MTV and the Disney Channel, to name a few. Sky alone now invests over £1 billion a year in UK content.

And it is this sector which has delivered so many innovations: from multichannel television in the first place, to the launch of digital, personal video recorders, high definition and soon 3D TV in the home.

All this – despite the dampening effect of a massive state-funded intervention which reduces the scope for programme investment and commissioning from independent production companies by private broadcasters. That is a major missed opportunity for the creative industries. And yet the authorities in the UK continue to seek more control and greater intervention.

There are many examples. First, the amount of detailed content regulation in UK broadcasting is astonishing.

Two or three times a month, Ofcom publishes a Broadcasting Bulletin – a recent version weighed in at 119 pages. Adjudications included judgments on whether it is fair to describe Middlesbrough as the worst place to live in the UK; and 20 pages on whether a BBC documentary on climate change was fair to two of the participants. Every year, roughly half-a-million words are being devoted to telling broadcasters what they can and cannot say.

Next, the UK and EU regulatory system also tightly controls advertising: the amount of advertising per hour, the availability of product placement, the distinction between advertising and editorial and so forth.

These rules often seem to have little connection with protecting people from real harm. As an example, Star Plus – one of News Corp's Hindi language entertainment channels – has been unable to show in the UK the Indian version of 'Are you smarter than a ten-year old?' because the logo of an Indian mobile phone company, which does not even operate in this country, appears on the set. What exactly are they afraid of?

Excessive regulation can also have more serious consequences. The latest EU-inspired rules on scheduling of advertising restrict the number of ad breaks permitted in news programming. Television news is already a tough enough business. If implemented, these proposals could undermine the commercial viability of news broadcasting even further.

In addition, the system is concerned with imposing what it calls impartiality in broadcast news. It should hardly be necessary to point out that the mere selection of stories and their place in the running order is itself a process full of unacknowledged partiality.

The effect of the system is not to curb bias – bias is present in all news media – but simply to disguise it.

We should be honest about this: it is an impingement on freedom of speech and on the right of people to choose what kind of news to watch. How in an all-media marketplace can we justify this degree of control in one place and not in others?

Content control, advertising regulation and restrictions on freedom of speech. We have been brought up in this system. It probably seems as natural and inevitable as rainfall. But is it really necessary? Is there no alternative?

Other areas of the media have been able to get by without it. There is a strong alternative tradition with at least four centuries behind it – first of pamphlets and books, later of magazines and newspapers. From the broadsides of the Levellers, to the thundering 19th century *Times*, to *The Sun* fighting for the rights of veterans today – it is a tradition of free comment, of investigative reporting, of satirizing and exposing the behaviour of one's betters.

Yes, the free press is fairly near the knuckle on occasion – it is noisy, disrespectful, raucous and quite capable of affronting people – it is frequently the despair of judges and it gets up the noses of politicians on a regular basis. But it is driven by the daily demand and choices of millions of people. It has had the profits to enable it to be fearless and independent. Great journalism does not get enough credit in our society, but it holds the powerful to account and plays a vital part in a functioning democracy.

Would we welcome a world in which The Times was told by the government how much religious coverage it had to carry?

In which there were a state newspaper with more money than the rest of the sector put together and 50% of the market?

In which cinemas were instructed how many ads they were allowed to put before the main feature?

In which Bloomsbury had to publish an equal number of pro-capitalist and pro-socialist books?

And, of course, we had to pay for an Ofpress to make sure all these rules were observed?

No, of course we would not. So why do we continue to assume that this approach is appropriate for broadcasting: especially as one communications medium is now barely distinguishable from another?

There is a word for this.

It's not one that the system likes to hear, but let's be honest: the right word is authoritarianism and it has always been part of our system.

It is hardly a secret that the early years of British broadcasting were dominated by concern about the potential of the new technology for creating social disruption. To deal with that perceived threat, there were two responses: to nationalise broadcasting through the BBC, and to ensure that any other provider was closely controlled and appropriately incentivised.

The greatest divergence between the rest of the media and broadcasting is the unspoken approach to the customer. In the regulated world of Public Service Broadcasting the customer does not exist: he or she is a passive creature – a viewer – in need of protection. In other parts of the media world – including pay television and newspapers – the customer is just that: someone whose very freedom to choose makes them important. And because they have power they are treated with great seriousness and respect, as people who are perfectly capable of making informed judgements about what to buy, read, and go and see.

The all-media world offers great opportunities for our society. We could take the approach of trust and freedom and apply it through the whole of the media, broadcasting included. But we are doing the opposite. We are using the interconnectedness of the media as a way of opening the door to the expansion of control.

This is already happening. There is a land-grab, pure and simple, going on – and in the interests of a free society it should be sternly resisted.

The land grab is spear-headed by the BBC. The scale and scope of its current activities and future ambitions is chilling.

Being funded by a universal hypothecated tax, the BBC feels empowered and obliged to try and offer something for everyone, even in areas well served by the market.

This whole approach is based on a mistaken view of the rationale behind state intervention and it produces bizarre and perverse outcomes. Rather than concentrating on areas where the market is not delivering, the BBC seeks to compete head-on for audiences with commercial providers to try and shore up support – or more accurately dampen opposition – to a compulsory licence fee.

Take Radio 2 as an example. A few years back, the BBC observed that it was losing share of listening among the 25 to 45 age-group, who were well served by commercial stations. Instead of stepping back and allowing the market to do its job, the BBC decided to reposition Radio 2 to go after this same group. Performers like Jonathan Ross were recruited on salaries no commercial competitor could afford, and audiences for Radio 2 have grown steadily as a result.

No doubt the BBC celebrates the fact that it now has well over half of all radio listening. But the consequent impoverishment of the once-successful commercial sector is testament to the Corporation's inability to distinguish between what is good for it, and what is good for the country.

Of course, this problem is compounded by the fact that there is no real oversight of this £4.6 billion intervention in the market, as the abysmal record of the BBC Trust demonstrates. So the breadth of intervention is striking and it is continuing to expand unchecked.

The negative consequences of this expansion for innovation and development in the creative industries are serious.

The nationalisation of the Lonely Planet travel guide business was a particularly egregious example of the expansion of the state into providing magazines and websites on a commercial basis. It stood out for its overt recklessness and for the total failure of the BBC Trust to ask tough questions about what management was up to.

Others in other sectors can tell similar stories: and they observe that if the BBC suffers any setback in expansion, it is merely temporary: there will soon be another initiative requiring yet more management time to fight off.

As new entrants like Joost discovered, operating alongside the BBC, without access to its content or cross-promotional power, is not a task for the faint hearted. You need deep pockets, sheer bloody-mindedness and an army of lawyers just to make the BBC Trust sit up and pay attention.

Most importantly, in this all-media marketplace, the expansion of state-sponsored journalism is a threat to the plurality and independence of news provision, which are so important for our democracy.

Dumping free, state-sponsored news on the market makes it incredibly difficult for journalism to flourish on the internet.

Yet it is essential for the future of independent digital journalism that a fair price can be charged for news to people who value it.

We seem to have decided as a society to let independence and plurality wither. To let the BBC throttle the news market and then get bigger to compensate.

Most policy-making is however pre-occupied with the supposed malign intervention of capitalists focused on profit, and is blind to the growth of the state.

Nearly all local authorities already publish their own newspapers with flattering accounts of their doings. Over 60% of these pocket-Pravdas carry advertising, weakening the local presence of more critical voices. I saw recently an article in which the editor of *The Guardian* suggested that the government should fund local news coverage of court proceedings and council meetings, a profoundly undemocratic and ruinous idea.

Just ask yourself whether Camilla Cavendish's award-winning campaign to open up the family courts would have occurred in a state-funded newspaper? The investigation would never have been allowed to take place.

For hundreds of years people have fought for the right to publish what they think.

Yet today the threat to independent news provision is serious and imminent.

More broadly, it must serve as a warning of what happens when state intervention and regulatory micro-management are allowed to go unchecked in the all-media marketplace. For the future health of our industry and our society, we must not allow these creationist tendencies to go on limiting the opportunities for independent commercial businesses, whether in journalism or any other form of content.

The private sector is a source of investment, talent, creativity and innovation in UK media.

But it will never fulfil its full potential unless we adopt a policy framework that recognises the centrality of commercial incentives.

This means accepting the simple truth that the ability to generate a profitable return is fundamental to the continuation of the quality, plurality and independence that we value so highly.

For that to happen our politicians and regulators need to have the courage to leave behind their analogue attitudes and choose a path for the digital present. So far, they have shown little inclination to do so.

V

Thanks to Darwin we understand that the evolution of a successful species is an unmanaged process. I have tried to show tonight that interventionist management of what is sometimes called the broadcasting ecology is not helping it – it is exhausting it.

Broadcasting is now part of a single all-media market. It brings two very different stories to that bigger market. On the one hand authoritarianism: endless intervention, regulation and control. On the other, the free part of the market where success has been achieved by a determined resistance to the constant efforts of the authorities to interfere.

I have argued tonight that this success is based on a very simple principle: trust people.

People are very good at making choices: choices about what media to consume; whether to pay for it and how much; what they think is acceptable to watch, read and hear; and the result of their billions of choices is that good companies survive, prosper, and proliferate.

That is a great story and it has been powerfully positive for our society.

But we are not learning from that. Governments and regulators are wonderfully crafted machines for mission creep. For them, the abolition of media boundaries is a trumpet call to expansion: to do more, regulate more, control more.

Sixty years ago George Orwell published *1984*. Its message is more relevant now than ever.

As Orwell foretold, to let the state enjoy a near-monopoly of information is to guarantee manipulation and distortion.

We must have a plurality of voices and they must be independent. Yet we have a system in which state-sponsored media – the BBC in particular – grow ever more dominant.

That process has to be reversed.

If we are to have that state sponsorship at all, then it is fundamental to the health of the creative industries, independent production, and professional journalism that it exists on a far, far smaller scale.

Above all we must have genuine independence in news media. Genuine independence is a rare thing. No amount of governance in the form of committees, regulators, trusts or advisory bodies is truly sufficient as a guarantor of independence. In fact, they curb speech.

On the contrary, independence is characterised by the absence of the apparatus of supervision and dependency.

Independence of faction, industrial or political.

Independence of subsidy, gift and patronage.

Independence is sustained by true accountability – the accountability owed to customers. People who buy the newspapers, open the application, decide to take out the television subscription – people who deliberately and willingly choose a service which they value.

And people value honest, fearless, and above all independent news coverage that challenges the consensus.

There is an inescapable conclusion that we must reach if we are to have a better society.

The only reliable, durable, and perpetual guarantor of independence is profit.

9

It Was Payback Time

It was no secret that James Murdoch was not universally admired at the top table of News Corp. Executives who had served the company for decades competed for Rupert's attention and approval, while James, the heir apparent, enjoyed automatic privileges. In practice, it meant that some senior colleagues were not always receptive to his ideas; some had ideas of their own, too.

In 2009, the vast industrial conglomerate General Electric (GE) let it be known that it was considering a sale of NBC Universal, the national television network and major Hollywood studio. Entertainment was a strange sideline for a company better known as a maker of jet engines, and GE chief executive Jeff Immelt wanted out. Comcast, the massive cable operator with lucrative broadband monopolies in major cities across the United States, was very much interested.

Comcast had tried and failed to break into Hollywood before. In 2004, it mounted a $54bn takeover bid for Disney, which was down on its luck at the time, but was knocked back. Major studios and broadcasters were not available for sale often, but Comcast had bided its time and five years later got another opportunity.

Comcast's manoeuvres triggered a debate at News Corp about the best use of the company's financial firepower. James wanted to buy Sky to create a powerful pan-European operator alongside Sky Italia and Sky Deutschland. News Corp executives in Los Angeles and New York, who knew little of Sky or the European market in general, argued that instead Comcast should be stopped with a rival bid for NBC Universal. News Corp owned no significant pay-TV distribution channel of its own in the United States and relied on cable operators for much of its income. The thought that Comcast, the biggest of them, might become a direct competitor in television and film production, as well as in network television, was a serious concern.

Peter Chernin, the chief operating officer based in Los Angeles, was on his way out too, after 12 years as Rupert's right-hand man. For American News Corp executives, a takeover of Sky threatened a major shift in the centre of power toward Europe and James.

The return of Chase Carey tipped the debate in James's favour. Carey had continued running DirecTV following the handover to John Malone, but Rupert tempted him back into the News Corp fold as deputy chairman. The move served to calm the nerves of independent shareholders who feared that Chernin's departure might herald the complete Murdoch domination of the company.

The appointment was seen as a sign that James was not quite ready to move to the centre of the action at News Corp. However, Carey fell in line with James's campaign to bid for Sky, and by late 2009 the wheels were in motion in New York as the company got its finances in order. Like Sky, News Corp had ridden the economic downturn and was sitting on $8bn in cash.

At the Leveson Inquiry into phone hacking, Murdoch said: "In 2007, the company acquired Dow Jones for $5.5bn in cash, and to contemplate a transaction of this size in the immediate aftermath of that, and given what happened in 2008 and 2009 with respect to the global financial crisis, would have been difficult. So in 2009 and 2010, we realised this was something that we could actually do."

By March 2010, rumours were swirling in London that News Corp was ready to pounce, aided by the weakness of sterling. A general election was imminent, however, and there was little point in making a bid just before the machinery of government and regulation was due to be shut down for campaigning. News Corp waited, and despite the Conservative failure to win an overall majority, got the result it wanted. Cameron became Prime Minster albeit of a coalition government, on a manifesto that had included plans to slash quangos such as Ofcom, ease regulation and challenge the BBC.

Murdoch said the plan was to "wait until the election was completed, regardless of the outcome, such that a transaction of this size . . . didn't become a political football".

"But the primary driver for the timing was really the affordability of it, being able to do it. We had taken some time to really husband our resources carefully. It was contemplated that it would be an all-cash offer and that took a little while to save up."

A month after the Coalition was formed, News Corp made its move. The Sky board was due to meet for its annual discussion of strategy and long-term planning in mid-June, which made the ideal forum for Murdoch and Carey, both Sky directors as well as News Corp executives, to discuss the bid with their colleagues. The independent Sky directors receiving the News Corp approach, including Darroch and Griffith, were led by Nick Ferguson, an experienced dealmaker with a private equity background.

The Sky side were baffled when News Corp came up with a figure of 675p per share, a premium of less than 20% on the share price that valued Sky at about £12bn. The independent directors knew that their credibility, as well as the future of the company, was at stake. The likes of Allan Leighton were unwilling to be bounced into accepting what they saw as an attempt to take ownership of Sky at a bargain price. The bid was lower than Sky's share price before the financial crisis, and the business had continued to grow through the recession.

"It was a classic News Corp thing," says one insider close to the discussions. "They had a strategy that was very sound around bringing together the Sky businesses in Europe, and the Asian businesses.

"It was the idea of needing to own content and distribution, the idea that as well as distribution Sky had skills indirect to consumer retailing that News Corp didn't have and would never be able to build. News Corp had content assets that Sky would be able to take and monetise. All of that was smart.

"But when it came to pursuing the strategy, they equivocated on price. Which I suspect was because within News Corp there was a whole set of different factions. Some thought it was a good idea because it was James. Some thought it was a bad idea because it was James. So they ended up supporting it in a very narrow way. They thought it was okay, so long as the price was low. It was to be purely a financial transaction whereby they restructured their balance sheet.

"Our side said we absolutely can't accept 675p because the directors' whole reputations and careers would have been finished."

It looked initially as though the talks would collapse. Sky's directors insisted that News Corp would have to pay at least 800p per share for the 61% of the company it did not own. A few days later, on 14 June, news of the approach was leaked to *The Daily Telegraph*, along with a warning that "there is still a meaningful gap between the two companies in terms of price".[1]

The situation was fragile. Darroch was acting as a go-between, shuttling between News Corp and his fellow Sky directors in an attempt to keep the talks alive. Ultimately, he and James Murdoch stitched together a compromise that would effectively make a deal without agreeing a price.

"Jeremy basically took the initiative, with James's cooperation, and basically stitched together a compromise where we would agree to cooperate with News Corp to secure regulatory clearance and price would be discussed once we were through that," says a source close to the talks.

"It's a very unusual situation to get into in M&A but it kept everyone together. Jeremy was doing shuttle diplomacy between News Corp and the board, and trying to make sure everyone in the business wasn't going mad with distraction."

On 15 June, Sky announced the unusual accord. News Corp raised its approach to 700p, but Ferguson said that, based on "careful advice" from investment banks UBS and Morgan Stanley, it still "significantly undervalues" the company. Nevertheless, Sky said it would cooperate with News Corp to secure regulatory clearance, prompting fears among independent shareholders they were being set up to accept a low price later.

Inside Sky, Darroch felt the company had little choice but to cooperate and that it was in the shareholders' interests. The alternative was embarrassment for News Corp and potential chaos. This way, News Corp did not have to commit any cash up front, reducing the perceived risk for its shareholders.

"They would have gone back to America in a sulk and we would have been God knows where," says one senior Sky executive. "We would've had an irretrievable breakdown."

Instead, News Corp was able to begin seeking approval for the bid from UK and EU regulators. Early on, there was little sign of serious opposition. Over the summer of 2010, commentators focused mainly on the price and suggestions that the Murdochs aimed to muscle their way to a bargain. Rupert warned that News Corp might find another use for its cash if the Sky board continued to demand more than 700p.

The atmosphere changed completely at the end of the summer, however, as News Corp prepared its formal submissions to regulators. At the Edinburgh International Television Festival, Mark Thompson, the Director-General of the BBC, rebuked Murdoch and Sky in his own MacTaggart Lecture. He challenged Sky to "pull its weight" and invest more in British creative talent and production. More significantly, Thompson used the platform to sound the alarm over the potential dominance of News Corp as a result of the planned takeover.

"If News Corp's proposal to acquire all of the remaining shares in Sky goes through, Sky will not just be Britain's biggest broadcaster, but a full part of a company which is also dominant in national newspapers as well as one of Britain's biggest publishers," Thompson said.[2]

He suggested that Ofcom and Ed Richards, a longstanding opponent of the Murdochs and their dreams of cross-media ownership, might intervene.

"Clearly it may be possible, at least in principle, to put regulatory safeguards and remedies in place to ensure that all of these media markets work fairly – though it will require strenuous work and real courage from all of those involved, as Ofcom has discovered in recent years."

Thompson cited a private report on the potential effects of the transaction by Enders Analysis, a leading media consultancy. It soon emerged that Claire Enders, the founder, had written to the new business secretary, Liberal Democrat Vince Cable, urging him to block the takeover of Sky. He had the power to trigger a media plurality investigation by Ofcom, a procedure only ever used once before, when Sky bought its stake in ITV.

In a scathing 20-page memo, Enders, a high profile and well-connected figure in the British media, described a News Corp takeover of Sky as Britain's "Berlusconi moment". She compared the level of power it would give Rupert Murdoch to that wielded in Italy by Silvio Berlusconi and argued it would mean "a reduction in media plurality to an unacceptably low level", particularly as News Corp would gain full control of Sky News.

It signalled the start of a rearguard action against the deal that would delay and frustrate Murdoch until, ultimately, they were humiliated by the enormity of the phone hacking scandal.

Fleet Street was next to rise up against News Corp. The left-leaning *Observer* newspaper published twin opinion pieces by Will Hutton, a former editor turned political economist, and Henry Porter, a senior columnist, both calling for intervention against the takeover of Sky. James Murdoch read the articles as the first to draw an overt link between the deal and phone hacking at News International and knew that he was in a real fight.

Unbeknown to him, further manoeuvres against the takeover were underway. At the Liberal Democrat party conference the following week, Cable held a private dinner with Alan Rusbridger, the editor of *The Guardian*, and Guy Black, which helped to convince him that Ofcom should review the deal.

Black went to work assembling an extraordinary coalition of media companies to make a formal submission to the government. By mid-October 2010, the campaign also included Trinity Mirror, DMGT (the publisher of *The Daily Mail*), the BBC, Channel 4 and BT. Rival newspaper owners were particularly concerned that Sky's vast customer base and marketing firepower would be used to give *The Sun* and *The Times* a powerful advantage, now that both newspapers were also attempting to build subscription businesses online.

Murdoch was enraged. The smartphone boom was well underway and he had been attempting to create a 'Spotify of news' joint venture with rival publishers that would allow readers to subscribe to a bundle of digital newspapers along with football clips and other shared material. He believed the talks were progressing well, but now the whole of Fleet Street had turned against him and News Corp.

James Murdoch learned of DMGT's involvement in the Media Alliance while on a business trip in Mumbai and immediately rang Jonathan Harmsworth, Lord Rothermere, head of the publisher's controlling dynasty to ask "what the fuck do you think you are doing?" Harmsworth replied that he was merely defending his commercial interests. Murdoch's aggressive tone was not appreciated by the blue-blooded proprietor, but he was in no mood to care.

In early November, Cable duly triggered an Ofcom investigation, setting Murdoch against his old foe Richards once again. The regulator had long believed that the Murdoch press held too much sway over politicians, but did not have the power to launch an investigation off his own bat. Now the question had been asked by a government minister, Richards was able to revisit his long-held concerns about Murdoch influence.

It would be the business secretary's last intervention, however. On 21 December, *The Daily Telegraph* published a conversation between Cable and undercover reporters posing as constituents. He described a "constant battle" behind the scenes with Conservative ministers and boasted that "if they push me too far then I can walk out and bring down the government".

The Daily Telegraph omitted to publish an explosive part of the conversation in which Cable indicated he was implacably opposed to the News Corp takeover of Sky. However, the recording was leaked from the newspaper to Robert Peston, the BBC's business editor, who immediately ran the story on his blog the same day, describing his source as a "whistleblower".[3]

"I don't know if you have been following what has been happening with the Murdoch press, where I have declared war on Mr Murdoch and I think we are going to win," Cable told the reporters.

"I have blocked it using the powers that I have got and they are legal powers that I have got. I can't politicise it but from the people that know what is happening this is a big, big thing.

"His whole empire is now under attack . . . So there are things like that we do in government, that we can't do . . . all we can do in opposition is protest."

The revelations were highly damaging for Cable, who held a supposedly impartial quasi-judicial role in the process, and embarrassing for *The Daily Telegraph*, which faced allegations that it had suppressed parts of the recording to protect a fellow opponent of the Sky takeover.

Downing Street was forced to issue an emergency statement reprimanding the business secretary for "totally unacceptable and inappropriate" comments and removing him from the process entirely. The newspaper meanwhile protested that it was not particularly interested in media stories and had taken a normal editorial decision to focus on other issues raised by the recording.

To James Murdoch, the scandal was confirmation that News Corp was the target of an establishment conspiracy.

At Sky, executives watched the mounting political tension around the takeover with frustration. The more pragmatic, less ideological culture that Darroch had sought to create could not understand some of the moves being made by News Corp.

"For all of Murdoch's so-called political influence, they are absolutely tone deaf when it comes to this stuff," says one insider close to the deal.

Sky believed that Murdoch's provocative MacTaggart speech less than a year before the bid had created unnecessary and powerful enemies.

"It was a stupid mistake by the BBC to allow itself to get involved but it was payback time, pure and simple," says one executive.

"If you had been thinking about this in a sensible political way, you would not have ended up giving that speech. You would have done the opposite. You would have tried to warm everybody up.

"You wouldn't have given the speech in 2009 when you knew the following year you were going to bid. You'd just set the whole of the media establishment against you. There was no effort to cultivate any friends. It was hardly surprising that when it came to make the bid, the media establishment were against it."

The removal of Cable gave News Corp a boost. Ofcom's plurality investigation would instead report to a Conservative, the culture secretary Jeremy Hunt, who was already on the record as sceptical that full Murdoch control of Sky would have any impact on its output.

In June, Hunt had said: "It does seem to me that News Corp do control Sky already, so it isn't clear to me that in terms of media plurality there is a substantive change, but I don't want to second guess what regulators might decide."

Hunt had also been also a regular text message correspondent of Fred Michel, a News Corp lobbyist whose over-familiar style would later make him a comic star of the Leveson Inquiry. Michel was given to calling the secretary of state 'daddy' in an attempt to build rapport. At Sky, he was viewed as a buffoon with little grasp of British political culture.

"The man just wasn't capable of having a sensible conversation," says a Sky executive. "When you then saw what happened with Leveson and it all came out what he'd been saying to James, it all made total sense because he was a complete fantasist."

"He basically talks at people loudly and incessantly and when they don't answer he assumes they have agreed with him," another former colleague confirmed.

Ofcom was already in the late stages of its investigation when Cable was removed. Ed Richards did not feel that attacks on the deal from Fleet Street eased the political pressure on him at all. His Whitehall intelligence network would report back every week that Murdoch or his executives had complained to ministers about Ofcom.

"Politicians just wanted it approved," says an Ofcom insider.

"Obviously, Cameron wanted it approved. Obviously, James thought it would be. If he was angry before about the pay-TV competition investigation, he was off the scale now. Absolutely furious. He tried seriously hard to undermine us."

Richards' report was delivered to Hunt on New Year's Eve. The conclusion was couched in the indirect language of Whitehall but the meaning was clear. Ofcom sought to make it impossible for the government not to refer the deal to the Competition Commission, which had powers to impose restrictions or block it entirely. Ofcom said "it reasonably believes that the proposed acquisition may be expected to operate against the public interest since there may not be a sufficient plurality of persons with control of media enterprises providing news and current affairs to UK-wide cross-media audiences".

Richards was impressed by Hunt's response. After New Year, Hunt called the Ofcom man into the Department for Culture and, with a panel of officials, spent hours grilling him over the detailed content of the report. Days later Hunt rang Richards to tell him that unless News Corp could give undertakings that would deal with the concerns identified by Ofcom, he would indeed refer the bid to the Competition Commission.

The news was delivered to Murdoch at a meeting on 6 January 2011. Notes prepared for Hunt confirm Richards' success: "I have carefully read the Ofcom report and I find it very difficult on the basis of what I have seen to date to see any grounds which would allow me to not refer this case to the

Competition Commission, especially given that the threshold for referring is relatively low."

News Corp and its lawyers, Allen & Overy, scrambled to respond. They attacked the Ofcom report, accusing the regulator of closed mindedness and bias towards the company's media rivals. Hunt rejected those concerns. Within a fortnight of the first meeting News Corp came back with an indication it was willing to spin off Sky News as a separately-listed company in order to gain control of Sky. Hunt said he would consider the "pretty big offer", but would want advice from both the Office of Fair Trading and, once again, Ofcom.

He would later describe it as "a very difficult meeting" with a "very cross" James Murdoch.

"I said I was going to ask for Ofcom's independent advice as well. This was not welcome to Mr Murdoch, because ... he considered Ofcom to be an organisation that was hostile to the interests of News Corp," Hunt told the Leveson Inquiry.

"From Mr Murdoch's point of view, he considered that was tantamount to wanting to kill the deal, because he believed that Ofcom would use every mechanism at their disposal."

There followed weeks of wrangling over the details of how Sky News would be spun off. Richards insisted that Murdoch could not be the chairman of the new company, in which News Corp was due to retain a 39% stake.

"That was a very, very significant thing for Mr Murdoch," Hunt said. "News Corporation thinks that one of its primary functions is what it says on the tin, is news.

"He first of all didn't think he should have to spin off Sky News at all because he didn't believe there was a plurality issue with the original proposal, and this was going to cost him hundreds of millions of pounds more; but secondly, he was at the time chairman of Sky, and that included being chairman of Sky News ... he wanted to continue to be chairman. I think that was pretty important to him."

The plan to spin off Sky News with a separate governance structure to avoid a Competition Commission inquiry was not finalised until March. It would, however, face further consultation and opposition from the Media Alliance. Newspapers remained opposed to a combination of Sky and the Murdoch press. Within days, Slaughter & May wrote to Hunt insisting that the proposal "entirely fails to address plurality concerns".

The consultation ran until the end of June, when Hunt announced he planned further safeguards for the independence of Sky News, including an independent monitoring trustee. He showed no sign of buckling to pressure from Tom Watson, his counterpart on the Labour front bench, to take into account the growing weight of evidence that there had been phone hacking on an industrial scale at *The News of the World*. Hunt relied on legal advice that the issues were separate.

Murdoch believed he was days away from winning approval for the takeover. Then, on 4 July, *The Guardian* revealed that, in 2002, *The News of the World* had hacked the voicemail of Milly Dowler, a 13-year-old girl who had been murdered in Surrey. The story catapulted the phone hacking scandal to the top of the national agenda and plunged News Corp into a full-blown crisis.

Within three days, News Corp announced the closure of *The News of The World*. It then tried to save the Sky bid by withdrawing its offer to spin off Sky News, hoping that the resulting Competition Commission inquiry would provide time for the crisis to pass. The outrage was simply too great. On 13 July, the bid was abandoned before a Labour motion in the Commons against the deal was due to win support from all parties. Murdoch was consumed by the corporate emergency at News International, leaving Chase Carey to admit it "is too difficult to progress in this climate".

Inside Wapping there was complete disarray. In the days after the Milly Dowler revelations, James Murdoch fought to protect Rebekah Brooks on behalf of his father. He was advised by lieutenants that as chief executive of News International and editor of *The News of the World* during the Dowler inquiry, she had to be sacked. Murdoch slammed the table and growled that "over my dead body does she leave this business". Brooks wound up leaving a week later, immediately after the withdrawal of the Sky bid by Rupert, who flew into London to take control of the situation from his son.

Rupert brought Wendi Deng with him on that visit, who by this stage was viewed by James as something of an unwelcome influence. James's older brother Lachlan, who was not at that point a News Corp executive, came to help in looking after their father through the crisis. James may have been fighting for his own survival but Lachlan was received by Rupert and staff at News International as a welcome calming presence amid the storm. He breezed into London from Australia and took up his place at his father's side. The rapprochement appeared temporary, but was the start of a process that would ultimately lead to the eldest son inheriting the crown.

For Sky, the end of the bid saga was mostly welcomed with relief. Nobody wanted to be associated with the hundreds of skeletons being uncovered on Fleet Street. Yet frustration with the way News Corp had conducted the process rankled with Sky's upper ranks.

"I remember a point of frustration was that it just took a long time for them to come out of the blocks with regulators," says one senior executive. "And because they had not got the recommendation from Sky, we were not that able to help. If it's a recommended bid, both managements can get out there on day one and sell the story and the vision. If they had just paid something north of 800p, there wouldn't have been a problem."

"It took them far too long to offer to spin out Sky News," says another. "Then by the time they did have approval, phone hacking was happening. If they had done it when they first filed in December, they would have got the deal away before phone hacking. They were their own worst enemies."

"The process took so long because News Corp, advised by its lawyers, never would believe that the arguments around media plurality actually stood up in law. At Sky, we believed it wasn't about the law – it was about pure politics."

Murdoch remained chairman but faced yet another investigation by Richards as to whether Sky, with him at the head of its board, was a fit and proper holder of a broadcast licence. By April 2012, with the Leveson Inquiry well underway, his position was untenable. He had already been forced to step down as a non-executive director at the drugs giant GlaxoSmithKline. Now James could see, with diplomatic nudging from Darroch, that he had become a political lightning rod and a distraction for Sky, the company he cared the most about. James Murdoch stepped down as chairman.

"I believe that my resignation will help to ensure that there is no false conflation with events at a separate organisation," he said, as he prepared to face Leveson.

An insider recalls the discussions: "Jeremy took him aside. They were talking all the time and to be fair to James he knew it wasn't helping him ... to stay because it created more of a target on his back. He needed to keep a low profile and go back to America.

"It was obviously pretty sad for him and ultimately he feels unfairly maligned."

Murdoch today believes that the Dowler story was deliberately timed to cause maximum damage to the Sky bid as it was on the verge of approval.

Richards may have been emboldened, but Ofcom's fit and proper review allowed Sky to keep its broadcasting licence and found no basis to conclude that Murdoch engaged in any deliberate wrongdoing. Nevertheless, it found he "repeatedly fell short" of the conduct expected of a chief executive and chairman at News Corp.

Murdoch's hope that the regulator might be scrapped by the Cameron government was meanwhile dead and buried. At Sky they believed – "no two ways about it" – that the two men had effectively done a deal that was never delivered, although this is something that both sides have always denied.

10

The Whole Organisation Was in a State of Shock

Ofcom's decision in 2010 to impose an obligation for the wholesaling of Sky Sports was a major victory for BT.

Three years into its attempt to challenge Sky in pay-TV, BT had a customer base of fewer than half a million subscribers. With Sky Sports and top-flight football now on offer at a controlled price, it believed it could make a real dent in the market dominance of its former partner. Murdoch and Darroch were furious but agreed a deal with Ofcom under which BT would pay the difference between the capped price and the price they wanted to charge for Sky Sports into an escrow account, pending a High Court challenge.

The man in charge of BT's renewed attack on Sky was Gavin Patterson, the new head of its retail division. Ian Livingston, who remained bitter about Murdoch's plotting on broadband when he was in the job, was promoted to BT chief executive and was determined to strike back against Sky.

"Not having Sky Sports has cost us customers," Patterson said.[1] "We reckon one in two customers we have approached in the last two years turned us down, saying 'Great service but sorry, pal – no Sky Sports, so we're washing our hands of you.'"

Sky Sports did not prove to be the boost that BT's fledgling television business required, however. Over two years it grew by just 200,000 subscribers, in part because the BT Vision set-top box, based on a system provided by Microsoft, was already proving to be outdated. It was not as user-friendly as Sky and, perhaps more importantly, lacked integration with mobile apps. In late 2011, to make matters worse, Netflix made its UK debut, its slick menus and smart recommendations only serving to underline the lack of progress that BT Vision had made.

Livingston's faith in pay-TV as a central plank of BT's strategy was nevertheless as strong as ever. It had to be. In the depths of the recession that followed the financial crisis, he had convinced the BT board to invest £2.5bn in a nationwide broadband network upgrade programme. New street cabinets would provide faster and more reliable links to local telephone exchanges for millions of homes.

The plan was bold but soon met with some significant challenges. BT's network division, Openreach, struggled to convince the company's rivals in the retail broadband market to sell the new services. Sky and TalkTalk had invested in their own equipment in local exchanges that delivered juicy profit margins. They forecast that most consumers would be happy with their existing broadband connection for years to come and that there was no reason for them to help BT recoup its outlay on network upgrades.

BT needed to sell faster broadband to its own customers, and quickly, and Livingston believed pay-TV offered the answer. He planned to replace BT Vision with a new service based on YouView, a set-top box joint venture alongside the BBC, ITV, Channel 4 and TalkTalk, among others, which aimed to leapfrog Sky's satellite technology with advanced features only made possible by video streaming.

YouView was an unwieldy corporate structure riven with conflicting interests and egos, but when bundled with faster broadband it offered Livingston a way to convince BT subscribers to upgrade. He might even be able to steal back some customers from Sky.

Yet there was a flaw in the plan. The Ofcom ruling that guaranteed access to Sky Sports at a controlled price applied only to BT Vision. There was no regulatory protection for YouView, and Livingston and Patterson knew that a pay-TV service without most Premier League football was doomed to failure. Relations with Sky remained strained and with £2.5bn already staked on broadband upgrades, in the spring of 2012 they decided BT needed to take drastic action.

"Sky was telling BT that we couldn't have Sky Sports and it sent us down a strategic cul de sac," says a senior BT insider. "While mobile and broadband weren't yet bedfellows, TV and broadband were coming together. The big thing for TV was sport and the big thing for sport was football. That was the logic."

A tiny group of senior BT executives were drawing up an audacious plot. Livingston and Patterson, together with his right-hand John Petter and Marc Watson, the head of BT TV and a veteran of sports rights sales, aimed to hit Sky where it would hurt the most – at that summer's auction for Premier League rights.

Over the course of a couple of months they developed plans to usurp Sky as the dominant broadcaster of top-flight football, a position it had occupied since the foundation of the Premier League 20 years earlier. Absolute secrecy was paramount for the ambush to succeed, so preparatory work on bidding strategy was carried out at Petter's kitchen table in Battersea. BT prepared false trails in case it was being watched.

"It was very secret. It's amazing how, if you don't tell people, things don't leak," says one BT executive involved in the work.

Petter later said:[2] "We'd read the history of Premier League auctions, about people being trailed home and leaks ... we weren't going to take any chances, so we did it at my place."

The maths would be difficult. At the last auction in 2009, Sky and Setanta had agreed to pay a record total of £1.8bn over three years for Premier League rights. Setanta promptly went bust, to be replaced by ESPN, the US sports broadcaster owned by Disney, and Sky's dominance remained unchallenged. It would go into the bidding again with millions of pay-TV sport subscribers under its control and ready to deliver a return on its investment in rights. BT had no more than a few hundred thousand subscribers, which meant it might struggle to compete in a bidding war.

Marc Watson provided the insight that convinced Livingston to give the go-ahead. Regulations meant that any broadcaster could demand distribution of its channels over the Sky satellite. That meant BT could insist on access to Sky's 10 million homes without having to provide its channels as part of a Sky pay-TV package.

"There was a realisation that the one bit of regulatory support we did have was that we could force Sky to carry BT Sport on their set top boxes," says a BT insider. "That meant we didn't have to wait until we had built up a big enough fibre broadband base to justify the expense."

BT also embarked on a private charm offensive in the run-up to the auction to convince the Premier League that it should be taken seriously despite its complete inexperience as a broadcaster. David Kogan, a longstanding adviser to the Premier League and a former boss of Watson's, acted as cheerleader for the interloper. He convinced Richard Scudamore, the Premier League chief executive, that a company of BT's scale and strength was required to stand up to Sky. After all, the European Union had barred Scudamore from selling all the rights to Sky, as had been his previous policy, and Setanta and ESPN had both struggled.

The auction was set for June and BT was ready to take its revenge for Sky's surprise acquisition of Easynet years earlier. Miraculously, the secret was kept. In Osterley, Darroch and his senior team had no idea that they were about to face an old enemy and a dagger aimed at the very heart of their business.

Sky was instead worried about a new bogeyman. Bein Sports, a broadcaster linked to the news channel Al Jazeera and backed by billions of Qatari petrodollars, had been picking up sports rights across Europe. Darroch feared that Bein might simply blow Sky out of the water to seize the Premier League. That would mean an end to 20 years of Sky control of top-flight football, hundreds if not thousands of job losses, and some explaining to do to the Murdochs and other investors.

Yet it would not necessarily be a disaster for the business. The Qataris would surely want to strike a deal to distribute their channels via Sky packages, so a loss at the Premier League auction might not mean major customer losses. It would change the shape of the business radically, but Sky by now prided itself on its ability to respond to new competition and technology.

The real challenger was not as rich as Bein but, in many ways, a greater threat. BT did not particularly want Sky to carry its sports channels, but it did want to use the lure of exclusive football coverage to encourage broadband upgrades. In the long run, BT wanted to be a pay-TV operator in its own right, too, and directly compete for control of the living room.

There were seven packages of live matches on the block, covering three Premier League seasons. BT planned to bid for the lot and hoped to come away with five in the first round by outbidding an unprepared Sky. In the end, Sky Sports was saved by the fear of Qatari billions.

"If we had just gone in flat, we would have lost – no question," says a senior Sky insider. "The reason they didn't win is we thought there was going to be someone there. We went in with a decent uplift on the previous auction because we thought the Qataris were going to be there. That was enough to take it to a second round."

The first round result came as a shock in Osterley, where executives gathered in a war room in New Horizons Court, the corporate centre. Sky was told on Friday that it had secured only one out of seven packages of matches. It had grown accustomed to dominating the Premier League auction and was now in uncharted waters. The fact that increased offers had not been accepted the first time was taken as confirmation that Bein Sports was bidding, and bidding aggressively. Sky had days to decide how to respond in the second round.

"For three days everyone is talking at each other and if you'd looked at the team on Saturday you'd be like 'fuck, these guys have got no idea what's happening," recalls one insider.

"We got into a tizzy that it was Al Jazeera. And then people said maybe it was BT or Virgin. In the end we realised we didn't know who it was, so let's not do anything based on trying to guess."

Darroch was under massive pressure; while nervous, he was calm in relation to some of his colleagues. As the weekend wore on, Sky gathered its thoughts and came up with a rational strategy.

"We realised that if it was Al Jazeera, well, they've got shitloads of money and we're just going to have to lose. So it was pointless worrying about that. Once you remember that, it was obvious that we didn't need to go mad."

Second round bids were due on Wednesday. Darroch was being advised by chief operating officer Mike Darcey, and Mai Fyfield, his highly regarded strategy chief, who had been involved in Premier League auctions since the Tony Ball era. He increased Sky's bids but declined to "sweep the corners" and offer the absolute maximum the company could muster.

It was a big decision for the chief executive. If Sky had then lost control of the Premier League, he knew that his own job would be under threat. The board would have demanded to know why he had not cleaned out the company bank accounts to save Sky Sports.

In the febrile atmosphere Sky also took another risky decision not to bid at all for one of the more attractive packages of matches in the second round. It aimed to ensure that if it defeated its new mystery rival, it would also saddle that rival with an expensive bill. Sky Sports knew the arcane details of the 'picks' system that determined which broadcaster got which matches each weekend and sought to exploit it to mean "they would be in for £200m or £300m with a first pick pack that was useless without any other pack".

Sky's calculations proved astute and highly lucrative for the Premier League. When the bills were issued on Wednesday afternoon, the total came to more than £3bn, a 70% increase on the previous auction. Sky won five out of seven packages, leaving BT disappointed with two, including packages of Saturday lunchtime matches that at £246m per season were expensive but not quite enough to build a strong challenge on.

Livingston anyway took the opportunity prior to the official announcement to call Darroch and reveal that BT was the mystery bidder personally.

"It wasn't that we hadn't gamed through a BT bid," recalls a Sky insider. "It just wasn't the number one view. If they think it was a master stroke, that wouldn't be right. They had hired people, they had talked to sports bodies. We weren't blindsided."

"The reaction was 'right, bring it on," says another. "Kill."

Now out in public, BT put a brave face on the auction result, but in private executives and the board were uneasy. Livingston and Patterson believed Scudamore had used his discretion to ensure Sky, his longstanding trusted partner, did not lose packages in the first round. BT was also forced to admit it had miscalculated.

"We bid for more and we definitely wanted a lot more, but we got our bidding strategy a bit wrong," says a senior BT insider. "We were naive first-timers who had very little time for planning and we were left with what could have been an extraordinarily embarrassing situation.

"We didn't even have a studio, we had no talent. We had no other content, and Sky really could have strangled us at birth but for whatever reason they didn't."

BT quickly got to work on a salvage operation. Now that its sporting ambitions were out in the open, it elbowed its way into stalled talks between Sky and rugby authorities to steal away exclusive rights to the Aviva Premiership and make its fledgling line-up of live sport significantly more respectable. It bought what remained of ESPN's UK operation, including FA Cup and Scottish Premier League rights.

As Livingston and Patterson scrambled to set BT up as a broadcaster, they were able to call on the advice of a seasoned sports pay-TV operator. In 2009, Tony Ball had joined the BT board as a non-executive director. The former Sky chief executive had served out his non-compete in Germany, building and selling a cable operator, and leapt at the chance to re-enter the fray in the UK. He cared little that BT had become enemy number one for his former employer.

Livingston's pay-TV ambitions and the audacity of the raid on the Premier League auction excited Ball, although he had cautioned against the strategy prior to the bidding. With the cheques signed, he joined the attack on his old team. "If you play for Manchester United and then you go to Chelsea, do you let the goals in? No," Ball thought. BT relied most on his experience and contacts at the sharp end of sports broadcasting. He helped Patterson bring in executives capable of setting up a credible sports broadcaster from scratch in less than a year.

To Rupert Murdoch, however, it seemed like a betrayal. Despite the expiry of Ball's non-compete deal, a degree of loyalty was expected of former lieutenants. He had not only joined BT but conspired in a direct attack on Sky.

The personal animosity between frontline BT and Sky executives also deepened. Livingston disliked James Murdoch and felt bitter at how Darroch, his own former deputy at Dixons, had continued the crusade against BT.

"Jeremy and I personally get on really well, we always have done," he nevertheless claimed in an interview.[3] In reality, suspicion was running high. On one visit to Osterley, ostensibly to discuss a potential mutual channel supply deal, Livingston found the Sky reception newly festooned with representations of all the sports rights controlled by Sky. He was told that Darroch was late for the meeting and offered a tour of Sky's production facilities.

The surprise of the auction subsided and Sky's staff soon were galvanised by BT's move into sport. Their enemy had come out of hiding at last and the real battle could now begin. Sky took BT seriously. In the month before the launch of BT Sport in 2013, senior executives across the business prepared to collaborate on "Project Purple", the codename for their response to the new challenger. Steven van Rooyen, now in the crucial role of head of marketing, led the charge, but Sky still had very little information on how BT would mount an attack.

Again, Livingston was playing his cards very close to his chest. Inside BT, internal documents were seeded with false information on pricing in case anyone was leaking to the enemy.

The answers came in May, when at a new state-of-the-art television studio on the Olympic Park in east London, Livingston revealed that he would offer BT Sport for free to broadband subscribers. It represented ample evidence of the escalating of the threat to Sky: BT was seeking to fundamentally undermine the value of pay-TV sport in order to increase the value of faster broadband. It positioned itself as the fans' champion, opening up access in the face of monopolistic and expensive Sky Sports.

Sky knew BT Sport would be cheap, but had not expected Livingston to be quite so aggressive. The sums did not add up, given the high cost of Premier League rights, and Sky was confident. James Murdoch, still on the board as a non-executive director, believed BT was acting irrationally and would not be able to make a business out of broadcasting given the cheques it was signing.

Project Purple began in earnest anyway, gathering intelligence in the press, from Twitter and from Sky's own call centres about the reaction to BT's offer. Van Rooyen launched an advertising campaign that emphasised the breadth of Sky Sports' rights to cricket, golf and other sports, as well as football. Sky refused to carry advertising for BT Sport on its own channels, prompting another complaint from BT to Ofcom.

"There was a sense across the business that was like 'okay, they have had to come out onto open ground now and it is going to be a fair fight;" says a colleague. "The consumer will decide who wins and loses. We weren't cocky but we knew our ground."

"We had a team of people tracking everything they did," recalls another senior executive at Sky. "We weren't going to miss a thing and we made sure we were always working with the latest information. It was the best marketing we have ever done and all joined up across the business. Sky is always best when there is a nemesis."

Despite the defensive manoeuvres and rumours that it had almost lost the Premier League auction, Sky remained convinced that BT was not seriously attempting to steal its pay-TV crown. Despite its rearguard marketing efforts, and acknowledgement that BT's challenger positioning made it a "£22bn gorilla in puppy's clothing", there was a degree of complacency at Sky. It publicly dismissed BT Sport as a "marketing gimmick".

"We thought it was just a marketing and regulatory exercise," says one insider. "They were doing the pay-TV complaints with Ofcom to get hold of Sky Sports and they were going to bundle it with broadband as a retention game. We didn't think they were trying to usurp our position in sport … anyway, we thought they were crap at running a customer business. So we weren't massively worried."

Livingston responded: "Sky called it a marketing gimmick but actually sport and TV and broadband are not separate products, they are the product. They're still thinking in the old-fashioned way."

After five years at the top and a major turnaround under his belt, and with BT Sport launched into the market by BT, Livingston stepped down and handed the reins to Patterson in September. Observers, including Ofcom, hoped a new chief executive might mean BT could agree a truce with Sky that involved the mutual supply of their sport channels. Like Livingston, Patterson was a former colleague of Darroch, when they had both been at Procter & Gamble. Unlike Livingston, he was cool-tempered and had maintained friendly relations with the Sky boss. Patterson and Darroch were even neighbours on the same exclusive private estate, St George's Hill in Weybridge, Surrey.

There was to be no end to the hostilities, however. Patterson definitely did not see BT Sport as a mere marketing tool. His first big move as chief executive gave Sky the biggest fright in its history and shook it out of any delusion that BT was not a threat to its status as the number one sports broadcaster. In November, a couple of months into his reign, Patterson agreed to pay the football governing body UEFA £897m for three years of exclusive rights to key European club competitions – the Champions League and the Europa League.

It was a stunning raid and the first time any broadcaster secured exclusive rights to the Champions League, which previously had been shared by Sky and ITV. The price, branded as "mad" by the media analyst Claire Enders, was more than double that of the previous deal. It massively boosted the BT Sport schedules, with up to 350 live matches per season, and completely deprived Sky of access to the top club competition in world football. Fans of top Premier League clubs would now face a real dilemma: do they stick with Sky and miss the Champions League, or transfer to BT?

Sky staff were shellshocked and its shares plummeted 10% in a day.

"We knew they were probably going to come after the Champions League," recalls one senior insider. "We put in a pretty good bid but we were still quite a long way behind them. We went to the limit of what we were willing to pay."

It was another big call for Darroch. During UEFA's auction, Barney Francis, the well-connected head of Sky Sports, received a tip-off that BT was poised to win everything. He appealed to Darroch to write a massive cheque. But after consultation with strategy experts, Darroch decided to walk away. The choice was complicated and also involved weighing the need to invest more in non-sport programming in order to meet the rising threat from Netflix, which by now was taking off in the UK.

Darroch also knew that while losing European football was bad, losing dominance of the Premier League at the next auction would be a disaster. If Sky had dug deep to retain the Champions League, its chances of defeating BT in that next battle would be damaged.

"We had a chance to come back in, of course we did," says one senior executive. "When you've got a relationship that runs that long, maybe the process says you can't come back in but it doesn't matter. If you want it and put enough money down, it's yours.

"We spent a day deciding we weren't going to do it. The conversation we had was that was more than the whole of the Sky One budget. It was just not worth it."

"Barney wasn't happy but for Jeremy it was his finest hour. He could have done it. An extra £100m here or there wouldn't have upset the City. It was braver to say no."

Darroch attempted to rally the troops once the news became public, but the loss of the Champions League was a heavy psychological blow. Sky Sports had not faced a genuine challenge in 20 years. Now a bigger, richer rival had demonstrated its power.

"There was a state of shock," recalls one executive. "This was an existential threat to Sky Sports. This was BT being serious. They wanted to be number one in sports. They had deeper pockets. I don't think anyone could do it based on their capabilities and execution. But we were very frightened of them financially.

"There was an email from Barney the day after that tried to calm nerves. But the whole organisation was in a state of shock. That lasted a few days. Then there was anger, then there was 'right, we are going to defeat these bastards.'"

Complacency evaporated. The competitive response moved into a higher gear with a larger budget. Sky moved quickly to secure deals for its other sports rights. It accelerated development of a new set-top box and launched Now TV, a streaming service for households who didn't want to commit to a dish. Van Rooyen aggressively discounted broadband to tie customers into contracts. That would make it difficult for them to defect to BT once it began broadcasting the Champions League.

Relations between the BT and Sky management teams were worse than ever. John Petter, the head of BT's consumer business, took to the role of insurgent, attacking Sky from conference podiums and in print. Sky executives were furious but mostly stayed silent.

By early 2015, there were signs that BT Sport had achieved at least part of its mission. BT was signing up lots of customers for faster broadband and had arrested the revenue decline of its consumer business. Sceptical investors began to give Patterson the benefit of the doubt over his broadcasting ambitions and BT shares were climbing to their highest level since the dotcom boom. There were few signs of an impact on Sky's business, in part because the company was reducing disclosure.

The scene was now set for what would become the defining battle. The Premier League's triennial auction was scheduled for February and there was no way that Sky could afford to let BT win. Unbeknown to Darroch, Patterson did not intend to take the majority of the rights. His focus had shifted to EE, the mobile network that BT had agreed to acquire for £12.5bn in December 2014. He planned only for BT Sport to consolidate its role as a strong number two to Sky Sports. Patterson feared that muscling in more on sport would bring regulatory action against the EE takeover, and in private he resigned himself to being Pepsi to Sky's Coke.

Sky bid very aggressively in a bid to head off BT and retain control of most of the packages. The result was extraordinary: the overall rights bill issued by the Premier League at the end of the process was a record £5.1bn over three years, up 70% on the previous auction. Sky bore the brunt of the increase. Darroch agreed to pay £4.2bn, an increase of 83% on its previous deal. Its annual bill of £1.4bn was more than £300m, even more than analysts had feared. In contrast, BT's bill for its two packages went up by just 18%.

"Jeremy would never admit this but he panicked," says a senior BT executive. "They somehow got into their head, their minds, that we were going to go in to crush them and they massively overpaid.

"We were shocked. You're not allowed to collude, obviously, but we had been trying to signal as much as possible that we weren't going in hard. I guess they must have thought it was a bluff because there was so much bad blood at that point."

Richard Scudamore, the Premier League chief executive, was thrilled. Once again he had delivered a massive increase in income for top clubs. He organised a televised 5pm press conference to make the announcement. At Sky there were cheers as staff gathered to watch the big moment when it was first revealed that they had retained rights to most of the packages. Then there was an audible gasp when the price tag was announced.

Sky had always prided itself on the quality of its auction planning, but this time it had got its tactics drastically wrong.

"It wasn't a great feeling," says one senior executive involved in the bidding. "We had thought we had to show them something to get them to back off. But we overdid it."

Darroch put a brave face on the result, which meant Sky would have to find hundreds of millions of pounds to hit its financial targets.

"We were the business that walked away with five packs," he protested,[4] as he sought to reassure investors that Sky would make £200m in costs and at the same time raise prices to bring in an extra £100m. "We were the business that walked away with the best picks, the best slots. If BT were happy with that, then good luck to them."

The cuts were sharp. The ambitious redevelopment of the Osterley campus had to be scaled back. Plans for a staff swimming pool were shelved. More importantly, hundreds of jobs were cut and budgets were pared back. Sky Sports was forced to reconsider its longstanding approach of seeking ownership of virtually all the rights available in favour of a more selective strategy based on hard-headed analysis of what subscribers valued the most. It dropped US Open tennis and, more painfully, gave up the Ashes cricket tour to BT.

Sky was in an unfamiliar position of making strategic choices on the defensive, and it was uncomfortable. Ultimately, however, the experience proved a useful "kick up the backside", according to senior executives. Sky slimmed down and sharpened up. The subscriber base for Sky Sports, at around five million, had not grown for some years, and there was good reason to fundamentally reassess its role in the business. The new Premier League bill meant that, as a standalone business, Sky Sports was a loss-maker; meanwhile Netflix was beginning to shake up pay-TV.

"It changed the philosophy of the sports business, from we need to own everything to what do we need to own to retain these customers," recalls one insider.

"A lot of the fat that was cut was good stuff to cut," says another top executive. "In the Netflix world you can't afford to have operating costs you shouldn't have. Their operating costs are non-existent. We started a mantra that you have to be thin to compete. Without that stimulus of BT threatening the business, we might not have done it."

Sky became more aggressive in its negotiations with third-party providers of smaller channels, such as Discovery and UKTV, chiselling their fees. Staff bonuses were cut. It may have been painful, but for Sky it was the low point of the battle with BT. Soon there was an opportunity for revenge, in the spirit of "throw rocks at our house and we will napalm your village".

Weeks after the damaging Premier League auction, Ofcom launched a once-in-a-decade review of the telecoms market on which BT relied. It was the first time the regulator had examined the structure since the creation of Openreach, the broadband wholesale monopoly, and Sky aimed to force change. Openreach had become a cash cow for BT, providing the financial breathing space for its expensive foray into broadcasting. David Wheeldon, Sky's public affairs chief, devised an attack campaign to urge Ofcom to break up BT and make Openreach fully independent.

The ensuing lobbying battle was fierce and put BT firmly on the back foot. The campaign drew support from TalkTalk and other rival broadband retailers, and quickly morphed into a push for investment in network upgrades as well as separation. BT responded angrily and ill-advisedly, putting itself into a long war with Ofcom that diverted management attention and killed the momentum behind its sport strategy. Sky had also become increasingly frustrated by Openreach's weak record on repairs and installations, which meant its customers suffered. The campaign was a triumph for Sky, as BT executives now privately admit.

"There was a lot of added poignancy because of our fight with BT but the actual reason for it was a naked commercial interest," says a Sky insider. "Maybe it wouldn't have even happened without sport.

"The underlying strategic play said that anything that makes life difficult for BT, and forces it to invest more in its network, gives it less to spend on content. That was in part driven by our assessment that BT had underinvested in its networks and by that had more firepower in sport.

"But it was also driven by frustration that we were spending hundreds of millions of quid with a monopoly supplier who was giving us shit service.

"Broadband is an exception for Sky because we pride ourselves on great customer service but in this case we're not in control of it. Over the years it built up into a head of real frustration. The structural separation campaign fortuitously met two objectives. It pinned BT down strategically and also helped us with a message about our customers being more important than anything else."

BT's fight with Ofcom to retain ownership of Openreach eroded investor enthusiasm for sport. Patterson then suffered a string of unexpected financial blows, including a massive accounting scandal in Italy, which meant BT's days of aggressive bidding were over. Most of the executives behind the expansion were cleared out in an overhaul demanded by angry shareholders.

By the end of 2017, with a new structure for Openreach finally agreed (still part of BT but with more independence) and another Premier League auction looming, he and Darroch were ready to sign a peace accord. They agreed to supply their sports channels to each other and effectively ended corporate hostility that had begun 12 years earlier when James Murdoch bought Easynet.

Both companies had wasted massive amounts of time and money, in a demonstration of the danger that a complete breakdown in trust can pose to businesses. BT and Sky destroyed billions of shareholder value in a dispute that was driven as much by ego and offence-taking as by genuine competition. The contest itself was brutal, and while consumers enjoyed better coverage and more innovation (BT was first to broadcast in ultra-high definition, for instance) as a result, they did not necessarily benefit from lower prices. Almost all of the extra money pumped into the Premier League has ended up in the hands of players and their agents.

The Premier League auction in 2018, weeks after the channel supply agreement, proved the point. BT and Sky both still cried up the packages, but the overall bill fell significantly for the first time in the history of the competition, despite flailing attempts by Scudamore to encourage bids from Amazon and Facebook. It would have happened earlier if negotiations between BT, Sky and Ofcom about the supply of Sky Sports had not been so riven with suspicion.

Sky believed BT was pulling the regulator's strings to gain an advantage; BT believed Sky was abusing its dominance. Tens of millions of pounds were paid out in lawyers' fees as they fought over the Ofcom 'must offer' rules, rather than pursuing serious commercial discussions. Ultimately, Sky 'won' the war, but only in the narrow sense that BT did not take its crown in sports broadcasting.

Sky showed how its ultra-competitive spirit could cut both ways. By casting BT as the enemy, it motivated and pushed itself to compete. But on a war footing, Sky then found it easier to keep fighting than to pursue peace. Estimates vary, but senior executives on both sides now privately admit that the conflict cost their shareholders billions of pounds.

11

We're Too Big and They Don't Like It

The phone hacking crisis was a heavy blow to Rupert Murdoch and his authority over News Corp. For years he had rejected calls from investors and his entertainment executives to separate the growing, profitable television and film business from the struggling newspaper and publishing assets. Murdoch was devoted to his newspapers and had long insisted that they benefit from the corporate and financial shelter provided.

The unfolding scandal in Britain meant that he had to listen seriously to critics of the vast network of companies he had constructed over decades of dealmaking. Investors were angry that wrongdoing in a financially insignificant corner of News Corp – the British newspaper industry – was costing them money. By 2012, the company had paid out $200m in lawyers' fees and settlements to victims of the practice. In the week of the Milly Dowler revelations, the stock price tumbled 14% and had to be propped up by a major $5bn share backpack programme.

Investors were openly questioning whether the Murdoch family should be allowed to continue to control the business. Reluctantly, Rupert gradually came around to the idea that News Corp should be split up. In June 2012, a couple of months after he and his son had been grilled by the Leveson Inquiry, the mogul summoned his top editors to a lunch meeting in New York and told them two new companies would be created.

The newspaper men would have to fend for themselves, just as smartphones, Google and Facebook were upending their industry, and they were justifiably worried. Murdoch said that he was tired of shareholders and analysts criticising, and the 'new' News Corp would benefit from its own dedicated management.

The other new company would be 21st Century Fox. It would inherit the old News Corp's entertainment assets, which accounted for most of its value, including its 39% stake in Sky. Murdoch, of course, planned to maintain control of both companies, but the plan represented the biggest shake-up of his empire yet.

Although phone hacking forced the issue, it partly reflected a broader trend. Many of the media giants assembled in the 1990s and 2000s were being pruned and reshaped as it became clear that the benefits of linking magazines and film production, or music and telecoms, or outdoor advertising and broadcasting, were limited. In the wake of the financial crisis, investors demanded more focus and growth from management teams, and the excesses of an unwieldly structure such as News Corp were deeply unfashionable.

Executives immediately began jockeying for position. After Rebekah Brooks had been forced out of News International, Murdoch called on Tom Mockridge, the trusted chief executive of Sky Italia and former non-executive director of Sky itself, to steady the ship. Having loyally walked into enemy fire, Mockridge was seen as a potential chief executive of 'new' News Corp. He was passed over, however, and quit in December.

Mockridge reemerged months later as the chief executive of Virgin Media, working for Murdoch's longstanding rival John Malone after 22 years as part of News Corp. In February 2013, his European cable holding company Liberty Global had swooped in to acquire Virgin Media for £15bn, putting it on the most stable financial footing in its history.

The complicated split of News Corp was eventually completed in the summer of 2013, immediately sparking speculation that the Murdochs would come back for Sky. Without a formal corporate link to the dirty world of newspapers and phone hacking, a takeover by Fox would surely be a relative doddle, City analysts suggested. But Sky had ideas of its own.

By the time James Murdoch stepped down as chairman and then ran the gauntlet of the Leveson hearings, attention in Osterley was firmly back on the task at hand. Sky was not, for the forseeable future, likely to become a fully integrated part of News Corp. Yet going through the motions of a takeover had convinced Darroch that he needed to do a deal. The new giants of Silicon Valley threatened not only newspapers, but pay-TV too, and they dwarfed even Sky.

There was also a growing sense that, 23 years after its market debut, Sky's core pay-TV business was finally approaching its limit. In the midst of the News Corp bid, in early November 2010, and two months ahead of schedule, it had hit the 10 million target set by Murdoch way back in 2004. By 2012, the number of satellite households was still growing, but at a slower pace. On top of that, BT had gatecrashed the Premier League auction and would soon mount a real challenge for the first time.

At the board's annual strategy day, two takeover options were discussed. Either Sky could buy Sky Italia and Sky Deutschland from News Corp and deliver the longstanding Murdoch vision of a pan-European pay-TV operator itself, or it could buy a mobile network and add another leg to its British business. Sky knew that Hutchison, the owner of the operator Three, was open to a sale.

"There was literally a choice," recalls one senior executive. "If we were going to be able to buy Italy and Germany we couldn't have afforded to buy Three."

Sky executives had been informally discussing both ideas for years. There were early discussions about European expansion by launching streaming services in the Netherlands and Scandinavia. When Murdoch was chairman, European expansion was always top of the agenda.

There had been a change of the guard on the board, however, partly triggered by phone hacking and partly by ordinary turnover of non-executive directors, which meant the case had to be made again.

Nick Ferguson, previously deputy chairman, was now the chairman. He brought the highly analytical approach of private equity to dealmaking, in contrast to Murdoch's more instinctive approach. Other newcomers included Martin Gilbert, the founder of the Scottish fund manager Aberdeen Asset Management, and Dave Lewis, a senior executive from Unilever who would go on to become chief executive of Tesco. All had their own reputations to defend, and knew that any deal with News Corp to buy Sky Italia and Sky Deutschland would be fraught with potential pitfalls. They insisted on an extremely thorough examination of whether UK mobile, rather than European expansion, was the best path for Sky to take.

The work was to be carried out by Andrew Griffith, the chief financial officer and former investment banker. He would spend the next 18 months carefully planning what, in any event, would be Sky's biggest ever deal.

"We went through all that with the board in a couple of years of strategy days," recalls a colleague. "They wanted to be sure that mobile had been properly looked at. Nick Ferguson started off being focused on the UK.

"News Corp were in such retreat in the UK after phone hacking, with their reputation where it was, that the new board directors were a lot more nervous about perception if we did a deal with them. Nick wasn't about to roll over and get ripped off.

"If you presented Europe or mobile, he would immediately be into the financials. It was completely the opposite to James, really. He would not pay any attention to the number if he thought it was the right thing to do. That wasn't Nick."

According to colleagues, Darroch was never keen on a takeover of Three, although talks were opened. Until the weight of phone hacking allegations eventually sunk the News Corp deal, he was lined up as the chief executive of the first pan-European pay-TV operator. While most Sky executives had worked only in the UK and were expert in the quirks of British consumers, his earlier careers at Procter & Gamble and then Dixons meant that Darroch had years of continental experience.

"Jeremy had really bought into the News Corp rationale for Sky Europe," says a colleague. "But it was quite tricky to get that signed off internally with the board."

He was sceptical, too, that providing mobile service would be a good fit with Sky's other businesses. While pay-TV and broadband were household bills, mobile tended to be a personal expense, and Darroch believed the opportunities for adding it to the bundle of Sky services would be limited as a result. There were cultural concerns too. Operating a mobile network would mean massive infrastructure ownership and thousands of new engineering staff in a company that prided itself on fleet-footedness and efficient deployment of capital. Sky was a world leader in marketing pay-TV to compete with free-to-air broadcasting, but had little appetite for the brutal grind of mobile.

"Those mobile guys are contemporaries of Sky in the sense of big business that grew from scratch late 1980s onwards," explains on senior Sky executive.

"But the difference is the market came to them and they are fighting for share of it. Sky was competing with free. We had an approach to marketing that was all about stimulating demand. We were converting people over quite a long timeline. They were in a quarterly street fight. It's quite a different skillset."

Sky's suspicion of the British regulatory system also played a role.

"There has always been a deep sense from our run-ins with regulators and politicians that Sky's ability to grow in the UK was restricted," says a senior executive.

"Growth by acquisition was going to be difficult. Even if we did it organically, there would be a regulatory price to pay. The establishment was not with us. Whatever we do on content investment or however brilliant Sky News is, it doesn't matter – we're too big and they don't like it. Therefore if we want to get bigger, we've got to go to other markets. That was definitely in our minds.

"When you start thinking that way it would be odd not to do the other Sky businesses first. They had the common brand and DNA. It was the best set of businesses available. And trying to buy Canal+ would be impossible because of the French."

By late 2013, the decision was taken: Sky would buy Sky Italia and Sky Deutschland. The split of News Corp was complete, so the vendor would now be 21st Century Fox. It owned Sky Italia outright and 57% of Sky Deutschland, which was listed on the Frankfurt stock exchange. The crucial question was what price would the Murdochs demand for the assets?

"We got to the start of 2014, everyone was bought in and there was a mandate to go and get the deal done," recalls a senior insider.

"Inevitably, once again, negotiating with the Murdochs and Fox is all take and no give. They were holding out for a very high price."

A few weeks into the talks, in May, news leaked that a deal was in the offing. The financial newswire Bloomberg broke the story on a Friday, when Darroch was in the air on his way to California to attend a Team Sky event. On landing his phone exploded with text messages and missed calls. The leak put the deal in jeopardy, as Sky Deutschland shares leapt. There was now a rush to agree terms with Fox before the price ran away from Sky.

"It started to get away from us financially," recalls one insider. "The only way we could afford it was for Fox to take less for its shares in Sky Deutschland. Eventually they took the minimum they were allowed to by the German takeover rules."

It was a tricky tightrope for Fox to walk. On the one hand it was a major shareholder in Sky and did not want to overload it with debt that might damage the business. Yet it also wanted as much cash as possible.

The Murdochs were resurgent and plotting their next deal in the United States. Lachlan, after a long absence in Australia, rejoined the family business in March as co-chairman with his father of both Fox and 'new' News Corp. James, meanwhile, was promoted to joint chief operating officer of Fox, alongside Chase Carey. The dynastic manoeuvres and buoyant share prices for both arms of the empire signalled that the clan had survived phone hacking and that Rupert remained determined to pass on what he had built to his sons.

At the same time as they were in talks to sell Sky Italia and Sky Deutschland, the Murdochs were planning an audacious $80bn takeover of Time Warner, the owner of the Hollywood studio Warner Bros and the maker of *Game of Thrones*, HBO. It would have been the biggest media deal in a decade, and Sky's cash would come in handy. It added a further layer of complexity and sensitivity to discussions in Europe: if it looked like Sky was generously funding a Murdoch war of conquest in the United States, City investors might protest.

The deal was finally unveiled at the end of July. The total price tag would be up to £7.4bn, depending how many independent Sky Deutschland shareholders took the offer. Fox was finally convinced to sell its stake in Germany at an affordable price by the inclusion in the deal of Sky's 21% stake in the National Geographic nature channel as a sweetener. Sky Italia cost £2.5bn. Sky Deutschland, smaller and loss-making but in a strong economy with plenty of room for pay-TV growth, accounted for the lion's share of the bill.

Sky did not have £7.4bn, so Griffith and Sky's advisers drew funding from everywhere possible. They cleaned out the company's cash reserves, issued new shares equivalent to a tenth of the value of the company and borrowed billions of pounds. Sky even sold off its remaining 6.4% in ITV, left over from its battle with regulators years earlier. It had been forced to sell most of its shares at a heavy loss, but now booked a profit on the final tranche, selling at 185p per share, compared with its 135p buy-in price in 2006. ITV had made a strong recovery by focusing on its programme production business.

In an ironic twist, the buyer was Liberty Global, the new owner of Virgin Media, the company that Sky had blocked from buying ITV in the first place. It had been tipped off that Sky was preparing to place the shares on the stock market and snapped up the whole stake.

Darroch got to work promoting his deal to the City. The new company would have 20 million customers across its territory, but the selling point was untapped growth, especially in Germany. Both of Sky's new subsidiaries were dragged by the British operation. By this point Sky UK had annual revenues of £7.6bn, compared with £2.3bn in Italy and just £1.3bn in Germany.

"Fundamentally it's about growth," Darroch said.[1] "We've got headroom today in the UK of about 14 million households. That will grow to 66 million households when you combine Sky Italia and Sky Deutschland.

"I think this really positions us well for the future. We see a sector that is becoming more international. I think to be at the forefront of that and shape the change as it manifests itself means we're going to be better placed."

Sky had been braced for a negative reaction. In an email to senior colleagues Darroch warned: "There are going to be people who don't like what we are proposing and who may be very chippy and challenging of us."

His fears were unfounded. In October, Sky shareholders waved through the takeovers of Sky Italia and Sky Deutschland by a resounding margin. Only 4% of investors opposed the plan to radically expand and internationalise the business.

In the meantime, Fox's attempted takeover of Time Warner had failed. Three weeks after the unsolicited approach was revealed, in early August, Fox walked away, complaining that its target had refused to negotiate. There had also been a sharp drop in the company's share price as investors worried that Murdoch would allow his ambition to control the assets to lead him to over pay, as it had years earlier when he bought *The Wall Street Journal*. Murdoch had planned to pay for most of Time Warner with Fox shares, so the maths became even more challenging as their price declined.

At Sky senior executives eyed the developments in the United States closely. Fox's swing and miss had been partly driven by the arrival as a shareholder of ValueAct, an activist investor known for triggering deals and sales at big companies. Time Warner had not worked out, but Darroch and Griffith detected a change in the weather at Fox. ValueAct would bring new impetus and scrutiny to Murdoch management of Fox. What that would mean for Sky was not yet clear, but more moves seemed inevitable.

Regardless, there was a job of integration to do. Taking control of Sky Italia and Sky Deutschland meant the company would have to step even further away from the strictly hierarchical, command-and-control style that had characterised its early years and adolescence. Darroch experimented with centralising corporate functions such as public affairs, but quickly changed tack to create Sky as a federation in which local management called most of the shots.

It meant Darroch himself became the main link for the operations as he sought to trim costs of £200m and find ways for them to share programme production and technology costs.

"Jeremy really believed in it so was a very convincing advocate for it," says a colleague. "Since then he is the one who has really tried to make it work. The other top executives have been more in and out of it. Jeremy also knew that having put his neck on the line he had to deliver. It's his legacy. It's the biggest thing he's done."

It helped that both the new additions were run by former Sky executives. In Germany, Brian Sullivan had been hard at work getting the old Premiere business back to growth after years of underinvestment under private equity ownership. He had always been closer to James Murdoch than Darroch and within a few months left to return to Fox in the United States. He was replaced by deputy Carsten Schmidt.

In Italy, Andrea Zappia, another former occupant of the crucial customer chief role at Sky, was chief executive after Tom Mockridge and took on the tough job of competing with Silvio Berlusconi's broadcaster Mediaset.

After a year of jetting between London, Munich and Milan, Darroch decided to delegate some of his domestic responsibilities by appointing a UK chief executive. The role was handed to Steven van Rooyen, the marketing and customer chief. He had thrived in the hard-charging, ultra-competitive atmosphere of the sporting clash with BT.

"The job he basically does is sales and marketing, which is the toughest job at Sky because it means keeping those customer numbers turning," says a colleague. "Everything else comes off the back of it."

It also meant a promotion for Griffith, who as well as head of finance was made chief operating officer, a role that had been vacant since 2011, when Mike Darcey got the call from Rupert Murdoch to take the hot seat at News International, after Mockridge's exit. Darroch effectively kicked himself upstairs, while retaining control of key decisions such as Premier League bidding.

The reshuffle reaffirmed a senior team highly unusual in its durability. Griffith and May Fyfield, the strategy chief, had been at Sky since the Tony Ball era. Van Rooyen joined in 2005 and worked his way up. James Conyers had been general counsel since 2005 and joined the legal department way back in 1993. Many other senior Sky executives were veterans by the time it expanded onto the continent. Both James Murdoch and Darroch inspired loyalty in their lieutenants.

Against expectations, Italy has proved the more fertile ground for Sky since the takeovers. In Germany, described by analysts initially as the "jewel" in the deal,[2] Sky found that the legacy of Premiere was harder to shake than it had hoped. Many customers had been signed up on short-term cheap deals that flattered the subscriber numbers. Sky Deutschland was still highly reliant on football too and not in control of the basic channels that it had mortgaged to keep the lights on in the private equity days.

"The hard bit in Germany is making the team feel like winners," says a Sky insider. "They can't leave their history behind. A load of things you think they would own they didn't and that made it hard to make the numbers work. It's a hard slog and I think we realised it is still quite early days there for pay-TV."

"There is still more opportunity in Germany than Italy, long-term. But there is unbelievable opportunity in Italy now. Netflix and Amazon aren't doing that well there and we're just getting going on broadband."

Another insider puts it simply: "Sky Italia is doing very well, Germany is doing less well."

Optimism in Italy is driven by the ultimate defeat of Mediaset, which had for years sought to compete with its own pay-TV service. Berlusconi ultimately overreached himself by paying too much for Champions League rights. After an attempt to offload the loss-making business to Vivendi in a deal that ended in acrimony, in 2018 Mediaset was forced to sell its pay-TV arm to Sky and grant its rival distribution over Italy's digital terrestrial broadcasting network. The agreement, the spoils of a long attritional fight, opens up millions more Italian homes to Sky.

As much as the takeover of Sky Italia and Sky Deutschland offered new opportunities for growth, its main benefits to Sky and its shareholders were more strategic and defensive.

It was clear that the future of pay-TV was competition with Netflix, Amazon and other streaming services. As well as the riches of the technology industry, they were bringing international scale to bear in negotiations with rights holders. Sky needed to expand to compete and hold its position. The underlying logic was the same as that developed by News Corp for its failed takeover bid four years earlier.

12

Netflix Is Just HBO with a Decent IT Department

In the 40th minute of the first half, captain Vincent Kompany turned the ball over the West Ham goal line to seal a comfortable two-nil victory for Manchester City, and with it the 2013/14 Premier League title. The celebrations at the Etihad Stadium lasted well into the evening.

The end of the season should also have been a day of triumph for Sky. Despite the strong challenge from BT, it remained Britain's dominant sports broadcaster and had just delivered another year of quality coverage.

Instead, Sky was in meltdown. Its new, low-cost streaming service, Now TV, had crashed, leaving thousands of fans cut off from the climax of a long Premier League season. Sky Go, the streaming service provided to satellite subscribers, also collapsed. Angry customers bombarded Sky's social media channels. The embarrassment for a company so intertwined with top-flight football was acute. Executives abandoned family dinners and scrambled to Sky headquarters at Osterley, but as far as fans were concerned the damage was done.

On Monday morning there was the inevitable reckoning. Jeremy Darroch, not given to outbursts of temper, was initially apoplectic. Executives discussed whether to abandon Now TV entirely. It was a sideline after all, and its failure showed that perhaps the technology was just not capable of delivering live broadcasts over the internet to large audiences.

"Everybody thought that we were going to basically put a pin in it," recalls one senior executive.

"It was a hard day that has ended up being one of those moments of proof about when we believe in something; we go after it and we fix it and we make it good. We don't just chuck in the towel."

Cooler heads soon prevailed, however. Rather than shut down Now TV, Sky opted to double down. Darroch ordered a programme of infrastructure investment to increase the resilience of the streaming network. It was a crucial moment and characteristic of Sky's approach to consumer technology.

Now TV was quick to market, only six months after Netflix made its debut in the UK, but was not ready for prime time. Delivering live video to hundreds of thousands of households at the same time over the internet was much more difficult than individual on-demand programmes, and far more challenging than Sky had imagined.

"It's one of Sky's strengths to go to the board and be able to launch things where we don't totally know what we're doing," says one executive involved in the launch of Now TV. "We don't wait to know all the answers. It's iterative."

By investing and rapidly cycling through improvements, it would ensure one way or another that it would not be embarrassed again by Now TV.

The Sky board had agreed to the creation of Now TV following a campaign by Mai Fyfield, the strategy chief, and Steven van Rooyen, the executive closest to Sky's day-to-day trading. They believed that the arrival of Netflix and Amazon as cheap streaming options demanded a response.

Sky customers were paying on average almost £50 per month and committed to long contracts, while Netflix arrived in the UK market at £5.99 with a month's free trial and no cancellation penalties.[1] Amazon's video service, then trading as Lovefilm Instant, was £1 cheaper still.

Reed Hastings, the Netflix founder, had already signalled his intent in the UK.

"The main rival is Sky, with Sky Movies and Sky Atlantic – they're the ones with big content," he said.

Internet video was not news to Sky. As long ago as 2000, Tony Ball was talking about a future in which Sky was not dependent on satellite distribution.

"I think it's inevitable that we are moving towards platform neutrality," he said.[2] "We've experimented with ADSL [the technology behind broadband], which is one way into the future, and there are others. But it is the general opinion that what the industry will be about is offering as much to your customers as possible."

Back in 2006, in the technological white heat of the James Murdoch era, it launched Sky By Broadband, a streaming service soon rebranded as Sky Anytime, then Sky Player and later again as Sky Go. It beat the BBC iPlayer to market by more than a year but for a long time made limited impact, in part because Sky charged a premium for the service.

By the time Now TV was under discussion in 2011, however, the consumer appetite for on-demand programming and internet video was exploding. Smart TVs, with built-in internet connections, were now on the market. Sky would soon rush to connect its existing estate of set-top boxes to rapidly improving broadband lines to ensure its customers were not tempted to spend more screen time outside the Sky menu.

"At the peak we connected a million homes in a quarter and I think we went from satellite broadcaster to the biggest on-demand platform in Europe in 18 months," says a senior executive.

"We overtook Virgin media in 18 months, which just shows that when the company makes a decision about something on the technology front and puts heft behind it, we can get it done."

The smartphone boom kicked off by the launch of the iPhone in 2007 was in full swing too, with the iPad also driving demand for video on the move. It was clear to those parts of Sky with an eye on the future that streaming would only accelerate.

But while connecting set-top boxes was uncontroversial, there was internal opposition to Now TV. For the first time, it would mean the Sky Sports, Sky Movies and Sky Atlantic channels would be available for less than Sky itself was charging for them. The risk of cannibalisation, whereby valuable Sky customers might cancel their expensive subscription in favour of a cheap Now TV deal, was too great for some. In the end the project got off the ground on promises of low costs and clever pricing and branding to protect the Sky subscriber base.

"At the time we said we can do this for about five pence, which was just not true," says an executive involved in the development. The Premier League debacle helped uncover the more expensive reality. Sky found Elemental, a Silicon Valley start-up, and used its video technology to underpin a much more robust foundation for Now TV.

The misjudgement and subsequent correction ultimately proved crucial to Sky's ability to fend off new competition. In fact, without Now TV Sky's core UK pay-TV business would now have been in decline for several years. Andrew Griffith, the finance chief, soon bundled Now TV figures with satellite figures, to take the spotlight off the slow erosion of traditional pay-TV.

The new business capitalised on a trend for 'pay-lite' TV. Households that had never committed to a satellite or cable subscription all of a sudden had a string of cheaper options with which to top up their Freeview channels. Now TV, when looked at with Sky eyes, was a growth opportunity as well as a defence against a shift in technology and the arrival of BT as a competitor.

"That was always the trick with the business," says a senior executive. "When one bit isn't working there is always something else to give it cover. If you look at the story of the last few years, the decline of the satellite base has been glossed over because we have had Now TV growing."

Now TV was initially under-powered in part because Sky was focused on the impact of streaming technology on its lucrative core satellite subscriber base. The old Sky+ HD set top box was proving amazingly adaptable for the on-demand age, but executives knew it would not last forever. At the same meeting at which the directors approved Now TV, they also backed the biggest update to Sky's set-top box technology since the shift to digital broadcasting in the late 1990s.

Sky assembled a development team led by Andrew Olson, a technology executive hired from Comcast, which had been at work on its own next generation set-top box. He brought a wildly ambitious vision to the project, codenamed Project Ethan after his son, including plans for recordings stored in the cloud rather than on a hard disk. For both recorded and on-demand video, the new system would make it possible for viewers pause on their main television and then pick up where they left off on another device, and vice-versa. Such 'side-loading' would require new rights contracts with studios and broadcasters. Compatibility with ultra-HD broadcasting was essential.

"It had to be so much better than BT's set-top box," recalls an executive close to the project. We knew it would need to be able to manage a ridiculous amount of choice. We also needed to link it to Sky broadband.

"We had all the building blocks early. It just took longer than we thought. The key bit was that this is not a vanity product. This is a product that lots of people are going to have. This is a mass market product that we need to roll out though our entire base quickly. There was no point having it in five homes. We needed to be able to get it into every Sky home quite quickly if we needed to."

Over time the cloud recording plans were dumped in favour of a more familiar hard disk, amid fears that Britain's broadband infrastructure was simply too unreliable.

"One thing that is very important for us is making sure all customers get the same experience," said Fyfield.[3] "So designing something in a way where only a small fraction of our customers would be able to benefit from it because you have to have an amazing broadband connection doesn't make sense."

The development schedule was also squeezed as BT dialled up the pressure on Sky Sports. Sky executives wanted to have their whizzy new system ready for the start of BT's Champions League rights deal in 2015, but the deadline was missed. As a result of the rush, Sky Q was technologically more conservative than many working on the project had hoped to create. More advanced features such as voice search and ultra-HD were not ready in time for the launch either.

When it was finally revealed in 2016, Sky Q was nevertheless revolutionary for Sky, which lived in fear of upsetting its loyal older customers with too much change.

"The basic big, long-term thoughts behind Sky Q were that interfaces are getting better and that people are going to want to be aggregating a whole range of stuff in one place," says a senior executive.

"We knew graphics quality on a connected TV was going to be better than what we had with Sky+ HD boxes. Our user interface was just going to look crap and we needed a new box."

Sky Q was designed to act as a hub for home entertainment, streaming programmes to multiple televisions and tablets over a wireless network. Watching Sky in a bedroom would no longer mean new wiring, and viewers would be able to pick up a recorded or on demand programme where they left off on any connected device in the home.

However, the most fundamental change brought about by Sky Q was philosophical. The technology towards which the system nudged Sky allowed internet video from third parties such as YouTube onto its set-top boxes for the first time. For a pay-TV operator that had always jealously defended its relationships with customers and its investments in infrastructure, letting outsiders in was a big step.

YouTube, free to access and mostly short clips of variable quality, was a long way from direct competition to pay-TV, but a line had been crossed. Sky had signalled that it was willing to open up and act as an aggregator of apps, at least on its own terms. A deal with Netflix became a possibility, although Sky was not yet sure that the streaming newcomer did not pose a direct threat.

Sky's cautious approach to the rise of Netflix, and many other technology shifts, was at odds with two elements of its corporate self-image. Executives would repeat mantras that the company was relentlessly focused on the interests of its customers and always willing to embrace change. While Sky has shown time and again that it is unusually adaptable for a large and dominant service provider, it has often taken decisions against the interests of customers and which involved the rejection of new technologies.

For instance, Sky Q does not have a 'backwards EPG' function to allow viewers to scroll back in time on traditional channel menus to catch up on-demand. The feature is very popular on those platforms that offer it, such as YouView. But it also gives a leg-up to the main free-to-air broadcasters, and Sky would rather focus on features that favour its own programming. Likewise, when it first added on-demand services to the Sky+ HD set-top box, services from free-to-air broadcasters, such as the BBC iPlayer, were initially frozen out. That decision was quickly reversed as monitoring showed viewers increasingly jumping out of Sky to use their smart TV.

"They do research the hell out of the consumers; they just every now and then choose to ignore them," says an industry consultant who has worked with Sky.

Taken on their own, such decisions are insignificant in the grand scheme of Sky, but the way in which the company has built and defends its presence in living rooms is now the essence of the company. The billions spent on building the subscriber base – in set-top boxes, in sports rights, in marketing – are at stake each time Sky makes a concession to a rival broadcaster or makes a new investment in its own programming.

The tensions were most obvious as Sky agonised over whether to open up and allow Netflix to join Sky Q, while viewers clamoured to access the streaming upstart's exclusive shows such as *House of Cards*.

"We didn't know whether they were or weren't a threat, because we didn't know what the business model was going to be," says a Sky executive involved in the discussions.

"Once upon a time with Netflix, the deal was they were going to buy all the shows from the US broadcasters and sell it to consumers for five bucks a month. That might have been a problem for Sky.

"But increasingly, Netflix has turned into a studio in its own right. They see that as their own destiny. So if they're their own studio, they're producing their own content; and if they want to produce their own content, then we can just see them as a channel partner the same as anybody else. They just happen to be the first that went direct to consumer. But now they can be part of Sky Q too."

Over time it became clear that streaming in general was not as big a threat to Sky's business as it was to the lucrative cable industry in the US. Americans, and young Americans in particular, were abandoning high-priced bundles of mostly little-watched channels in favour of a pick and mix of cheaper internet video subscriptions. Sky's satellite base proved more resilient, thanks in part – somewhat ironically – to the regulated UK free-to-air broadcasting market it had so often raged against.

The American pay-TV industry enjoyed a much higher penetration rate than Sky. Five out of six households paid for television, and to a large extent it was seen as a necessary utility, like electricity. In contrast, because of its relatively recent arrival and the strength of free-to-air programming, in the UK full-blown pay-TV was largely a discretionary expense. Sky's research showed that meant Netflix and its ilk were more likely to be viewed as additional rather than alternative services.

The way Sky had sliced and diced its channel packages over the years to tempt more price-sensitive customers to top-up the BBC and ITV also acted as a bulwark against satellite "cord cutting". US cable operators, which often hold a pay-TV monopoly within a city, meanwhile tended to offer few tiers of service in favour of foisting big bundles of channels on consumers.

For instance, Sky gave subscribers the choice of whether they wanted to pay extra for Sky Sports, but Disney's sports channel ESPN comes as standard in the US, inflating bills and increasing the appeal of cutting the cord.

When the time finally came to do the deal in early 2018, Sky was able to demand concessions from Netflix that no other pay-TV distributor had won. It would be offered to Sky Q customers only as part of an add-on bundle that also included access to Sky's own on-demand boxsets. The deal was designed so that some Netflix stardust might rub off on Sky's in-house productions.

It meant that, from a Sky perspective, Netflix has become simply 'HBO with a decent IT department'. As the streaming revolution has progressed, executives have instead become convinced that Amazon now poses the biggest threat to their platform in pay-TV.

These fears are stoked by Amazon's interest in live sport. Although it has only dipped a toe in the Premier League auction by buying rights to 20 matches per season, and has irritated tennis fans with unreliable streaming coverage of the US Open, Amazon brings to the battlefield a new armoury that Sky has never faced, even from BT.

The vast majority of Sky subscribers are reckoned to be Amazon customers too, with existing billing relationships for online shopping that make it easy to convert them into pay-TV subscribers. Amazon's commercial model also poses a novel challenge. Its pay-TV operation is mostly a loss-leader to encourage more retail transactions via Prime subscriptions. That means it could bring a much higher pain threshold in rights auctions than Sky, for which the Premier League must be worthwhile as part of a subscription business only.

Fear of Amazon means the Prime streaming app is not welcome on Sky Q. Executives almost religiously reject a business model in which entertainment is merely a marketing cost. The details of Amazon's app introduce practical objections that it would be a cuckoo in the Sky Q nest. It bundles third party channels, potentially usurping Sky's traditional role, and at the same time includes the ability to rent films, which threatens the lucrative Sky Store.

Amazon's scale and the pace of its technological innovation, including in the hardware required to colonise living rooms, is frightening to Sky too. Some

10,000 Amazon engineers, more than a third of Sky's total staff across Europe, work on the Alexa voice assistant alone. Sky Q has been playing catch-up on voice control and, so far, losing, despite the creation of an in-house artificial intelligence team in Leeds under long-serving chief technology officer Didier Lebrat.

"Amazon is innovating quicker than us, and that I think is a problem," says a Sky technology executive. "If you look from the launch of Alexa to now, there've been two or three versions of Echo hardware. Now they've got a set-top box with Alexa built in. The speed is a worry."

The future of Sky depends, in large part, on its ability to accelerate and gain scale as part of a larger company. Both Sky Q and Now TV would benefit from distribution in more territories, able to draw economies of scale in technology development and spread the costs of original and third-party programming over a bigger base of subscribers paying a wider range of prices.

In 2018, the average Sky bill fell for the first time ever, albeit by just £1, in a signal that Now TV was accounting for a great proportion of its pay-TV subscriber base.

One of the more optimistic versions of Sky's future has it stepping up to become a force in increasingly 'smart' homes, using its trusted relationships and boots on the ground to act as a guide to a host of new technologies around the house.

"Look at Apple," says one senior executive. "They make great products but they are 'fire and forget'.

"Our capability can be to innovate and to go into people's homes and network them up, make sure the broadband works, sort them out with the best sound experience and create a version of video-calling from your main TV that is better than anybody else."

Such ambitions compete with the current reality of Sky, which is that millions of its subscribers still use old set-top boxes that are increasingly difficult to adapt to the new technologies driving entertainment. It carries a legacy of decisions made years ago that made sense at the time but now hamper its progress.

When on-demand was first introduced to Sky set-top boxes, for instance, it was feared that the unreliable broadband connections were incapable of delivering smooth streaming. The answer, delivered in 2010 after a four-year development codenamed Project Darwin, was to use the hard disk as a buffer. Programmes would download and be played on a slight delay rather than streamed straight to the screen.

It was a clever solution but has subsequently proved costly, as it means on-demand services from commercial broadcasters such as ITV are unable to connect to modern advertising systems, which insert targeted advertising on the fly. It's a problem that has persisted with Sky Q, causing further tension between Sky and the commercial broadcasters.

Now that it has visions of competing with tech giants as a platform, Sky executives know the company must be a better collaborator, and become more open technically, commercially and culturally.

It is the defining challenge of the next era, yet Sky's faith in its own ability to solve technology problems and adapt to change only increases. These days, Now TV is 99.999% reliable, the same rate as for satellite broadcasting.

13

The Moment Has Come

For the better part of a decade, Rupert Murdoch lamented the rift between his business and his eldest son, Lachlan. For a media mogul who cast himself as a disruptor of old orders and Establishment tendencies, Rupert was obsessed with dynastic succession. It gnawed at him that his heir was estranged from News Corp and 21st Century Fox.

Lachlan walked out in 2005 after he was repeatedly outmanoeuvred in the battle for his father's favour by Roger Ailes, the former media adviser to Richard Nixon, who had turned Fox News into an influential profit machine. The split hurt Rupert, who had been signalling his intention to pass the empire to Lachlan since the 1990s, referring to him as 'the first among equals' in comparison with his siblings then already in the business, James and Elisabeth.

"I look forward to the day when Lachlan wants to return to News Corporation," Rupert said when he left.

Many News Corp staff worried about succession too. In the wake of the phone hacking scandal and split of publishing away from the more lucrative television and film assets in 2013, many wondered what would happen if Murdoch, who was well into his eighties, was unable to maintain his grip on the business.

After all, it was his love of newspapers that had protected titles such as *The Times* through years of losses. The very fact that News International, if not *The News of the World*, survived the phone hacking scandal was in large part thanks to the old man's affection for newspapers and journalists, together with the influence they had helped him wield over decades.

James was long gone too. After the Leveson hearings of 2012, he returned to New York, sold his British home and wanted as little as possible to do with newspapers. In the split of News Corp, James took an executive role at Fox, but downgraded his involvement in the 'new' News Corp to that of a non-executive director.

One journalist from *The Sun* asked Rupert directly, as News Corp prepared for its split:[1] "Will the company's support vanish overnight if you're not here?"

Murdoch's reply was revealing.

"Yes – if I wasn't here, the decision would be – well, it will either be with my son, Lachlan, or with Robert Thomson [News Corp chief executive]. And you don't have any worries about either of them."

It was the first sign that Lachlan was on his way back into the fold. He may have been out of the family business but not out of the family, and when both were threatened by the phone hacking scandal he rushed to join the defensive effort. Lachlan was at News International for the chaotic period that immediately followed the Milly Dowler revelations, and accompanied his father to the Leveson hearings the next year. Now his father just had to persuade him to take a full-time job in the new structure, and accept his inheritance.

It did not take long, even though Roger Ailes still held sway over Fox News. Lachlan's record as a quasi-independent media entrepreneur in Australia was not dazzling. An attempt at a debt-fuelled buyout of pay-TV investor Consolidated Media Holdings alongside fellow billionaire offspring James Packer collapsed as the financial crisis took hold. He invested in Ten Network, a broadcaster, which promptly lost nearly three quarters of its stock market value as part of a long slide towards bankruptcy.

In March 2014, the patriarch got his wish. Lachlan agreed to return to the front line at both 'new' News Corp and Fox. He became joint-chairman of both companies, alongside his father, catapulting him back to the head of the queue to take over.

James, who had been badly damaged by phone hacking and the withering criticism about his chairmanship of News International in the Ofcom report that followed, was also elevated. In a signal that, in the eyes of his father at least, his career was back on track, the younger son was promoted to joint chief operating officer of Fox. He would work alongside the longtime Murdoch loyalist Chase Carey, running the day-to-day operations of the television and film business, including its stake in Sky, where James remained a non-executive director.

As ever, business and personal matters were intertwined. It was not irrelevant that in 2013, Rupert's marriage to Wendi Deng ended abruptly. He was convinced by rumours of a string of affairs; most unbearably, Deng had grown close to Tony Blair, who Murdoch had supported politically and made godfather to his daughter Grace (Blair denies an affair). Deng's departure was hardly lamented by James and Lachlan. Some in the Murdoch orbit were convinced that Deng had been working for the Chinese government all along.

With Lachlan and James both in senior roles the message was clear: the Murdoch family were back in command and united. Within months they agreed the sale of Sky Italia and Sky Deutschland, and made their audacious bid for Time Warner.

Sky was busy integrating its European empire, fighting off BT and navigating the beginning of the streaming age, but the intrigue at the court of Murdoch and the new dynamism that came with it did not go unnoticed. The addition of the activist investor ValueAct into the mix suggested to senior Sky executives that, one way or another, the status quo would not persist. Darroch and Griffith, who were accomplished Murdochologists, could see that the ownership of Sky was likely to be revisited.

Their suspicions were confirmed by James in a joint interview with Lachlan in *The Hollywood Reporter* in late 2015. He rejected a suggestion that Fox was poised to mount a new takeover bid for Sky, but did little to quash speculation.

"The Sky businesses, we've only just brought them all together into one big European platform," James said. 'That integration is going really well. The company is moving at a very fast pace and has grown in value enormously.

"We've also been clear that, over time, having 40% of an unconsolidated asset is not an end state that is natural for us."

It was not 100% certain, however, that Fox would seek a takeover this time. The Time Warner bid had shown that it was thinking the previously unthinkable, as it sought success in a new era of entertainment. The presence of ValueAct meant the Murdochs were under more pressure to consider their fellow shareholders' interests and explore all options. In 2015, still that included the possibility that Fox could sell its 39% stake in the enlarged, pan-European Sky.

Word of such deliberations reached Vivendi, the French media giant behind Canal+. It had now come under the control of Vincent Bollore, a veteran industrialist and corporate raider who had developed dreams of media moguldom. The logic of the combination of Sky and Canal+ was as strong as it had ever been, but this was perhaps the first time that Rupert Murdoch had seriously considered giving up control of his prized pay-TV operator. Vivendi was meanwhile sitting on billions in cash brought in by a series of asset sales by Bollore.

Vivendi let it be known it would be interested in a conversation with Fox early in 2015 and a meeting was duly organised. Mr Bollore's advisers prepared presentations on the potential strategic benefits of the combination. Like BT, telecoms operators on the continent were entering the pay-TV market and Vivendi believed that greater heft across more markets would help it to compete more effectively.

It was a waste of time. The meeting confirmed that Fox had no real intention of selling its stake in Sky. The French were told that the price required to open serious discussions was £18 per share. Sky shares were riding high towards £11, their highest level since the dotcom fever, as investors had bought into the takeovers of Sky Italia and Sky Deutschland. But the Murdoch price represented a premium of nearly 75% and was effectively a 'not for sale' sign.

"Fox were never really sellers," says one insider.

"They never reached out to Vivendi. It was the bankers who were saying 'what if', so Vivendi came in and said 'would you ever sell Sky?'. The answer was it's not really for sale but if you offered us £18 we'd have to take it seriously."

The brief discussion with Vivendi was taken by investment bankers as the clearest sign yet that the Murdochs planned to return with another bid for Sky. James continued to deliver the line to Fox investors that a minority stake in Europe's leading pay-TV operator was not a 'natural end state' and, once promoted again to chief executive of Fox in June 2015, waited for his moment to strike.

There was still some phone hacking fallout to resolve. In August 2015, Rebekah Brooks was reappointed as chief executive of News International, rebadged as News UK in an attempt to draw a line under the scandal. She had been acquitted on charges of conspiracy to hack phones a year earlier, and her return to the head of the British newspaper business was, in Rupert Murdoch's mind, confirmation that everything was back to normal.

Next, in January 2016, James was reappointed as Sky chairman. He had stepped down over fears that he was a 'lightning rod' for phone hacking trouble. His return prompted familiar grumbling from the City, but not because of his damaged reputation. It was increasingly clear to many investors that Fox could soon make a new bid for full control, and they worried that James would not have their interests at heart.

The asset manager Royal London, which owned a £50m stake in Sky, led the protests. "Should Fox make a bid for Sky, investors need a strong, independent chairman to protect the interests of minority shareholders and negotiate the best possible deal," it said.[2]

The fear of an opportunistic bid from the Murdochs was justified. Through 2016, Sky's share price tumbled, from nearly £11 at the turn of the year to less than £8 by November. The battle with BT was finally taking a toll on Sky as investors feared that Premier League costs would continue to rocket and render profit forecasts too optimistic. A record-breaking deal for Bundesliga rights in Germany in the summer added to the gloom.

Meanwhile there were signs in the US that Netflix and other streaming services were becoming a real threat to traditional pay-TV operators. The phenomenon of 'cord cutting' was accelerating, as Americans abandoned their costly packages of cable channels in favour of a pick-and-mix of cheaper streaming subscriptions. There were good reasons to hope that Sky might be more resilient, but the fears persisted and the shares kept falling.

British politics also turned in favour of the Murdochs. Against expectations, David Cameron comfortably won the 2015 General Election outright, freeing the Conservatives from the bonds of coalition government and the requirement to work alongside Liberal Democrats such as Vince Cable. Next Cameron called a referendum on membership of the European Union, which he lost in 2016, sending the value of sterling into a tailspin as currency markets struggled to compute the economic impact of the vote. Rupert Murdoch watched the shock result in favour of Brexit emerge on the set of Sky News, with Sky public relations staff carefully manoeuvring him to ensure he stayed out of shot.

The fall in the value of the pound meant that for American tourists in London, and for American buyers of British companies, big discounts were suddenly available. By the summer of 2016, some in the City were openly predicting a Fox bid for Sky. "The moment has come", the Australian investment bank Macquarie told clients in August, as it calculated that the combination of the fall in Sky shares and the fall in sterling amounted to a discount of one third since the start of the year.

Yet another signal came in October, when the US telecoms behemoth AT&T agreed to pay $85bn for Time Warner, the media company that Fox failed to secure in 2014. It was viewed as the starting gun on a new round of consolidation and showed that the theory that had underpinned the idea of a takeover of Sky by News Corp or Fox was more valid than ever. To compete with Facebook, Apple, Amazon, Netflix and Google – the FAANGs – you had to be big. AT&T's bid for Time Warner also aimed to combine a distribution network, like Sky, with a film and television producer, like Fox.

Lorna Tilbian, an experienced media analyst at the stockbroker Numis, distilled the logic of AT&T's deal: "The old adage is that content is king. And content with distribution is King Kong."

Darroch and Griffith were frustrated by the way the stock market turned against Sky, despite its dominant position in pay-TV in Britain. They knew that a bid might be coming and also that a falling share price made the company more vulnerable. They called in investment bankers to prepare Sky's defence against a low-ball offer, and then in October summoned analysts to a presentation that aimed to convince investors that Sky's long story of growth was not finished.

They highlighted how Sky had grown through the recession, how it had broadened its business with broadband and the streaming service Now TV. Under Darroch, sales had increased from about £5bn in 2008 to £12bn. He argued that the investment in drama and other forms of entertainment had reduced Sky's reliance on expensive sports rights and that there was plenty of room for more growth.

The appeals fell on deaf ears, however. By early December, Sky shares were changing hands for about £7.70, the lowest level in four years. Five years after they had been humiliatingly forced to withdraw from a takeover of Sky, the Murdoch family were ready to try again.

For James Murdoch especially it was a case of unfinished business. He put the call in to Martin Gilbert, the deputy chairman of Sky, and invited him for a chat at Fox's New York headquarters. The outgoing Scotsman, founder of Aberdeen Asset Management and a veteran of dozens of deals, immediately guessed that a takeover bid was in the offing.

"I didn't think he was just inviting me in for coffee," Gilbert said later.[3]

At the Fox building on Sixth Avenue in Midtown Manhattan, Gilbert was met by the full set of Murdochs. James, Lachlan and Rupert sent Gilbert back to London with an offer of £10 per share, equivalent to a 30% premium on the Sky share price. James followed close behind, taking Fox chief financial officer John Nallen to help him seal the deal with Sky's independent directors.

It was a moment of extreme pressure for the Sky board. The Murdochs, once again, had shown their willingness to drive a very hard bargain. Under normal circumstances, a 30% premium might be acceptable, but after a tough few months on the stock market, Sky was cheaper than it had been for years. At £10 per share, the Fox approach represented less than the market price only nine months earlier.

Gilbert, Darroch, Griffith and Andrew Sukawaty, Sky's senior independent director, knew they could not accept. Even without the longstanding concerns in the City over Murdoch influence over the company, the price was simply too low given their firm believe in Sky's resilience and growth prospects. If they had urged investors to accept the initial offer, their reputations would have been at risk. Days of tense negotiation ensued, all conducted in strict secrecy.

As the price quickly edged up, the Sky directors decided that they could accept a premium of 40%, or £10.75 per share. They were convinced that investors would approve the price, influenced in part by the takeover earlier that summer of another great British public company, the microchip designer Arm Holdings. It had fallen prey to the Japanese telecoms giant Softbank in another deal partly driven by the Brexit discount on sterling. A few Arm shareholders had protested, but the takeover went ahead. Gilbert and his colleagues believed it would be hard for Sky's owners to reasonably demand a higher premium from Fox.

There were more details to thrash out but word of the discussions leaked into the market and spread among traders on Friday 9 December, forcing Sky to announce the price to its shareholders. It also said that it was willing to recommend the bid to shareholders, a crucial difference compared with the earlier bid, when the failure to agree a price before running the regulatory gauntlet was a serious tactical mistake by News Corp. James was better prepared this time.

The reaction from the City was predictable and fierce by City standards. Weeks earlier the majority of independent Sky shareholders had voted, impotently, against James Murdoch's reappointment as chairman. Now their worst fears were confirmed.

Over the weekend *The Sunday Telegraph* reported a Sky investor as saying "our initial reaction is one of serious disappointment that they have rolled over like this". Another, Jupiter Asset Management, criticised the speed with which Sky appeared to have accepted its fate, saying that the approach "ought to be the start of the process, not the conclusion".

By Monday morning some fund managers were in unusually open revolt. Standard Life appeared on Radio 4's flagship *Today* programme to attack the deal.

Its investment director said:[4] "We've got to represent the interests of our clients and our view would be no, this isn't a good deal.

"The share price clearly was at a low ebb on Friday when the bid was rumoured and, of course, we would be expecting a full value ... the question is whether the board is independent enough to represent the interest of all shareholders, not just the 40% that is owned by 21st Century Fox."

Analysts at the investment bank Citi said Sky was worth 25% more than Fox was offering. Nevertheless, six frantic days after the leak, Sky agreed to the takeover at £10.75 per share. The deal valued the company at £18.5bn and Fox would pay £11.7bn cash for the 61% it did not already own. In the final days Sky's directors secured what they hoped was a key concession. Conscious of the risk of more political trouble and slow regulatory approvals, Sky demanded that Fox allow it to pay a special dividend if the process were to drag all the way through 2017 and into 2018.

Investors were not satisfied, but knew there was a long way to go before the deal was complete. There would, they thought, be a chance to hold out for more money later.

14

James Fought Like A Tiger. Again.

James Murdoch was sure that, this time, he had cracked it. Fox's lawyers, the elite City firm Allen & Overy, were convinced that the company's split from News Corp meant there would be no problem with media plurality as he attempted, again, to take full control of Sky.

The media landscape had been radically transformed in the five years since the News Corp bid. Newspapers were in decline and *The Sun* especially was a fading political force. Meanwhile Google and Facebook were increasingly dominant in the distribution of news online. In the days and weeks after the Fox offer for Sky was accepted, it seemed that there would be no repeat of the media infighting that had played such a major role in News Corp's earlier failure.

Quickly, it became clear there was no appetite among Murdoch rivals in the newspaper industry to raise complaints. In 2011 they had feared the commercial threat of Sky subscriptions bundled with *The Times*, but News Corp and Fox were now separate listed companies. By 2017 the accelerating decline of print and slow growth of digital advertising was a much more pressing concern for DMGT, *The Telegraph* and Trinity Mirror. *The Guardian* remained opposed, but more out of political animus towards the Murdoch press than any concern over what full Fox control of Sky might mean in practice.

Similarly, the broadcasters who had opposed the News Corp takeover of Sky in 2011 had no appetite for another war against the Murdoch clan. The BBC and Channel 4 were already more concerned about Netflix than Sky. Even Sky's bitterest commercial and regulatory rival, BT, declined to protest against the Fox takeover. It had been part of the opposition to News Corp but by 2017 was in crisis over an accounting scandal in Italy that was forcing a rethink of its expensive battle with Sky.

Claire Enders, who had helped marshall the opposition first time around, endorsed Fox assertions that its separation from News Corp changed the equation on plurality.

"It's a different structure and a different regulatory environment," she said.[1] "The role of Rupert Murdoch has been redefined and there is more normal corporate governance."

Fox and its lawyers knew that the government was likely to refer the new deal to Ofcom for assessment, but they were convinced there would be no repeat of the tortuous process of 2011. They drew up a series of reassurances meant to soothe any fears. Sky News would be funded and impartial; the Osterley campus would continue to develop; Sky would keep investing in UK production and technology.

There was a new cast of characters that would take the political heat out of decision making, too. Murdoch's old enemy Ed Richards was no longer in charge of the media regulator. The new chief executive of Ofcom, Sharon White, was a career civil servant and studiously apolitical. It helped that David Cameron had been swept away by the Brexit vote and replaced with Theresa May, a politician with few friends in the media, who could not be accused of Murdoch cronyism.

The early signs for the bid were good and appeared to justify James's confidence that the deal would clear the regulatory hurdles in six months.

"We do think that this passes regulatory muster, and we think as the relevant authorities look at the facts set around both the competition and potential UK intervention issues, that no meaningful concessions will need to be made," he had told investors when the deal was unveiled.

Not everyone was convinced. When the bid was announced Sky shares leapt, but only to about £10, significantly short of the £10.75 offer price. The shortfall reflected fears among City institutions with long memories that something might go wrong.

For instance, there was phone hacking litigation still grinding its way through the courts and rumours that explosive new evidence might emerge. There was Brexit and instability in Westminster that might trigger another change of government. Meanwhile in the US, Fox was battling to contain a sexual harassment scandal at Fox News. Looked at from a certain angle, the Fox takeover of Sky still looked quite risky.

The Fox News ructions marked the swift end of a long era. Former anchor and Miss America, Gretchen Carlson, sued the channel, alleging that she had been sacked after refusing the advances of Roger Ailes. The Murdoch brothers, who both disliked Ailes, launched an investigation and after little more than a fortnight, as more women came forward with distressing allegations, ousted him after decades at their father's side.

They had acted swiftly in genuine revulsion at Ailes' behaviour and seized an opportunity to exile a corporate enemy within. The end of his empire opened the floodgates, however. Allegations of sexual harassment, and gender and racial discrimination against Fox News executives and personalities piled up as the focus turned towards Sky.

The bid situation attracted investors with an appetite for risk. Some City investors quickly cashed in their Sky stakes when the bid came in, offloading the shares to hedge funds willing to ride the rollercoaster of a big takeover in hope of making big returns in a relatively short time. If the Murdochs were thwarted again, the hedge funds would register losses in the tens of millions of pounds as the shares would tumble. It created a cottage industry of intelligence gathering in London, as newcomers to the Sky story attempted to get to grips with the complex history and future of the deal.

James's old political opponents no longer held power, but they remained implacably against any expansion of his family's business in Britain. Vince Cable had become leader of the Liberal Democrats, but the party had been almost wiped out in the 2015 election, punished by voters for its compromises while in coalition government with the Conservatives. Ed Miliband, who had tabled the Commons motion that triggered the collapse of the News Corp bid for Sky, had returned to the Labour backbenches after losing the election to David Cameron and the Conservative Party.

Though the wind appeared to be blowing in Fox's favour, in January 2017 Miliband began rallying opposition to the deal. He aimed to gather a cross-party group to put political pressure on the government and Ofcom to ensure the takeover could not simply be waved through in the absence of commercial objections.

It meant once again a focus on Sky News, which remained a small and loss-making part of Sky's business, yet the main concern in any media plurality investigation. Some at Sky thought the question should have been dealt with long ago. The failure of the first bid had exposed a strategic problem that could already have been addressed.

"Up until then everyone thought, 'Sky News is small but we invest a bit of money in it and it's nice, so what's the problem?'," says one senior executive. "It was never even discussed by the board. Nobody ever said in a board meeting can we have an update on Sky News. They just didn't give a shit, it was so small."

Another agrees: "If you were News Corp and thought you were one day going to be coming back for this asset, why didn't they insist Sky continue with the spin-off of Sky News?

"That would have been the strategic thing to have done. It was the impediment to ever doing a deal. Therefore get rid of the problem while you haver the chance. Or just close it down for Christ's sake. Then when you come back you haven't got the problem."

The scandal at Fox News put a new twist on the discussion. Miliband aimed to pin the allegations of serious sexual misconduct against Roger Ailes, the head of Fox News since its foundation, on Murdoch mismanagement. The former Labour leader believed he might be able to reopen the question of whether the family were fit and proper to control Sky News.

"The bid for Sky must not be waved through," Miliband warned.[2] "On the grounds of plurality and the record of the Murdoch empire, it should be resisted. This bid would mean significantly greater concentration of media ownership and it risks the 'Foxification' of Sky News."

Miliband was giving voice to a fear that had its roots in James's own MacTaggart speech of 2009. In it he had raged against the strict impartiality regulations that prevented the creation of a highly partisan news channel in the Fox New mould in the UK. Nearly a decade later that speech was still proving a barrier to ownership of Sky.

James had been advised not to become personally involved in the public debate. Fox's public relations firm, the elite City firm Brunswick, aimed to avoid association with the Murdochs as much as possible.

The decision to refer Fox's bid to Ofcom fell to the Culture Secretary, Karen Bradley. She was a former tax accountant who had risen through the Conservative ranks and a Theresa May loyalist. Bradley would later make an unfortunate mark as Northern Ireland Secretary by admitting a profound ignorance of the history and politics of Ulster ("I didn't understand things like when elections are fought, for example, in Northern Ireland – people who are nationalists don't vote for unionist parties and vice versa"), but she could at least be relied upon to stick to the rule book. This time there would be no 'daddy' texts between Murdoch lobbyists and government ministers.

To the astonishment of many at Sky, Fred Michel, the fabulist author of those texts to Jeremy Hunt, had made a quiet return. After his humiliation at the Leveson Inquiry, Michel worked as a consultant to Sky Italia; when Sky completed its European takeovers, he became part of the mothership. Michel's resurrection was a demonstration of loyalty by James that rankled with many at Sky.

In March, once Fox had formally submitted its intentions to the relevant authorities, Karen Bradley duly announced that she would ask Ofcom to investigate. The regulator was to look at the potential impact of the deal on the public interest in media plurality, just as it had in 2011. Bradley surprised many by also demanding a first-of-its-kind investigation into what effect full Fox ownership might have on Sky's commitment to broadcasting standards. In effect, the regulator was asked whether Sky News might end up 'Foxified'.

In a further boost to Murdoch opponents, Ofcom also announced that it would conduct the separate assessment of whether Sky would be fit and proper to hold its broadcasting licences if it was fully owned and controlled by Fox. For James, it would mean an uncomfortable repeat of the process that in 2012 found he "repeatedly fell short of the conduct to be expected of him as a chief executive officer and chairman". Ed Miliband and his allies successfully argued that the assessment should be repeated because while James held sway over just 39% of Sky shares in 2012, he was now seeking full ownership.

It was clear Bradley aimed to give the deal the most thorough probe possible. Politically cautious, she wanted to be sure that if she ultimately approved the deal she could not be accused of mishandling her quasi-judicial role. Fox and its advisers were not unduly concerned and had expected an investigation. Ofcom was due to report back in mid-May 2016, and they fully expected to be given the green light.

A real problem came out of the blue. In mid-April 2016, Theresa May called a snap election in an attempt to stamp her authority on Parliament as it prepared for Britain to leave the EU. Her campaign turned a 20-point opinion poll lead into a brush with defeat and cost the Conservatives their majority in the House of Commons. May was forced to cobble together a deal with Northern Ireland's hardline Democratic Unionist Party (DUP) to cling onto power, dramatically destabilising her administration. She was suddenly vulnerable to defeat on any issue of significant controversy.

The immediate impact of the snap election on the Sky bid was a delay of six weeks to Ofcom's investigations, as the machinery of Whitehall shut down during the campaign. The more damaging result was a sudden and irreversible change in the political weather. Fox had made its bid in the most benign climate for the Murdoch empire since Tony Blair left power. Without warning it now faced a maelstrom in which its controversial takeover ambitions posed a potential threat to the survival of the government.

For Bradley, the key was not to make a decision, or even to allow anyone else to make one, for as long as possible.

Ofcom finally reported back at the end of June 2016. On media plurality and broadcasting standards, it was due to advise Bradley on whether to refer the takeover of Sky to the more powerful Competition and Markets Authority (CMA) for further investigation and possible restriction.

Prior to the election, Ofcom's findings might have been good news for Fox. The regulator found its record of breaches of the rules was not out of line with rival broadcasters. Regulators paid particular attention to Fox News, which on average had only 2,000 viewers in Britain but represented the heavily slanted approach to television news that Murdoch opponents feared would be applied to Sky News.

Ofcom found plenty of problems at Fox News. The channel had no mechanism for ensuring its compliance with Britain's strict broadcasting code. Its approach to coverage of Hillary Clinton, for instance, was anathema to UK reporting standards and found to be in breach of impartiality rules. An alarmist segment on Islamic extremism in Europe was found to be 'materially misleading', including in relation to a baseless assertion that areas of Birmingham had become 'no-go zones' for non-Muslims.

Nevertheless, Ofcom said there were no concerns about broadcasting standards that would justify referring the deal to the CMA. Bradley had asked the regulator to investigate whether the sexual harassment scandal at Fox News might have any bearing on Sky's commitment to broadcasting standards. Ofcom said no.

There was more good news for James Murdoch in the repeat of the 'fit and proper' assessment that had been so personally damaging for him years earlier.

He and Lachlan had flown to London to give Sharon White full details of their response to the allegations against Roger Ailes and Bill O'Reilly, a firebrand Fox News presenter also accused of sexual harassment, a claim denied by O'Reilly.[3] The brothers had put in place new whistleblowing and independent investigation procedures that convinced White that she "cannot reasonably conclude that were Sky to be wholly-owned by Fox, Sky would not in future properly investigate and resolve misconduct, and take measures to prevent it from recurring.

"This in turn means that we cannot – on today's evidence – cease to be satisfied that were Sky to be 100%-owned by Fox, it would be fit and proper to hold its broadcast licences."

Fox effectively won the all-clear from Ofcom on its commitment to standards and its fitness to hold broadcasting standards. The only remaining hurdle was media plurality.

Despite the division of their media empire into separate publishing and entertainment companies, the Murdoch family failed to convince the regulator that anything had substantially changed since 2011. They remained the controlling shareholders of News Corp and Fox, and adding full control of Sky and Sky News would only increase their sway over Britain's media landscape.

Likewise Fox's carefully constructed arguments about the internet revolution in news fell flat. Google and Facebook were gaining strength, Ofcom conceded, but they were not producers of news and newspapers still wielded power.

"Analysing how the news agenda is shaped is not straightforward," Ofcom said. "However, evidence suggests newspapers may have greater influence over public opinion than consumption metrics alone might suggest, through the ability to set the wider news agenda."

The risk of damaging the public interest in media plurality was still present, according to the regulator.

"We have identified a risk that the transaction might allow news providers under the influence of members of the Murdoch Family Trust to have greater influence over public opinion, and to extend the influence of members of the Murdoch Family Trust over the political process.

"This could be done by choosing news stories that align with the interests of the Murdoch Family Trust, influencing the editorial position at Sky News or through the perception of their greater influence over the political process."

White agreed with Ed Richards' conclusion that a Murdoch takeover of Sky should be referred to the CMA for further investigation. It was a blow to the deal. A CMA investigation would take six months and mean Fox had no chance of completing the takeover in 2017. Many investors, who had misread the political atmosphere and bought into Fox's confidence that its arguments would win out, were shocked. The shares slid towards £9 as doubts arose over the deal and more long-term shareholders sold up.

There was a potential solution already under discussion, however. As part of its talks with Ofcom, Fox had offered to create an independent editorial board to guard against Murdoch influence over Sky News. White stopped short of recommending the arrangement to Bradley, but said it could mitigate the threat to media plurality.

At Sky they knew there was no way the government could accept the deal on the table. It was a behavioural remedy, and any minister signing it would effectively take the Murdochs on trust that they would not seek to influence Sky News. A strong Conservative government might have been able to ignore inevitable criticism from Labour and its own benches to take such a decision, but that was not the case now.

Theresa May's fragile administration would never dare stick its neck out on behalf of Fox and certainly not to accept less protection for Sky News than News Corp had offered in 2011, when the channel was due to be spun off as a separate listed company.

Bradley had little choice but to reject the offer of an editorial board for Sky News and refer the takeover to the CMA for a media plurality investigation, saying that she needed to hear further representations. The deal entered a form of Westminster purgatory involving months of delays, including the usual summer recess.

Miliband and other Murdoch opponents in Parliament – including the Labour deputy leader Tom Watson, the film producer Lord Puttnam, the former Labour Lord Chancellor Charles Falconer and the Tory grandee Ken Clarke – sensed the government's vulnerability. They lobbied hard for the question of broadcasting standards to be reopened. Bradley, without the authority to dismiss their concerns and follow Ofcom's advice, was bound to listen.

"Some people will argue that we couldn't end up with Fox News here because of our codes on broadcasting, including our impartiality rules," said Miliband, who had been a target of ridicule for *The Sun* while Labour leader.[4]

"But that is far too complacent. First, because the codes are limited, as Ofcom acknowledges – impartiality rules cannot take account of story selection, tone or prominence.

"Fox News has played a major role in polluting the well of public conversation in the US, stirring division and hatred. We know also that Rupert Murdoch has mused about making Sky more like Fox. We should not risk the Foxification of Sky News."

Fox News had now become a problem for the bid. In August 2017, and after a 15-year run, the channel was permanently taken off-air in the UK, in an attempt to contain the criticism.

It did not work. Bradley caved under pressure and decided to overrule Ofcom's advice. In September, she finally referred the takeover of Sky to the CMA for investigation of its impact on both media plurality and broadcasting standards. It was an extraordinary move that angered Ofcom.

In a pointed letter to Bradley, White said she had reviewed the new representations from the Miliband group and that in her view in relation to broadcasting standards "while we consider there are non-fanciful concerns, we do not consider that these are such as may justify a reference in relation to the broadcast standards public interest consideration".

Bradley had relied on a low legal threshold and the discretionary powers she had over the process to ensure that she could not be criticised for siding with the Murdoch empire.

At Sky there was a growing sense of frustration that history was repeating itself. Once again, the Murdochs had misread the political environment and caused problems for themselves by their determination to retain Sky News.

"It's because we're British and they're not," says one executive close to the process.

"News Corp and Fox have both ended up being advised by lawyers who are not across the political and media landscape here. So it took them forever to understand, again, what they were up against. It was infuriating."

Despite years of brooding, corporate restructuring and careful planning, the deal was threatened yet again. The double referral to the CMA and the months of delays that preceded it would probably not have happened without Theresa May's disastrous snap election, though Fox's arguments on media plurality were never likely to convince Ofcom to go against its own earlier judgement. Though Ed Richards had moved on, many of his senior officials remained.

Two days after Bradley triggered the CMA investigations, sending Sky shares to their lowest point since the deal was announced a full nine months earlier, James Murdoch was scheduled to appear on stage at the Royal Television Society's biannual conference in Cambridge.

The speech, his first major public intervention in Britain since the Leveson hearings, had been agreed months earlier. Fox intended it as victory lap that would allow Murdoch to reintroduce himself. Instead he was forced to defend his plans for Sky and lobby the government to move on with allowing the takeover to go ahead. With Britain's role in the world in question as a result of the Brexit vote, Murdoch believed he knew the buttons to press.

"If the UK truly is 'open for business' post-Brexit, we look forward to moving through the regulatory review process and this transformative transaction for the UK creative sector becoming an affirmation of that claim," he said.

"We're eager to provide Sky with access to the resources, reach, and creative sparks needed to keep pace against a new breed of competitors that now include some of the largest companies in the world, but none of whom have the local depth of investment and commitment to the UK and to Europe."

It was a slick performance and Murdoch handily dealt with phone hacking and sexual harassment questions afterwards. Privately he was furious, however, that concerted attempts to depoliticise Fox's takeover of Sky had failed. Even without a coalition of commercial rivals lined up against him, he had been stymied by what he saw as a British establishment that had never welcomed his family.

Fox was being treated differently to any other media company, and to Murdoch that was deeply unfair rather than a reflection of his father's political entanglements or his struggles with phone hacking. He decided to stop broadcasting Fox News in Britain in an attempt to blunt the attacks from Miliband and his allies, but the damage to the Sky bid was already done.

"It has proved impossible for James to fully grasp the situation of his father and the Murdoch Family Trust," says Claire Enders.

"So it has been impossible, it is still impossible today, for James Murdoch to acquiesce to the view that the family brought this upon themselves. It is impossible for him to understand this, and yet it is the absolute truth."

"Fox could have had this wrapped up by June if they offered to sponsor off Sky News right away and raised the price.

"Instead James fought like a tiger, again, against the view that he somehow had any responsibility to bear for past mistakes, that his integrity had been diminished. It was something he could not bear, he still cannot bear."

Yet as he stood on the stage in Cambridge, James knew there was a better chance than any of his audience realised that he might not end up with control of Sky. Thousands of miles away, his father was already at work on a deal that would send shockwaves through the global media industry and trigger one final battle for Sky.

15

Protect the Content Budget

On a brisk spring evening in March 2015, the Tower of London was lit up with flame. Sky had seized the castle to host the starry world premiere of the fifth season of its blockbusting fantasy saga, *Game of Thrones*, and projected a giant fire-breathing dragon onto the ancient walls.

The lavish event signified a change in Sky's business. Where once almost all its promotional muscle went into sport, subscribers were now demanding big dramas and there was none bigger than *Game of Thrones*. The series had become the lynchpin of Sky Atlantic. The premium drama channel was launched just four years earlier and had already overtaken Hollywood films in the list of Sky attractions most cited by customers as a reason to subscribe, behind only live sport.

The Tower buzzed with celebrities and press, confirming that, for the first time in its history, Sky had a genuine original cultural phenomenon on its hands. It was a moment of triumph, but also of frustration. *Game of Thrones*, alas, belonged to the US broadcaster HBO; Sky was merely the UK retailer. HBO's perma-tanned chief executive Richard Plepler jetted in to the premiere to optimistically declare the cast "one of the greatest ensembles in the history of either film or television". Jeremy Darroch wanted Sky to produce its own hits, and now he was more determined than ever.

Such dreams were nothing new in Osterley, however. Elisabeth Murdoch had persuaded Sky to invest more in original programming under Sam

Chisholm and Mark Booth in the 1990s. She had built a mini-empire, Sky Networks, to be in charge of commissioning and scheduling for flagship entertainment channel Sky One, and others. Sky Networks also included Sky Pictures, a film unit inspired by the early US success of HBO.

The arrival of Tony Ball and departure of Elisabeth Murdoch meant Sky's original production ambitions were sharply curtailed.[1] Sky Pictures was shut down and Sky One stagnated. Ball was focused completely on sport, the digital rollout and hitting his financial targets. As far as he was concerned, it was war time and original programming was nowhere near a top priority.

"Since I arrived, I've done quite a lot of restructuring, and while we obviously have good people who will look after the programming side, I don't think I'll be looking for a straight replacement for Liz," Ball said.

Into this environment stepped Dawn Airey, becoming programming chief. Known as 'Scary Airey' for her hard-charging style, she had been due to join ITV, but was poached by Ball as part of his victory lap after crushing ITV Digital. She was joined by Sophie Turner Laing, as Airey's deputy, an equally formidable character with a background in US rights deals and, unusually for Sky at the time, the BBC.

They were two of only three senior women at Osterley's boys' club (the other was legal chief Deanna Bates) and initially seemed to make little headway. Airey's popular touch – she had run Channel 5 to a strategy she infamously summarised as 'the three Fs': football, films and fucking – nevertheless produced some palpable hits. *Ross Kemp on Gangs* made its debut just as James Murdoch was appointed chief executive, and ran for five years. But there was little consistency and Sky's analytical culture did not tend to support creative risk-taking.

"The thing used to be we'd get people in they'd do one good thing and then we'd give them more money for another thing and of course it would be rubbish and we'd get rid," recalls a colleague.

"I think we had six heads of Sky One within five years. We'd pull investment and have to start again a year later. We didn't stick with it because people just didn't have the conviction it was something we should be doing."

Turner Laing spent most of her early years at Sky renegotiating film deals, which had been badly designed to allow Hollywood studios to extract large fees for unpopular films.

Under Murdoch, campaigning by Airey and Turner Laing for a more ambitious approach to commissioning won a more sympathetic hearing. They convinced Sky to commission and heavily market the Terry Pratchett adaptation *The Hogfather* for Christmas 2006, and were vindicated with good reviews and record-breaking viewing figures on Sky One. It proved that Sky could make high quality, original programming of the type traditionally dominated by the BBC and ITV.

Airey eventually left Sky, leaving Turner Laing to continue the fight for funding. Original programming would always have to compete with Sky's more established strengths in sports rights, marketing and technology. Turner Laing had a t-shirt printed that said 'Protect the Content Budget' and gave it to Darroch, then chief financial officer.

Turner Laing's contacts in US television proved pivotal in Sky's zig-zagging path towards serious investment in entertainment programmes. At the BBC she had been responsible for bringing *24*, one of the first of a new wave of big-budget serials, to British screens. She had also forged a production partnership with HBO on *Band of Brothers*, the landmark Second World War drama.

HBO had since repeatedly raised viewer expectations with an extraordinary run of programming that kickstarted a new golden age of television. *The Sopranos*, *The Wire*, *Deadwood* and *Six Feet Under* set new standards; other US programme makers responded with the likes of *Mad Men* and *Lost*. Sky, able to outbid terrestrial broadcasters as it realised drama could help release the 'female handbrake' that had prevented some households from subscribing, became home to most of them. By 2010, Turner Laing had won support within Sky for the creation of a dedicated channel.

Turner Laing felt very strongly that Sky's reputation for quality in sports and news increasingly clashed with its cheap entertainment programming. Sky, she argued, should not spend its money competing with primetime BBC One with soaps and quizzes, but on exclusive, expensive dramas that might convince viewers to subscribe.

Technology trends were behind her. The take-up of Sky+ and on-demand services were changing viewing habits in favour of drama series, allowing episodes to be watched at any time, as well as stacked and binged. The shift allowed more word-of-mouth hits, as viewers could catch up halfway through a series. It also boosted the argument for original commissioning, as the shelf life of a hit was radically increased.

The foundation stone for the new venture would be an exclusive deal for HBO shows. However, HBO did not make enough series to fill the hungry schedule of a whole channel. Sky planned to gradually ramp up its own commissioning to match, and to call the channel Sky HBO. That plan was quickly blocked by HBO, which did not want to share its brand.

The project had been codenamed Sky Atlantic as a private joke based on a poster for the *Band of Brothers* follow-up *The Pacific*, which hung in Turner Laing's office. It stuck. Sky Atlantic made its debut on 1 February 2011, in the midst of the News Corp takeover.

The scale of the financial commitment was not revealed until June 2011, weeks before the bid collapsed. Darroch revealed that Sky's spending on original UK programming would increase by more than 50% over the following three years to £600m. The figures included the cost of Sky News and producing live sport, but it was nevertheless a statement of intent and a retort. Months earlier, the BBC director-general Mark Thompson had attacked Sky over its failure to invest in British creativity and raised doubts over the impact Sky Atlantic would have.

"It's great that Sky is going to make the HBO archive of outstanding programmes available to British viewers over the next few years," said Thompson.[2] "It's great that they're announcing a few more drama commissions. But it's time that Sky pulled its weight by investing much, much more in British talent and British content."

Darroch replied that British television, by which he meant the BBC, suffered from "the misconception that good outcomes only happen because they are ordained from above and enacted through some form of intervention".[3]

In increasing its programming budget, Sky was following wider global trends. In the US, producers were increasingly merging with broadcasters, who would often keep the best productions for themselves. Such marriages challenged the old Sky model of simply buying up programmes in Hollywood. The situation has only become more acute since the emergence of streaming. The heavy spending of Netflix and Amazon has inflated prices for independent productions, making it more economical for Sky to come up with and fund its own ideas.

Turner Laing left in 2014 and was replaced the following year by Gary Davey, a News Corp and Fox lifer who had been running programming for Sky Deutschland until its takeover by Sky. Davey had earlier been part of what he describes as the "planeload of hooligans" that arrived in London from Australia to set up Sky in 1989. He remains a confidante of Rupert Murdoch, one of very few at Sky in latter years.

Davey was in place for the launch of *Fortitude*, Sky's first determined attempt to produce the sort of landmark drama at which HBO and latterly Netflix have excelled. At £30m for the first series, it cost four times as much as any previous in-house drama, and it set a frustrating pattern that Sky has struggled to break. Reviews were encouraging, but ratings quickly tumbled and *Fortitude* failed to make the impact of Netflix's *House of Cards*, let alone HBO's *Game of Thrones*.

'Tentpole' series had become Netflix's most powerful marketing tool, garnering acres of favourable press coverage and positive word-of-mouth promotion. Though Sky executives argue with some justification that in an era of on-demand programming, ratings mattered little to a subscription business, they privately admit that their failure to land a big hit has been a cause of concern. Sky News, a loss-making free-to-air channel, remains their calling card to this day.

Later efforts, such as *Young Pope* and *Patrick Melrose*, have won more critical acclaim, but the prized 'water cooler TV' label has proved elusive, even as its spending has continued to rise. Sky's Italian arm has had more success in a market poorly served by global streaming players and low quality free-to-air television.

Senior executives blame the clash of Sky's analytical brain with the randomness of successful creativity.

"Creating a company where the marketing and retail people can sit side by side as equals with creative people is really difficult," says one senior executive.

"If you think about how you run a subscription business like Sky, it is all numbers. It's daily sales reports, analytical updates. You ask, say, why didn't this or that initiative work and there are usually clear answers. It's never just a punt.

"Content is totally different. It's about trusting someone and giving them a shitload of money one day and them coming back three years later with something that is not what they said and you cross your fingers that it works."

Another agrees: "Unlike us taking a view on something more mechanical like broadband penetration rates or broadband speeds or shipping boxes to people's homes or updating software on people's boxes, it's far more mechanical and in control.

"What happens in that industry is you sign up for scripts then it takes two years, which is a long time, before it gets on air. You don't know what else is on screen two years from now, whether it's still relevant. Whether a while away through the production process it met its vision. It just takes a bit more time."

The lack of a breakout success has led Sky to view its original programming more as a means of retaining existing subscribers than attracting newcomers. It has persisted with *Fortitude*, for instance, although its marketing support for the programme has been drastically cut.

"In content, cutting through with a new programme brand is really challenging and expensive. So, as a growth tool, it's challenging," said Gary Davey in 2017.[4]

"As a retention tool, it is in my view the most powerful weapon we have. That is why for us returning series are so important. Of our 11 dramas this year, I think five of them are returning. That is a sign of the maturity of our investment strategy. If we can get our customers engaged in a series and then keep bringing it back, we build a relationship between the TV show and the customer. A show would not return on our platform unless we believe that the customer base was engaged with it."

The planned takeover by Fox, or later by Disney or Comcast, was nevertheless viewed by some inside the company as a relief in the search for a big hit. All the potential owners had more experience of programme making. "That's where they can help us, hopefully," says one executive.

Sky aims to launch a new drama every six weeks so that before one ends the next one starts.

"The important part of my job going forward is to make entertainment a primary reason to get Sky. If we get our storytelling in entertainment right, it's just as engaging as football," says Davey.

Executives are increasingly confident that Netflix does not pose an urgent threat, especially now it is available as part of a Sky package. More serious near-term challenges may come from Amazon and Apple, who as well as spending billions producing programming are owners of vast technology platforms that could usurp Sky in living rooms across the world.

16

Pivoting at a Pivotal Moment

In 2017, Rupert Murdoch turned 86 years old. To most of the outside world he remained the master of one of the biggest and most influential media empires the world had ever known. In reality, his powers were waning and he knew it.

He was – inescapably – old. After the trauma of his divorce from Wendi Deng, Murdoch had married Jerry Hall, the former wife of Sir Mick Jagger. At 60, she was still more then quarter of a century his junior, but brought a new sense of calm to Murdoch's life as he started to lose his battle with time.

Murdoch was no longer as mentally sharp as he used to be and was easily tired. In 2000, after successful prostate cancer treatment, he had declared that he was "convinced of my immortality". Then it was only half a joke. The better part of 20 years later, even Murdoch had to admit he was beginning to fade.

Neither was Fox the commercial force it once had been. For a number of years, it had been clear that entertainment and pay-TV companies would be challenged by the giants of Silicon Valley as television and the internet merged. To stand a chance of defending their businesses against the FAANGs (the common term used to describe Facebook, Amazon, Apple, Netflix and Google), they had to become bigger. Fox had a market valuation of less than $50bn, compared to numbers well into the hundreds of billions as the tech giants raced to become the world's first trillion-dollar company.

Such numbers were allowing Netflix and Amazon to pile billions of dollars into big budget series to attract subscribers. Apple and Google were following suit, each with half the world's smartphones and a growing number of televisions under their control. As a result, the price of programme making was rising, and broadcast networks like Fox were finding life harder.

Rupert had already tried getting bigger, however. In 2014 he tried, and quickly failed, to tempt Time Warner into a merger. The price was simply too high for Fox, which aimed to buy Time Warner using its own falling stock. Instead the prize fell to the telecoms behemoth AT&T for $85bn, in one of the biggest takeovers of all time. AT&T aimed to ensure that it was not relegated to a mere provider of broadband and mobile pipes, while Netflix and others cashed in with the content that consumers wanted.

The Time Warner deal prompted much soul-searching across the US media and telecoms sector. Murdoch confronted his own mortality and the vulnerability of Fox and saw it was time to cash in his chips. It was a momentous realisation that demonstrated the fundamental nature of the change underway. Over decades he had parlayed a single tabloid in South Australia into a global juggernaut of film and television. However, there would be no more conquests for Murdoch in an age of streaming.

Murdoch plotted his moves over summer at his vineyard in Los Angeles, the Moraga Estate. In early August, Bob Iger, the boss of Disney, the biggest and most successful of the six main Hollywood studios with a stock market value approaching $160bn, made a visit. Over chicken salad and a couple of glasses of chardonnay, they discussed the new forces faced by the industry and Iger detected Murdoch's restlessness. They flirted with the idea of a merger, but neither made a direct statement of intent.

Iger was the biggest fish in Hollywood, but wanted to be bigger still. He had come to the conclusion that Disney needed to compete directly with Netflix for consumer subscriptions, rather than merely supply films and television wholesale. Years earlier, when Netflix was beginning its transition from a

DVD-by-post rental business to a pioneer of subscription streaming, the Hollywood studios had granted it access to their vast libraries at bargain prices.

By 2017, Neflix had used the leg-up to persuade tens of millions of Americans to subscribe and abandon the expensive cable packages that sustained Disney. Iger wanted to fight back with Disney's own streaming service, which meant the more programming he could control the better. If Murdoch was indeed planning to sell up, Iger was definitely interested in owning *The Simpsons*, *Family Guy* and the *X-Men* franchise.

Sky would be a valuable addition too, as Disney had virtually no experience in running a pay-TV business or dealing directly with consumers (outside of its theme parks).

Iger did not know it, but Murdoch was studying his enthusiasm. Fox had already had a takeover approach from another big player in the game of chess triggered by the swoop for Time Warner. Within days, James and Lachlan were due to meet the leadership of AT&T's telecoms rival Verizon in New York to discuss its interest.

Few in Fox believed a combination with Verizon made much sense. The telecoms operator was determined not to pay any premium for control of Fox, which without any compelling or proven strategic rationale would be hard to accept. The approach stoked conversation among the Murdochs about selling up, however, and Iger soon called again to begin real discussions.

The family was divided. Rupert was convinced a deal could deliver a lucrative end to his 30-year career in entertainment. James, who since his earliest days at News Corp always had an eye on the impact of new technology on the business, thought it was a good time to sell and that Disney would be the best buyer. Lachlan was against it. He had only been back in the family business for three years, after nearly a decade away, and was not immediately keen to see the most profitable part of his inheritance sold off.

The majority quickly prevailed, however, and detailed talks with Disney began. The deal would be complicated. Both companies held powerful positions in US sports broadcasting and competition regulators would not probably allow Disney to become more dominant. The two sides also agreed that Fox News should not change hands. Instead a 'new Fox', radically smaller and focused on sport and news, would be hived off as a separate company, allowing Disney to buy the rest of the assets.

That included the Murdochs' film studio and its library, most of their cable television channels, the Asian pay-TV operator Star, their stake in the streaming joint venture Hulu and their stake in Sky.

There was other logic to 'new Fox' too. Scale was essential to compete with tech giants in general entertainment, but sport and news appeared to be different. They were live, meaning traditional broadcast television was still the best way to deliver them to a large audience. Sport and news were territorial too. Sports rights sold on a country-by-country basis were not much use to the likes of Netflix, as it sought to conquer the world with hit series capable of crossing borders and attracting subscribers in Europe as well as the US.

By late October the two sides were ready to talk price. Iger initially offered about $60bn in a mixture of cash and Disney shares. The following day Rupert rang him with bad news: Fox would turn down the bid as too low. Months of careful, secret work appeared at risk. More importantly Murdoch's exit plan was under threat.

Not for the first time in his long career, the deal was resuscitated by a leak. A week later, CNBC revealed the discussions between Fox and Disney to astonished investors and media watchers.

"The two sides are not currently talking at this very moment, but given the on again, off again nature of the talks, they could be revisited," said the report.[1]

The news was a bombshell to Wall Street, to Hollywood and to Sky. It signalled, out of the blue to most observers, that after decades of expansion Murdoch was at the very least considering retrenchment. A UBS analyst wrote of his "shock and awe"[2] at the hitherto secret talks, "especially given how tied to these assets the family has been".

For Sky, the future was transformed. The Murdoch takeover was under investigation by the Competition and Markets Authority in the UK, but it appeared that after years of political wrangling the company could be immediately sold on to Disney and become part of the world's biggest entertainment business. What this meant for Sky senior executives who had benefited from Murdoch support was not clear.

When news of the aborted talks between Fox and Disney broke, one reader, the ultimate boss of CNBC, had a very clear idea of what it meant. For Brian Roberts, the chairman of Comcast, it was an opportunity. If the Murdochs were willing to sell to Disney, they might be willing to sell to him. He picked up the phone the same day and told Rupert that Comcast would be interested in a discussion.

Roberts and the Murdoch patriarch, 28 years his senior, had much in common. Like Rupert, Roberts inherited a successful business from his father and turned it into an empire. Comcast turned over less than $1bn when Roberts took the helm in 1990; by 2017, annual revenues were nearly $85bn. Both men kept tight control over massive public companies via minority stakes and a small group of trusted lieutenants.

Comcast and Fox had very different corporate DNA, however. Excluding international distribution businesses such as Sky, Fox was primarily a creative business. Its expertise was in taking risks on new ideas for films and television programmes, and exploiting successes such as *The Simpsons* as aggressively as possible.

In essence, it was in the hits business, with boom and potential bust dependent, to a large extent, on how good its ideas were when they had received the green light two or three years earlier. On that basis Fox was a good match for Disney, which with the Marvel and Star Wars franchises has created the closest thing in Hollywood to a hits machine while remaining a creative business.

Meanwhile Comcast is, at heart, a telecoms company. It invests billions in broadband infrastructure with reasonable certainty that it will make a good return over a long period. Its headquarters are in Philadelphia, not the media hubs of New York and Los Angeles.

Roberts used the riches of the broadband boom to build America's biggest cable operator. In 2001 he bet big on the long-term future of the industry amid the rubble of the dotcom crash, and acquired AT&T's broadband business for $52bn. Next he turned his attention to programming, and made his audacious 2004 attempt to seize control of Disney. Eventually, in 2009, Roberts settled for another major broadcaster and Hollywood studio, NBC Universal.

Comcast was not welcomed by the US entertainment establishment and faced more than 150 conditions on the deal imposed by competition watchdogs, but in time proved itself a canny media operator.

Roberts left NBC Universal largely to its own devices, joining its forces with the Comcast cable business only when, on major projects such as broadcasting the Olympics or promoting major film releases, it made commercial sense. Over five years of Comcast ownership, cash flow doubled at NBC Universal, convincing Roberts that he had discovered the "secret sauce"[3] to profit from the combination of media and telecoms, even as Netflix and others challenged the traditional pay-TV model.

It meant the chance to acquire Fox was too good to miss, especially if he could deny his old enemies at Disney. Roberts' personal style is low-key and guarded, with little of the passion and frankness that characterises public interventions by members of the Murdoch clan, but he is no less ambitious and determined to win. Comcast had a deserved reputation as a ruthless operator. In carriage fee disputes with channel providers it had been known to publish the personal phone numbers of enemy executives. Within days of Roberts' first call to Murdoch, negotiations were underway.

Meanwhile, Iger knew the leak put Disney under pressure. It got back in touch with Fox to suggest it could improve its earlier offer of $60bn and restructure the deal to reduce the tax bill for shareholders, including the Murdochs. By a combination of luck and cunning, Fox had engineered what was, in effect, a bidding war for its assets between two wealthy rivals. They may have been selling up, but had ensured they would get best possible deal.

Quickfire negotiations followed in a frantic few weeks of shuttle diplomacy by bankers and lawyers. In purely financial terms, Roberts blew Disney out of the water. He offered the equivalent of $34.41 per share, paid for with Comcast stock. Iger's improved offer was $28 per share in Disney stock, valuing the Fox assets at $66bn including debts.

For the Murdochs, the decision was more complicated. Most of the family's wealth was tied up in Fox shares. They would be swapped for shares in either Disney or Comcast. Given that the decision to sell was founded partly on doubts about the long-term prospects of the traditional pay-TV subscription model, it seemed perverse to become Comcast shareholders, when pay-TV still accounted for the biggest share of its revenues. Bankers from Goldman Sachs showed Fox share price forecasts that suggested that in the emerging streaming landscape it would be more lucrative to own a slice of Disney.

There were also cultural barriers to a deal with Roberts. James Murdoch, with his experience in driving Sky's technology roadmap and overseeing its slick customer operations, disdained Comcast's reputation for terrible service and slow innovation.

The debate was firmly tipped in Disney's favour by the regulatory backdrop. AT&T's takeover of Time Warner was under attack from the Trump administration's Department of Justice.

The battle lines were drawn on the campaign trail soon after the deal was announced in 2016, when Trump branded it "an example of the power structure I'm fighting" and "too much concentration of power in the hands of too few". Unusually for a 'vertical' merger that combined a supplier and a distributor, competition officials had taken their cue from the President and challenged the deal in court.

To Fox it meant Comcast's bid was unacceptably risky. It would also be a vertical merger, combining cable distribution with Fox programming. Disney offered comfort against risks that regulators would erect hurdles to its offer, including by paying a $1.5bn fee to Fox if the deal was blocked. Comcast refused to agree a similar backstop for its offer. To the Murdochs, it was a sign that Roberts shared their fears that the row between AT&T and the Department of Justice was a threat. Comcast "carried a qualitatively higher level of regulatory risk, including the possibility of an outright prohibition, than such a transaction with Disney", Fox later told investors.

On 6 December, exactly a month after Comcast made its approach, the Fox board met to agree the way forward. The next day Rupert Murdoch called Roberts and told him there would be no deal. He wanted Disney shares, not a stake in Comcast.

Defeated and angry, Roberts issued a statement that effectively accused Murdoch of using Comcast's interest as a negotiating weapon against Disney.

"When a set of assets like 21st Century Fox's becomes available, it's our responsibility to evaluate if there's a strategic fit that could benefit our company and our shareholders," it said.

"That is what we tried to do and we are no longer engaged in the review of those assets. We never got the level of engagement needed to make a definitive offer."

Over the following week Fox put in place the final touches to the Disney deal. Rupert Murdoch and Bob Iger met in London to shake hands on the deal and pose for photographs on the high terrace at the News Corp building at London Bridge. The final terms were unveiled to Wall Street on 14 December 2017, confounding those who still struggled to believe Murdoch would sell.

The consequences were huge. It was irrefutable confirmation that the rise of streaming meant the end of an era and of the old Hollywood oligopoly. In Britain it meant the Murdoch family would not only not be in full control of Sky, but they would cut ties with it entirely. There would be a split in the dynasty, too, as James signalled he would not be involved in running News Corp or the 'new' Fox.

James was not interested in returning to an executive role at News Corp, and the new Fox, with its focus on sport and Fox News, did not appeal either. He had never publicly aired his views about Fox News, but in private he chafed against its attacks on climate science, its devotion to Donald Trump and its indulgence of populism and 'alt-right' movements. The break-up of Fox, which he had championed, offered a chance for him to make a break with what he viewed as toxic assets. Lachlan, who had inherited more of Rupert's politics and pragmatism, would be handed the keys to kingdom.

"This is returning to our roots, which is news and sports," Rupert said in an interview on Sky News on the day the deal was announced. His speech faltered, but the mogul retained his strategic clarity.

"You've got huge companies going into this area now like Amazon, Facebook, Apple, Netflix of course, all spending fortunes on making scripted programmes and putting up the cost enormously," he said. "It's strategically the right time and the right move. We're pivoting at a pivotal moment."

Having done the big deal, he was almost indifferent to the fate of Sky and the regulatory process in which it remained mired. If Fox wasn't allowed to buy it, Murdoch believed, Disney would still take control of 39% and could mount its own takeover without his political baggage. Iger certainly wanted Sky, desiring it as a 'crown jewel' of the deal.

"We think it'll go through," Murdoch said. "If it doesn't, then I'm sure Disney will [buy it].

"There's no reason to knock it back. Ofcom turned upside down and around for months, and said we were fine ... but you just never know. If anything's controversial they [the government] don't want to touch it. That's just the state of politics at this moment."

The truth was considerably more complicated. In Philadelphia, Roberts and Comcast may have been down – but they were certainly not out.

17

The Knowledgeable
Cab Driver

After the NBC Universal takeover, it appeared Comcast would not be allowed by regulators to become much bigger in the US. In 2014, Brian Roberts made a $45bn bid for Time Warner Cable but after years of legal wrangling saw the deal shot down by competition regulators. Comcast needed to broaden its horizons.

Its roots in the American regional cable industry combined with conservative investment approach meant risky overseas conquest in the Murdoch style did not come naturally. Roberts knew, however, that to continue expanding Comcast would one day need break into Europe, and there was no better asset than Sky.

Roberts' interest built gradually. In 2015 he was in London when Sky launched the Sky Q set-top box, and paid a private visit to the demonstration event on the South Bank of the Thames. By then Comcast already had a comparable service, Xfinity X1, in the market. Sky was world famous in the pay-TV industry for its ability to market and deliver new technology to its customers, however, and Roberts came to gather ideas. It was on that visit that he met Jeremy Darroch for the first time.

The following year, Roberts and Steve Burke, the head of NBC Universal, had dinner with Darroch and Andrew Griffith, Sky's chief operating officer.

The idea of a Comcast takeover was not discussed, but it was clear that Sky was on Roberts' radar. In fact, he was making secret overtures to James Murdoch, even suggesting that Fox and Comcast could collaborate on a joint venture to take Sky private.

Murdoch had his own plans for Sky and rebuffed Roberts, who backed off and said that he would not seek to challenge Fox. Comcast was forced to examine other options for its European expansion. Its bankers and in-house takeover team crunched numbers on an array of targets, including BT. They opened informal talks about a potential bid for John Malone's Liberty Global, the owner of Virgin Media. Then, apparently out of the blue, it emerged that the Murdoch family were willing to sell most of Fox, including Sky.

"To Brian's mind that meant all bets were off," says a deal insider. "His priority was obviously getting the whole of Fox, but that didn't work out, so then Comcast came for Sky.

"They obviously liked all of the Fox assets. But I think the internationalisation of Comcast through Sky was a very logical thing. If you look at what Comcast is and does, the match with Sky is extremely close."

"In Europe what are your choices? Liberty is difficult to do for all sorts of reasons to do with debt and other things. But Sky is quite similar in lots of ways. So they really liked it. I don't think you do this just because you believe you have to go and steal a balloon from someone else's party."

At one point in negotiations for the Fox assets, Comcast even signalled to Disney that it would be willing to divide the spoils. It suggested it would buy international distribution with Sky and Star, while Disney could take control of Fox's US production and channels business. Iger did not bite, however.

Taking Sky away from Fox and Disney would not be easy. Comcast was entering the fray at a steep disadvantage against an opponent that already owned 39% of the target and was ahead in securing many if not yet all of the necessary regulatory approvals. Roberts needed help, and found it in the form of Robey Warshaw, the leading London 'boutique advisory'.

Most of the big investment banks already had a role in the complex situation, whether working with Fox, Disney or Sky. Robey Warshaw, a tiny firm of only a dozen staff working out of a nondescript townhouse in St James's, were not yet involved. Despite its modest size, Robey Warshaw was perfectly suited for the task of helping Comcast to gatecrash Fox's takeover.

In five years it had established a reputation for discrete and canny advice in the biggest, most complex and most politically sensitive takeover situations. Its two founders, Simon Robey and Simon Warshaw, were among the best-connected bankers in London and had helped the pharmaceutical giant AstraZeneca fend off an unwanted bid from its US rival Pfizer. They steered the energy giant BG Group through a $52bn merger with Shell, and the Peroni brewer SABMiller through its $79bn combination with AB Inbev.

Robey and Warshaw had quickly become the bankers of choice for corporate chieftains with a takeover problem. Even better, as far as Comcast was concerned, they were both veterans of the News Corp bid that failed in 2011, in their previous roles as senior dealmakers at Morgan Stanley and UBS, the investment banks that advised Sky. Better than most people, Robey and Warshaw knew the lay of the land.

Robey Warshaw had done some theoretical work on Comcast's European options in 2017. After Disney prevailed in the tussle for Fox and the year turned, in February Roberts engaged the firm to begin work in earnest on a bid for Sky.

The first question was whether it would even be possible for Comcast to elbow its way into a deal that was already more than a year old. Fox's existing Sky stake meant that in a straight race to 50%, it would start within yards of the finish line. However, Fox's agreement with Sky prevented it from buying any more shares until the deal was finally done. It had also bid on the basis of a takeover by a court-backed restructuring process known as a scheme of arrangement, which meant that it required approval from three-quarters of the independent Sky shareholders.

Robey Warshaw advised Comcast that these two restrictions on Fox meant, unlikely as it seemed, that it had a chance. It could make a simple takeover bid with an acceptance threshold of 50% plus one share. Detailed analysis of Sky's independent shareholder base suggested that it might be possible to hit the target within the 61% of the company not controlled by Fox.

Such an approach brought risks. Comcast might end up with a controlling stake in Sky with Fox as a troublesome and powerful minority. But it was the only way Roberts could signal the seriousness of his interest to Sky shareholders.

The next question was whether Comcast could catch up with Fox in terms of the regulatory process. Sky shareholders had already waited 14 months for their money, and would probably be frustrated by any further delay. If Roberts was to be a successful interloper, he would need to match the Murdoch timetable.

Fortunately, politics was on his side. In January 2018, Karen Bradley was replaced as Culture Secretary by Matt Hancock, an energetic and ambitious Cabinet first timer; he was no more likely to rush the approval for Fox than his predecessor. The Competition and Markets Authority's (CMA's) provisional verdict, repeatedly delayed by the sheer volume of public consultation responses, eventually came in late January.

In line with Ofcom, it cleared Fox on its commitment to broadcasting standards but found the deal was a threat to the public interest in media plurality because – even though they intended to sell Sky on to Disney – the Murdoch family would gain full control of Sky News. It meant months more horse-trading over remedies to protect Sky News, and further opened the door to Comcast.

By late February 2018, Roberts was ready to show his hand. Comcast stunned the stock market by issuing an announcement known as a '2.4', a non-binding intention to make a takeover bid. The requirements for secrecy and speed meant there had not been time to draw up a full, firm offer with finance in place, but Comcast went as far as it could to show Sky shareholders that it was in the fight to win.

As well as the low acceptance threshold, the 2.4 included plans to match the reassurances Fox had given around the continued operation of Sky News, investment in technology and the maintenance of Sky's Osterley headquarters.

"The UK is and will remain a great place to do business," Roberts said. "We already have a strong presence in London and Comcast intends to use Sky as a platform for our growth in Europe. We intend to maintain and enhance Sky's business."

The aim was to make the comparison of the Comcast bid to the Fox bid as simple as possible; the main substantial difference would be the price.

Comcast announced that it would pay £12.50 per share for Sky, or about £22bn – 16% more than Fox's £10.75 offer. The shares were already climbing after Sky secured a deep cut to its Premier League bill, raising hopes that Fox could be forced to renegotiate. Now, with the prospect of an all-out bidding war between Comcast and Fox acting as a proxy for Disney, excited hedge fund speculators piled in again to force the price above £13.

They did not appreciate at this stage the significance of the valuation Comcast had placed on Sky. The 16% gap between its bid and Fox's was identical to the gap between its bid for Fox and Disney's. Comcast had used the same calculations to set its offer for Sky.

In a further signal of intent, Roberts toured the offices of major newspapers to promote his deal and introduce the British media to Comcast, which despite its size and power was an unknown quantity to most editors. At the offices of *The Times*, deep in Murdoch territory, he asked to be shown to the terrace where Rupert and Bob Iger had posed for photographs.

The charm offensive included an unlikely origin story. Roberts said he had been seduced by Sky on a visit to London the previous November, when a black cab driver regaled him in impressive detail about the superiority of Sky services compared with those of Virgin Media. Such was the taxi driver's enthusiasm that Roberts decided to visit a Sky outlet on the high street, where a demonstration of its services set the ball rolling towards his attempt to gatecrash a Murdoch takeover.

"The cab driver was incredibly knowledgeable about the difference between Virgin and Sky in every feature," he said. "We were learning a lot there."

The media lapped up the tale of cockney wisdom, regardless of its loose relationship with the truth. Roberts had in fact lusted after Sky for years and was no stranger to Sky Q. Nevertheless, he was in London that November, on a mission to poach Virgin Media executive Dana Strong to work in Philadelphia. The cabbie story was a masterstroke of media tactics. It immediately humanised Roberts and took the edge off his aggressive corporate manoeuvre.

The Sky board could only wait to see what happened next. Without a firm offer from Comcast, the company's agreement to be acquired by Fox still stood, yet the publication of the 2.4 allowed the new bidder to begin seeking the approval of regulators.

It was a race. Comcast's lawyers, the big City firm Freshfields, immediately made contact with European authorities in Brussels and with Ofcom. If all went smoothly, they could secure the necessary approvals by summer, around the same time as Fox, and reduce the battle for Sky to a straight bidding war.

James Murdoch had other ideas. He intended to sell Sky, but not to let Roberts buy it. As Murdoch saw it, Comcast's bid was a broken promise.

To his mind, Comcast should have been given the same treatment Fox had faced from the British regulatory system. Media plurality was unlikely to be a concern, however. Comcast had very little sway in the UK market, just a handful of niche pay-TV channels and a stake in the news website Buzzfeed. But if Fox had a case to answer on broadcasting standards and corporate misbehaviour, then so did Comcast.

NBC Universal had been swept up by the wave of allegations of sexual misconduct in the entertainment industry unleashed by the #MeToo movement. Its star breakfast television presenter Matt Lauer was forced out after a number of women accused him of a catalogue of harassment over many years.[1] Lauer later admitted inappropriate behaviour but said claims of "coercive, aggressive or abusive actions" against him were false. Even more damagingly for Comcast, NBC's news executives were accused by the reporter Ronan Farrow of suppressing his agenda-setting investigation of the powerful Hollywood producer Harvey Weinstein. Farrow took the story to *The New Yorker* and subsequently won a Pulitzer Prize.

In the weeks after Comcast announced its intention to make an offer for Sky, Fox lobbied hard for Ofcom to investigate such matters, just as it had investigated sexual harassment at Fox News. It engaged the public relations firm Portland, which had once campaigned against Murdoch's appointment as Sky chief executive, to lobby politicians and journalists. Comcast's record of violating the conditions imposed on its takeover of NBC Universal was also highlighted, as Fox fought to slow down its new rival for Sky.

The campaign was a complete failure.

"Fox could never take on board the uniqueness of the Murdochs," says a Sky executive. "They genuinely believed they were going to get Matt Hancock to refer Comcast to Ofcom for a fit and proper test. They just couldn't see that as far as the political system was concerned, they would always be different."

"We kept saying to them the whole idea was madness. Comcast, far from being a problem for Matt Hancock, was his way out of a decision he didn't want to make to approve the Fox bid. It meant the market would decide who got to own Sky. He really couldn't believe his luck."

Comcast's plan to copy Fox's reassurances on the long-term future of Sky News had convinced politicians that it was a benign force. By the end of April it was ready to make its firm offer and turn its reassurances into legally binding commitments.

"Comcast knew that this was how to get the regulatory red carpet rolled out," says Claire Enders. "Nobody had to twist their arm."

In May 2018, Hancock duly gave Comcast the green light, saying "the proposed merger does not raise concerns in relation to public interest considerations which would meet the threshold for intervention".[2]

It was yet another blow to the Murdoch family from the British establishment. Although the Disney deal meant Fox had no intention of owning Sky in the long term, it had every intention of completing its unfinished business in Britain. Comcast's accommodating tactics and swift regulatory success served as a sharp contrast to Fox's unyielding approach and the obstacles placed in its path.

The firm offer from Comcast also allowed Sky's independent directors to abandon their support of the Fox bid. Martin Gilbert and the rest could no longer be accused of selling to the Murdoch family at a bargain price. Sky was being set up for an auction.

Fox ultimately won approval for its takeover plans by agreeing to substantially the same concession as it had agreed seven years earlier. Under a deal with the CMA and the UK government, Sky News would be spun off as a separate company beyond the reach of Murdoch influence. Disney agreed to 'buy' the unit – in reality it offered to fund its losses – so that if and when it won full control, Sky News could be reunited with its parent.

Still fearful of attacks from Labour, Hancock held out for a guarantee of funding for the channel for 15 years, an increase from the 10-year commitment initially proposed by Fox and Disney. Finally, a full 18 months after it first returned for Sky, Fox would be allowed to complete a takeover, but only if it could defeat Comcast in the bidding.

Before the future of Sky could be resolved once and for all, Roberts spied another chance to disrupt Disney's deal with Fox. The Murdochs had rejected Comcast's $35 per share bid on grounds that the US Department of Justice was seeking to block the comparable takeover of Time Warner by AT&T. Fox told its shareholders that taking Roberts' money was just too risky: the US government might take it away.

For instance, a deal with Comcast would hand Roberts majority control of the popular subscription streaming joint venture Hulu. When he bought NBC Universal, the Department of Justice imposed conditions to prevent Comcast from curbing Hulu to protect its traditional cable business. Surely competition regulators would not allow Roberts greater power over this venture?

However, when the AT&T case came to court in Washington DC, it became clear that the federal judge Richard Leon was unlikely to overturn precedent to agree with the Trump Department of Justice. It had claimed that the takeover of Time Warner would cause major damage to competition and higher prices for pay-TV subscribers, even as a 'vertical' merger of a programming supplier and retailer that would not reduce choice. On 12 June, Leon cleared the takeover without conditions, throwing the door open again to a Comcast bid to snatch Fox's assets from Disney's grasp.

Roberts was prepared. As well as sprinting over the regulatory hurdles in its bid for Sky, Comcast had spent the previous few weeks in clandestine talks with Wall Street financiers, building and gathering the firepower for the biggest all-cash takeover bid in corporate history.

When Fox was originally on the block, Roberts had suggested to the Murdochs that he could pay for Fox's assets with Comcast stock. Now, with the threat his bid would be blocked by regulators apparently reduced, he was planning a hostile campaign of conquest with $65bn in hard cash as his weapon. The day after the AT&T ruling, Comcast publicly announced its offer, in an attempt to drive a wedge between the Murdoch family and the rest of Fox's shareholders. At $35 per share, it valued the assets at about the same level as Roberts' private approach months earlier, equivalent to a 19% premium on the deal agreed with Disney. Comcast bought 1,000 Fox shares so that it could demand a list of other shareholders and begin contacting them to make its case directly.

The approach was calculated to set Fox shareholders against the Murdoch family. Under the Disney deal, Rupert and his children would not be liable to pay any capital gains tax, as they would accept stock for their stake in the Fox assets. Comcast's higher cash offer would be highly attractive to other shareholders, but for the Murdoch family it would crystallise a hefty tax bill.

The conflict was publicised by the British hedge fund manager Chris Hohn. He revealed he had built a 7.4% stake in Fox and demanded that, as the regulatory risks of a Comcast bid were now "equal and low" when compared with Disney's offer, it must be considered regardless of the Murdoch family's finances.

"The personal tax position of the Murdoch family must be an irrelevant consideration for the board, in order for the board to comply with their fiduciary duties," he warned in a letter that was widely publicised prior to Comcast's announcement.[3]

The battle for Fox's assets had effectively become a public auction, and Roberts was still the highest bidder. At Disney, Bob Iger knew that he would have to respond. Though Fox's lawyers still believed a takeover attempt by Comcast would trigger an intervention by competition watchdogs, enough shareholders were convinced by Roberts' approach that Disney knew it would be forced to improve its bid.

Iger moved quickly. On June 15, just two days after Comcast's offer, the Disney board agreed to a new bid at $38 per Fox share, valuing the Murdoch assets at more than $71bn. As well as beating Roberts by more than $6bn, Iger aimed to satisfy Fox shareholders keen to receive cash rather than stock. Disney's new bid would be half cash, half stock, simultaneously allowing the Murdoch family to avoid a tax bill and many other shareholders to take the money and run. In a further sweetener, Iger added a mechanism to ensure that any fall in the Disney share price would be accounted for, so Fox shareholders were guaranteed to receive $38 per share regardless of how long the deal took to complete.

On June 19, Iger met Rupert Murdoch in London to present his improved proposal. For Fox shareholders it was a bonanza. Their board had originally expected to sell the assets for $52.4bn, but Comcast's intervention had added nearly $20bn to the price tag. The following day, the Fox board met and publicly approved the revised deal with Disney.

Roberts was not yet defeated in the US, but the action returned to the UK and to Sky.

Comcast was still in the lead. Roberts had caught up with the Murdochs by securing regulatory clearances and at £12.50 per Sky share was the top bidder, ahead of Fox on £10.75. That figure dated from December 2016, before Sky had sued for peace with BT, driving down the cost of Premier League rights, and before it had neutralised much of the perceived threat from Netflix by striking a groundbreaking deal to include the streaming service in Sky Q subscriptions. There could be no doubt that Sky was worth more than Fox had originally intended to pay for it.

The extraordinary tussle in the US between Comcast and Disney meant Sky's performance would be only one of many factors in its price.

The transatlantic situation had drawn the interest of the UK's Takeover Panel, an obscure organisation billed as City's regulator of takeovers but in reality a self-regulatory body staffed by investment bankers on secondment. Its basic task is to ensure that all shareholders are treated equally when companies are bought and sold.

In the case of Sky this presented a complex challenge. Disney's takeover of Fox assets meant that it was due to acquire 39% of Sky. Under Britain's takeover rules, as Fox had already agreed to acquire/buy the remaining 61%, Disney was also obliged to make an offer under rules known as the chain principle. The question faced by the Takeover Panel was at what price it should have to pay as a minimum. In effect, panel members had to decide what value the $71bn deal for Fox implied for Sky, so that Disney would pay a fair price for all the shares.

In the midst of the Takeover Panel's deliberations, the Government was due to issue the final formal approval of Fox's bid for Sky. It was a trigger to improve the price and leapfrog Comcast. On July 11, Fox unveiled a £14 per share bid that valued Sky at £24.5bn. Sky's board agreed to the offer and gave a concession. In anticipation of an all-out bidding war, Fox demanded the right to abandon its earlier plan to execute the takeover via a scheme of arrangement. Sky agreed Fox could, at a later date, switch to a simple takeover bid, potentially requiring approval by shareholders representing a simple majority of the stock.

This would mean that if Comcast and Fox came up with similar final offers and moved into a race to buy up Sky shares, then Fox's existing 39% stake would have a massive headstart. A scheme of arrangement would have needed approval from shareholders representing three-quarters of the remaining 61%.

The new Fox bid also revealed a fundamental shift in control. Disney was bankrolling the offer and therefore pulling the strings. It signalled that, in whatever came next, Fox and the Murdochs were taking direction from Bob Iger. The final battle for Sky would be not Fox versus Comcast, but Disney versus Comcast.

The decision to leap from Comcast's £12.50 all the way to £14 per share was a result of the chain principle. The Takeover Panel had not yet ruled, but was under heavy pressure from the hedge funds that had piled into Sky shares to set a minimum that would reflect the steep price Disney had agreed to pay for Fox. A bid of around £13 would now be unlikely to win the recommendation of the Sky board.

Even at £14, Fox's position as top bidder lasted less than a day. That night, as the England football team crashed out of their first World Cup semi-final since 1990, Comcast fired back with a bid of £14.75, valuing Sky at £26bn. The agreement with Fox was immediately torn up as months of cold war turned briefly hot.

The Takeover Panel ruled days later that the minimum price for a Disney takeover of Sky should be £14. The decision angered hedge funds, who believed that at the very least they should have been guaranteed £14.59 by projecting the increase in the price for Fox assets in the US onto Sky. Comcast and Robey Warshaw appeared to have anticipated this logic at least. Their £12.50 bid for Sky represented the same premium on Fox's £10.75 bid as Roberts had offered Murdoch in his first attempt to gatecrash the Disney deal.

Sky itself called for a higher floor price, as Martin Gilbert and the other independent directors were emboldened by the prospect of a bidding war and keen to show that they were defending the interests of shareholders. Elliott Advisors, the notoriously aggressive activist fund run by Paul Singer, hired a top barrister to appeal for £15.01.

Fox and Disney found themselves talking down the valuation of Sky, playing down Iger's comment in a television interview months earlier that it was a "crown jewel" in their deal. Disney found itself arguing that it had never attributed a separate valuation for Sky in its bid for Fox. The claim drew derision from Sky and its investors.

The Takeover Panel stuck to its guns. Its decision was a mixture of maths and politics. Disney argued in hearings that its internal valuations pegged Sky's value at £11.80 per share but had approved and helped a Fox bid at £14. That was to be the minimum.

Ultimately, the arcane wrangling had little impact on the fate of Sky. It did, however, help make up Roberts' mind in the US. Comcast had been weighing whether to go for broke and outbid Disney yet again for the Fox assets. Investors were becoming nervous about the level of debt that Roberts would load on the company. Confirmation that the chain principle would be enforced firmly – if not quite as firmly as hedge funds might like – meant that if Comcast bid up for Fox, it would also have to bid up for Sky. Roberts decided it was time to walk away from Fox.

On July 19, little over a month since AT&T won approval to acquire Time Warner, Comcast formally conceded Fox to Disney, but warned it was ready to focus its energy and financial firepower on Sky.

The move prompted speculation that peace would break out in a transatlantic carve-up of Murdoch assets by Roberts and Iger. Yet through August, Disney kept Comcast guessing. When the time came on 8 August for Fox, its proxy, to publish a formal offer document to Sky shareholders, it held its price at £14. Disney gave no signal of whether, having stretched itself to win in the US, it would do so again in the UK.

Comcast was still in the lead on £14.75, but there remained no clear winner. Fox may not have declared £14 as its best and final offer, but had started a 60-day clock. If neither side would back down, then two weeks before time was up, the Takeover Panel would compel them to face each other in an auction. The implications were extraordinary. Sky's fate – nearly two years after Fox made its approach, more than eight years after News Corp made its initial attempts, and after multiple regulatory inquiries and political bust-ups – would be decided over just a few days of quick-fire bidding.

Such auctions were so rare that few investment bankers in London, including those running the Takeover Panel, had any direct experience. Nobody had known an asset of Sky's value – £26bn and counting – go to final round sealed bids. In the most recent precedent, PTT won control of Cove Energy after Shell dropped out of a head-to-head in 2012. Before that, Tata paid £6.2bn in an auction of Corus steel in 2007 against CSN of Brazil, in what turned out to be a disastrous deal.

Just like the Premier League rights auctions in which Sky was itself expert, the risks of overpaying would be high.

After Shell had walked away from the Cove Energy auction, the Takeover Panel had sought to clarify the rules with a default auction design. It called for five rounds of bidding over five days, but as deadline day approached for Sky, neither the target nor the bidders were in favour of such a drawn-out process. The rules allowed them to agree to a shorter, three-round process lasting just 24-hours. Such an intense battle would make it easier to maintain confidentiality.

The three-round structure made matters simpler all round. As the trailing bidder going into the auction, in the first round only Fox would submit an offer to the Takeover Panel, which would act as umpire. In the second round Comcast would respond. In the final round, if neither side had thrown in the towel, they would both make their best and final offer and hope for the best.

The deadline for normal bidding came and went on Friday 21 September 2018, without movement from either side. At 5pm the auction clock began ticking, with Sky shares resting at £15.85 – comfortably above the best offer to date.

As the City geared up for climax of the biggest, longest takeover battle on record, Jeremy Darroch sought to reassure staff.

"Having three of the world's best and largest media companies seeking to own Sky is a major and positive endorsement of our strategy and the execution of our plans," he said. "A process like the one announced today doesn't happen very often and is therefore likely to generate coverage and speculation in the media over the coming days."

The Takeover Panel had set up a dedicated secure online system for the event, to allow the two sides to submit their bids remotely. When the real action began on a drizzly Saturday morning, Brian Roberts and his Comcast lieutenants based themselves at the five-star Stafford Hotel in St James's, footsteps away from the Robey Warshaw townhouse. They were joined by the eponymous investment bankers and Philip Apostolides, the third partner in the firm, and holed up in the hotel's vaulted wine cellars, built in the 17th Century for Sir Francis Godolphin. The bankers would shuttle across to their office to make the actual bids.

The opposition, led by Disney chairman Bob Iger, but also including Fox finance chief John Nallen, opted for the more corporate surroundings of the City law firm Allen & Overy, near Liverpool Street station on the other side of town. The Murdochs stayed at home in New York, on the phone but mostly as spectators who stood to gain regardless of who emerged victorious.

The Sky team of Darroch, Andrew Griffith and Martin Gilbert, with their own phalanx of bankers and lawyers, set themselves up in the boardroom in

Osterley. They nominated a banker from PJT Partners to monitor the auction from a terminal in an adjacent glass-walled office. "He had everyone staring at him," says one attendee. "It was like some sort of gameshow."

Fox made the first move at about midday but showed nothing of its hand. It improved on Comcast's £14.75 offer by only one pence. The bid told Roberts nothing of Disney's appetite for Sky or what it might do in a final round of blind bidding.

After three hours of debate, Comcast responded with a second round bid calibrated to test Disney's resolve for a risky final round of blind bids. Iger had stretched the company's balance sheet to secure ownership of Fox; if he was bluffing on Sky and did not want to be stuck with the bill, Roberts wanted to flush him out. No such luck.

By late afternoon, it was clear the bout would go the full three rounds. In Osterley the tension tested even the coolest heads. It would all come down to who had the nerve to write the biggest number and send it blind to the Takeover Panel.

For Roberts and Robey Warshaw, there were further tactical considerations. A narrow victory was far from desirable. Fox already owned 39% of Sky, which meant a takeover was intrinsically more likely to succeed than a Comcast bid from scratch. If the final bids were close in value, Sky's directors would probably urge shareholders to accept the Fox offer.

Disney had avoided sending any signals over its intentions throughout the summer, however, and ultimately the advice to Roberts was to offer for Sky what he believed it could be worth to Comcast. Financial analysis would be part of the analysis, but Roberts was also conscious that a Murdoch exit from global entertainment was a one-off event from which he did not want to walk away empty-handed.

The number he came up with, £17.28 per share, was a knockout blow. At a total of £29.7bn, or £37bn including debt, the price represented a 125% increase on Sky's valuation before Fox made its initial approach in December 2016.

Disney had allowed Fox to go only to £15.67, less than the market value going into the auction and almost £3bn short of Comcast's bid. James Murdoch would have gone further if it had been up to him, but Iger had a reputation for prudence to restore. The crown jewel in the Fox deal had slipped through his fingers, though he had succeeded in forcing Roberts to pay up in revenge for their bidding war in the US.

After a nerve-wracking few minutes, shortly after 7pm the Takeover Panel revealed the results of the final round on its website. There was short-lived jubilation and high-fiving at the Stafford Hotel. Roberts quickly rang Gilbert to demand the recommendation of the Sky board for his offer. About an hour later it was formally issued as Darroch hailed the new boss, saying "Brian and his team have built a great business and we are looking forward to bringing our two companies together". Iger skipped town immediately.

Those who had watched events unfold in Osterley could see that for Darroch and Andrew Griffith, it was bitterly sweet. "In their heart of hearts they hoped Fox would win," says one eyewitness. "They did all the right things for shareholders but they were emotionally and historically tied to Fox."

Comcast immediately instructed bankers at Bank of America Merrill Lynch to begin buying up Sky shares from the hedge funds that were itching to cash in on the auction. Roberts still had little idea about Iger's plans for Fox's 39% stake. There had been speculation that he might cling on and make trouble, or hope to extract concessions on a separate deal involving the US streaming joint venture Hulu.

In the wake of defeat, Iger was giving nothing away, though in the US investors quickly celebrated the fact that Disney would not take on more debt to add Sky to its empire. On Thursday, as Comcast swept up even small individual shareholders in its pursuit of the magic 50% threshold it needed to pass to control Sky, Iger yielded. Fox announced it would sell its Sky stake, now valued at £11.6bn, to Comcast.

There was tidying up to do but finally the years of uncertainty over Sky's ownership were over. Bankers, lawyers, accountants and other hangers-on were in line to collect hundreds of millions of pounds in fees. Robey Warshaw alone was due to receive nearly £39m for its work guiding Roberts through unfamiliar British waters to turn the tide against Fox. Some 13,000 Sky staff cashed in shares and hundreds became overnight millionaires.

Above all, as Sky joined a new era of global competition, the deal signalled the end of the Murdoch family as a force in British television.

18

The Biggest and Most Dangerous Gamble of All

The formal end of Sky as a Murdoch company was as dizzyingly quick as the political battle over its ownership had been grindingly slow. On 7 November 2018, little more than six weeks after Comcast's dramatic auction victory, the company's 24 years as a public company came to an end as the shares were delisted and Brian Roberts returned to Osterley to introduce himself to staff.

He aimed to calm nerves. Years of vague uncertainty over the future of the company were replaced with urgent questions over Comcast's intentions. Sky had only ever known life as a Murdoch company, and remained suffused with an idea of itself as a fleet-footed challenger and innovator, shaking up the establishment on behalf of the consumer.

The reputation of the new landlord could scarcely be more different. Comcast, to many minds at Sky, was a lumbering monopolist that charged Americans hundreds of dollars a month for famously bad service. When they first travelled to Silicon Valley to build bridges with technology start-ups, Sky executives had been at pains to explain that their company was not like Comcast, despite being in the same businesses of pay-TV and broadband.

Roberts' message was simple. Comcast the conquerer came in peace. After all the tumult, Sky could look forward to stability and support. Roberts certainly had a strong claim as a fan of Sky. He had paid nearly £30bn for the company, more than double its stock market valuation before Fox bid in 2016.

"Sky has been getting taken over for five years basically," he says, underestimating how long Sky had operated under a cloud. News Corp had begun hatching plans for its failed takeover bid nine years earlier, in the late summer of 2009. "I've been in the same company since 1981. I'm looking for the very long term."

"Today everyone says we got a really great deal from General Electric on NBC. And GE has had its own troubles so it looks even more right. But at the time our stock was down 30%. I remember talking to the head of Time Warner and asking why didn't you buy NBC? He told me they didn't want it at that price."

At a gathering in the vaulting eco-friendly atrium at the heart of the Sky campus, figuratively if not geographically a million miles away from the cigarette smoke-filled Portakabins of the company's early years, Roberts urged hundreds of staff to adopt a new creed. As part of Comcast, he said in his gentle tones, the task for each employee was to take decisions as if "you own the company 100% and you're not selling it".

It was a far cry from the buccaneering Sky of the early 1990s, when it looked like Rupert Murdoch's attempt to break into British broadcasting might threaten his entire empire. At times the company appeared to be days from disaster. Back then, 'the long term' sometimes meant next week. Likewise, Roberts' style was a world away from the restlessness and ideological aggression of the James Murdoch years of the mid-2000s.

Aware of both Comcast's reputation and Sky's self-image, the new boss was keen to highlight Comcast's own credentials as a force for change. Under founder Ralph Roberts, his father, the company had played a central role in America's cable revolution, which broke the grip of the telecoms company and the broadcast networks.

"The perception may be that we're an incumbent but we view ourselves as the disrupter," says Roberts. "When my dad started the company we had nothing. The phone company owned the poles and if we wanted to put a cable on them they said, 'you can't'. The broadcasters had all the viewing too."

In any case, Roberts planned to treat Sky as he had treated NBC Universal. When Comcast bought the broadcaster and Hollywood studio, critics claimed that its creativity would be suffocated by the staid, financial culture of the cable industry. They were wrong; NBC Universal had maintained an independent identity and thrived under Comcast. Robert wanted to assure Sky it would receive the same treatment.

Darroch, despite the £38m in Sky shares that he had personally cashed in during the takeover, would stay on. Although he was always one of the best-paid chief executives in the FTSE 100, even his competitors never believed he was in it for the money. Power, winning and constant change motivated Darroch, but his biggest material extravagance is a self-built chalet for walking holidays in Italy.

At a meeting soon after the auction, Darroch presented Sky's business plans to Roberts, and won his endorsement. He would be in charge of the 'third leg of a stool', alongside the core US cable business and NBC Universal.

"There is no risk we will make [Sky customer service] worse because we're not going to be telling Jeremy how to do his job. Jeremy is going to be helping teach us how they were successful," said the Comcast man.

"Different organisations have different philosophies and my dad's philosophy was get an expert and let them do their job," he says. "My job is to go get the money to give to Jeremy to let him innovate and focus on the customer."

As with NBC Universal, collaboration between Sky and Comcast would be modest. In Italy, where Sky is a partner in an ultrafast broadband rollout, Darroch aims to make use of xFi, Comcast's advanced Wi-Fi service.

Sky Q, the set-top box, would be promoted in the run up to Christmas with an advertising campaign based on the new Universal animation

The Grinch. Darroch suggested that for major US news events such as the mid-term elections, Sky News would be able to draw on hundreds of NBC reporters. None of these initiatives should pose a threat to Sky's culture.

In time though, Comcast has promised its investors $300m in cost savings and $200m in extra sales. Bigger ideas will be required. Executives who have worked with and competed with Comcast in the US doubt it will be able to resist the urge to change things.

"To me, Sky got fat and lazy and there are too many private planes and too many people with Mercedes," says one former senior executive. "I mean, it's really changed from those early years, and I think Comcast are going to go for it like a bloody dose of salts. Believe me, because there's a lot of money to take out of Sky now."

Sky has unarguably changed in character under Darroch. It became more pragmatic and focused on its trading performance, partly out of necessity as it leant into the storm of the financial crisis, and partly as the natural result of leadership with a background in accounting. It developed more formal and complicated corporate structures as a result of its expansion onto the continent. Doubtless there is fat for Comcast to cut.

Darroch's achievements should not be underestimated, however. Steering Sky through a major consumer recession and ensuring it was unscathed, while at the same time profitably navigating the generational shift in technology to on-demand television, places him among the top rank of British corporate leaders. Meanwhile Darroch also assembled a team of able senior executives that, despite egos and rivalries aplenty, remained loyal to the cause and gave the centre of Sky a stability that enabled it to make the changes required. Andrew Griffith, technology boss Didier Lebrat, and chief lawyer James Conyers have all been at the top table through Darroch's tenure. Other more recent additions to the executive board, such as Steven van Rooyen and Gary Davey, have long histories within Sky.

Equally unusually, of the core management team, only the strategy chief Mai Fyfield chose not to stay on through the takeover.

"We always talk about how we do things better, and that will pretty quickly turn into a group discussion," says a core member of the group.

"I mean if there's one thing that's true about Sky, which you may not have heard, is we spend time as a group together, probably more than anybody would imagine. We are constantly in a group, constantly in a group.

"One of us'll have a thought and will wander in next door and go, 'What do you think about this?' And they go, 'Oh, that's a good idea.' And then we just wander two doors down and go, 'Jeremy, what about this?' He goes, 'Oh, sounds good. Work it up.'

"You have to remember that we've worked together as a team for a long time. So compatibility, chemistry, capabilities; they all match quite well. And so when we talk about things, there's normally a reasonable confidence that, when we think we've got something, we can push on with it."

Arguably more impressive than any of that, Darroch survived the Murdoch family and the controversy that follows its members. His political skill in avoiding 'tall poppy syndrome,' while maintaining friendly relations with the dominant shareholder and credibility with independent investors for a decade was remarkable. Potentially damaging events such as the News Corp bid, the takeovers of Sky Deutschland and Sky Italia, and the final melee with Comcast and Disney, were handled with deft diplomacy.

"You've got all the strategic stuff that you're making decisions about what the company should be doing," says a friend.

"All that interpersonal stuff of managing an executive team that are jockeying. But also dealing with the board, James, Rupert, News Corp, the independent directors. Keeping all of those things aligned is hard work. You're effectively the only person doing it. It is a lot of pressure but the wheels never came off. The right decisions were nearly always made; despite some very difficult situations there was never an irretrievable breakdown between News Corp and management."

Sky has been on a more pragmatic path ever since Jeremy Darroch was appointed as chief executive. Rows with regulators became more private and less frequent. The Comcast era promises more of the same, particularly as technology giants, largely unencumbered by the regulation that Sky spent decades fighting, compete more in the pay-TV business. For the first time, Sky finds itself calling for tighter regulation of television, not less.

It has been executing this uncomfortable reversal for a year or so, but having cut ties with the Murdoch family, Sky is now taking public positions that would once have been unthinkable. In a recent move to curb gambling advertising on Sky channels, Steven van Rooyen said that "thanks to regulation, TV has long been a safe space".

Such an utterance would never have escaped Osterley until very recently. For regulators and long-term Sky observers, there can be few more stark demonstrations of the new challenges faced by the company. Under Comcast, if the realpolitik of competing with the FAANGs requires Sky to undergo a personality transplant, so be it, even if some find it incredible. Darroch once said "the day we become an incumbent is the day we've lost",[1] yet now finds himself taking some very incumbent-like positions as he appeals for technology giants to be reined in.

"The next bit is they have to ally with the BBC against the internet companies," says a Sky antagonist. "That is very difficult for them. They are in a much more culturally difficult position. They hate the BBC."

The success of Netflix in building a UK subscription base of more than 10 million in a few short years in some ways demonstrates why Rupert, and then James, railed against regulation for so long. Free from Ofcom rules such as the watershed and prominence for public service broadcasters, Netflix is able to meticulously craft its service in a way that best suits its business. It is no coincidence that Sky only began serious investment in original programming once it was possible to distribute it on-demand and beyond the reach of many regulations.

Sky's own marathon to 10 million was, of course, hobbled mainly by technology. Convincing consumers to fix a satellite dish to their house and commit to a long contract to cover the cost of a set-top box was difficult. Getting them to enter their credit card details in an online form to sign up for a month of Netflix is not, in relative terms. In launching satellite television, Sky used new technology to elbow its way into the broadcasting industry. Streaming technology bypasses broadcasters entirely.

The incredible flowering of high quality programming in the pay-TV and streaming era is confirmation of Rupert's analysis of British television when he launched Sky. His prophecies have proved eerily accurate, while the claims of Sky's opponents that it would lead only to an explosion of trash were embarrassingly wrong.

In his 1989 MacTaggart lecture, Rupert told assembled BBC and ITV executives: "I do not dispute that there will be a future role for public broadcasting, though in a scaled-down form. But I suspect that the market is able to provide much more variety, and risk-taking, than many of you realise."

And: "The television set of the future will be, in reality, a telecomputer linked by fibre-optic cable to a global cornucopia of programming and nearly infinite libraries of data, education and entertainment."

James Murdoch told Ofcom officials something similar in 2006: "One simply cannot plausibly argue that choice has been narrowed or that plurality is under threat in the universe of possibilities that the connectedness of media now affords. And this ultimate diversity has not led to quality being driven out."

The uncomfortable reality for political enemies of the Murdoch family is that their basic arguments were right. The punt News Corp took on Sky did lead to an unrecognisably wider choice of quality entertainment and a greater diversity of news coverage. Sport in Britain has been transformed, especially football. Some fans lament what has been lost to pay-TV money, but much more has been gained.

Sky has employed tens of thousands of people, paid its taxes and funded creativity. None of that would have happened without Murdoch aggression and risk taking. As Rupert said on a visit to Osterley after the auction for the opening of a new building in his name (advisers flapped over whether he would be well enough to appear in public, but the event went ahead), founding Sky was "the biggest and most dangerous gamble" of his business career. It paid off spectacularly . . . eventually.

Sky's success was not guaranteed at any stage. Again and again it took risks to transform its business in line with shifting technology and markets. The hefty investment in free set-top boxes that crushed ITV Digital, spending on HD when there were very few homes with a capable television and creating Now TV all required an appetite for the unknown.

Sky's ability to repeatedly make such investments reveals another crucial aspect of the Murdoch influence over the company, and an uncomfortable reality, for Britain's stock market. Without News Corp as a dominant shareholder, able to strong-arm other investors, Sky would not have been able to take many of these decisions.

The way in which City institutions dumped their shares when James Murdoch presented his new strategy in 2004 demonstrates the predicament many UK companies find themselves in. Long-term, risky projects are punished in favour of next year's bonus.

Darroch firmly believes that without Murdoch support, Sky would not have been able to shape-shift as it needed to, or push through the European expansion that secured its scarcity value to Comcast as an international beachhead. Sky, through its risk-taking, gradually eroded its UK investor base in favour of more imaginative American funds. It was they who enjoyed the massive payday in the end.

"The City always misunderstood Sky's ability to shape-shift," says a senior executive. "They look at Sky and think 'well, you've got 10 million but there's no more'. But Sky just shifts its shape. There's Now TV, there's film rentals, there's mobile. It's what the City always got wrong. Sky just finds new ways to grow."

There is even a view within Sky that with more support from the City it might have been able to maintain its independence, and become a champion for the UK on the global stage. It is certainly one of very few genuinely innovative big companies of international significance that the country has produced in the last 30 years.

In its own way it stands alongside the mobile pioneer Vodafone and the dominant smartphone microchip designer ARM Holdings as a home-grown giant in an industry partly of its own creation. It was always likely to fall into American hands, though perhaps, at one time, another future was possible.

Sky's founding chairman, the broadcaster Andrew Neil, told the competition investigation into the Fox bid: "We are in danger of ending up in the situation where nearly all our commercial broadcasters will be foreign owned. We will have given away the crown jewels."

James Murdoch may have flashes of similar thoughts. He spent several years in pursuit of Sky and a vision that ultimately will be executed by Brian Roberts and Comcast.

For at least the last decade, in Murdoch terms, Sky was really his company. Rupert's interventions have been limited to occasional vague exaltations to senior executives to push harder and move faster. The foundations of growth that allowed it to stand firm though the financial crisis were laid when James was chief executive. Unlike James's disastrous leadership of News International, his subsequent chairmanship of Sky was a success and he maintained a close working relationship with Darroch. It is clear to friends and colleagues that Sky is close to his heart; visitors to his New York office are greeted with memorabilia from his days in Osterley.

Yet Murdoch could never have Sky. The traits that made him an effective leader of the business were also lethal to his hopes of gaining full control. Murdoch's resistance to compromise with regulators, with competitors and with his own family history led to bad decisions in both the attempted takeovers. He could not, or would not, accept that the political baggage of decades of newspaper ownership, including the phone hacking scandal, meant News Corp and Fox would be treated differently to a company like Comcast.

For instance, his own MacTaggart speech, delivered even as the first bid was germinating, was a needless attack. It lashed out at a time when News Corp should have been making friends. It helped galvanise the unprecedented coalition of media rivals that opposed the takeover of Sky. The speech also created an enduring impression that Murdoch wanted to make Sky News more like Fox News. In the minds of political enemies it lasted until the Fox bid for Sky, which created a link too with the unfolding sexual harassment scandal across US media.

As well as his own misjudgements, James Murdoch was thwarted by a dose of bad luck and a degree of genuine injustice. Theresa May's botched snap general election was a major factor in both.

The way in which Karen Bradley overruled Ofcom to trigger an investigation by the Competition and Markets Authority (CMA) of Fox's commitment to broadcasting standards was extraordinary and appeared to be the cowardly act of a government focused on self-preservation. She aimed to take no decisions. Likewise, Matt Hancock had no mandate from the CMA's investigation to demand 15 years of funding for Sky News, rather than 10. He did so because it was politically expedient.

It is possible that a stronger Conservative administration would not have referred the takeover to the CMA at all. Ofcom, its specialist regulator, had suggested that an independent editorial board for Sky News could deal with any issues concerning too much Murdoch influence.

Yet regardless, Fox could and should have anticipated opposition, and sought a swift deal on Sky News. For the Murdoch family to protest that a regulatory process was politicised would never carry weight in post-phone-hacking Britain.

Ultimately, all the delays only made the denouement more lucrative. If the Sky takeover had been completed as planned, there would have been no opportunity for Roberts to gatecrash the deal when it emerged that Fox was in talks with Disney. There would have been no Comcast, no auction and no cheque for £30bn.

The sale of Sky was, in the end, a sub-plot in the end of an era for the Murdoch dynasty. When it came, James was satisfied and preparing to make a break with the family business. He wrote a farewell letter:

To all my former colleagues and friends at Sky

The last few weeks, leading up to the auction process and then the aftermath of the acquisition of Sky by Comcast, have gone by very fast and I apologise for not writing sooner.

To be perfectly honest, even with all the preparation in the world, things seemed to move very quickly and it has taken a little while for me to get my head around it.

While I knew – and have been open about since early this year – that we would be parting ways one way or another, with our pending transaction with Disney looming, or in the event of a successful Comcast offer, nonetheless it was a little jarring to sign my resignation letter to the board of directors and to suddenly step away from my role as the Chairman of the company.

That said, I'm enormously excited for you all as this new chapter for Sky takes shape, and I'm also proud of what we've achieved. So I wanted to take this moment to thank each of you for your hard work and commitment in making Sky the extraordinary company it is today.

We transformed the business together, that's for sure, and we did it by serving our customers with consistently world-leading products and services and extraordinary storytelling both made by us, and by our many valuable partners.

We invested more in programming, we invested more in technology, and we created new services, like Sky Broadband, that were game changers for our customers.

We continued to invest in Sky News and TG24. From Romanzo Criminale and Gomorrah, to A League of Their Own and Babylon Berlin, we showed the world that Hollywood or White City aren't the only places where amazing stories can be told and great entertainment can be made.

We raised the bar in sports broadcasting across Europe, and were first out of the gate with true tv-everywhere, OTT experiences. We believed in our customers and our future customers, especially when many thought we would fail.

And also we believed in ourselves. Aiming high, and aspiring to be better than we are, has made Sky the company it is.

It takes a weird combination of grit and joy to improve by changing and challenging with zeal every day, but we've shown how and I know you'll continue to.

Nobody outside thought we could grow to 10 million customers. Most doubted that Sky Italia could be a commercial and creative force. Folks didn't understand why a company would want to be carbon neutral. People wondered why we should care about plastic. Winning the Tour de France? No way. This list could go on for a while. You killed it.

When we launched the Bigger Picture initiative at Sky, we articulated an aspiration to be better – for companies to be better, and to behave in the way that we imagined we would want to and be expected to in the future. An idea that companies should embrace what their customers and people care about, and that by doing so, it makes them stronger. This made us a better company, and better for our communities. I will carry this spirit to every enterprise I build in my own future, and will be forever grateful to all of you for proving that always striving to be better – genuinely believing in better – brings great rewards to shareholders, to customers, and to the communities and cultures we serve.

It has been unbelievably fun to share the last fifteen years with you and a privilege to call you colleagues.

Best,

JRM

The future of the Murdoch empire is now in the hands of Lachlan. Rupert's involvement, such as it is, is ceremonial. James, with $2bn in hand from the sale of Fox, is preparing independent ventures and plans to have no involvement in either Fox or News Corp. Lupa Systems, his new holding company, is likely to invest from the socially progressive and environmentalist standpoint of James and his wife Kathryn. Already he has signalled his opposition with the hardline conservative agenda pursued by Fox News, making a personal donation to the gay Democratic presidential hopeful Pete Buttigieg.

Despite Roberts' assurances that he will not impose change, Sky and Comcast are moving together into a new era.

In response to the rise of Netflix, the major Hollywood studios, including NBC Universal, are developing their own subscription streaming services. Rather than providing films and television wholesale for operators such as Sky to package up as channels and box sets, they aim to build their own direct relationships with consumers. The likes of Disney and HBO owner Time Warner, controlled by Comcast rival AT&T, plan to transform their businesses to match viewing habits.

The effect this will have on Sky is uncertain. What will it mean when those Disney films are only available as part of a branded streaming service? Will Comcast be able to do a deal to bundle it in a Sky subscription? The massive value it has attributed to Sky as a distribution platform will be tested. Relationships with longstanding partners such as HBO could be strained as they are tempted to choose the streaming future over lucrative but declining traditional channels. Bob Iger, for instance, Sky's most powerful supplier, is staking his legacy on creating a global 'Disneyflix' subscription streaming service, Disney+. Sky is in line to lose its exclusive access new films from the House of Mouse, a privilege it has enjoyed since the dawn of pay-TV in the UK and one which has become more important as Pixar, Marvel and Star Wars have joined the Disney fold. Iger's takeover of most of Fox means an even closer tie may also be cut, or at least weakened.

Darroch believes that Sky's power as a retailer and marketer of television will endure, particularly now that it is part of Comcast, with a total customer base of 50 million. Studios will still have to go through Sky to get access to consumers, he believes. The groundbreaking deal with Netflix, under which customers are effectively shared, could serve as a template.

"Broadly the way rights have been sold traditionally has disconnected with how people are consuming content," he says. "Over time that's where you start to get leakage and the ecosystem starts to get disrupted. Now the opportunity to shape that for ourselves and the industry is an interesting big picture topic."

Roberts, too, is in the foothills of exploring what international scale means for Comcast's power as a distributor and producer.

"Some organisations may say 'we love access to the whole 50 million, that's unique'. Others may say, 'no, we have a special relationship in London that is very different to what we have in Philadelphia' [with Comcast]. We're going to respect that."

Sky and Comcast have very different approaches to Amazon, for example. Comcast has allowed the online giant's streaming service onto its set-top box in the US. In Osterley, meanwhile, Amazon has emerged as the new nemesis to replace BT. Sky executives see Amazon's dabbling in live sport and focus on using cheap consumer hardware to open the door to the living room as a rising threat. They have no intention of allowing Amazon access to Sky Q households.

"Maybe it's harder for a big company to sync up all of it on that platform," says Roberts.

"But if you're a start-up and you want to get access to 50 million households, or an animated movie and you want to get marketed better than anyone else, or you're Steven Spielberg and you want to make the next *Jurassic World*, why do you work with our company and not with another? Because we have a capability to deliver something nobody else can. Not in all instances will that capability be taken advantage of but over time in the long term I think that will be what distinguishes."

Darroch adds: "There may be some stuff where we can come together and do a deal because we can say to a rights holder, or a technology company or an advertiser, this is what we can give you."

It is clear, however, that in the coming years Sky's investment priorities will change. It is already squeezing the providers of niche channels such as Discovery, pushing them to accept lower fees. Their cheap and cheerful programming once buttressed the vast choice that was the basis of Sky's marketing pitch, but in the streaming age quality is the top priority and Darroch would rather spend the money on original drama that can compete with Silicon Valley.

Sky, which has struggled to establish itself as a drama hitmaker, is keen to build a relationship with NBC Universal. Its own production efforts, such as literary adaptation *Patrick Melrose*, have won critical acclaim and underpinned Sky Atlantic. As part of a giant such as Comcast, the opportunities to share costs and distribution are much greater. More than anything, Sky wants its own calling card hit to rank alongside HBO's *Game of Thrones* or Netflix's *House of Cards*.

"We've got an organisation with 50 million households, some of the most valuable households in the world, and many of those are English-speaking," says Darroch. "In time we will start to say, right, there could be some big things we can do that really utilise that asset base."

The upheaval in television makes it easy to forget that Comcast is a telecoms company first and a media company second. Roberts' approach to Sky's broadband business is being closely watched by old enemies such as BT. Sky could become an investor in full-fibre broadband infrastructure. Openreach, the newly independent network subsidiary of BT, would like nothing more than to share the cost of upgrades with a rich partner.

Openreach also sees in Sky a player capable of stimulating demand for the higher speed and capacity offered by full-fibre broadband. Pumping ultra-high-definition television through new networks could meanwhile allow Sky to make a gradual exit from satellite distribution.

The arrival of a wealthy new player in Europe already has London's investment bankers imagining more deals for Comcast. As an infrastructure investor it might prefer to own a mobile network such as O2 rather than rent capacity from it. In broadband Roberts could even revisit his talks with Liberty Global, some believe, although a combination of Sky and Virgin Media, still its biggest pay-TV rival, would face serious competition hurdles.

A cheaper option for expansion would be to introduce Now TV to more new markets. Sky has already made steps into Spain, where it has no satellite pay-TV business. As NBC Universal joins the fray of Hollywood studios seeking to replace traditional channels and programme wholesaling with streaming distribution, Sky offers expertise and infrastructure.

Roberts is under some pressure to address these big questions sooner rather than later. Including debt, he has invested £37bn in a company facing technological turmoil based in a country facing economic disruption from Brexit. It was, says one rival media mogul, "ballsy". Unfamiliar Wall Street investors immediately compared Sky with ESPN, Disney's struggling sport business, or with a traditional US pay-TV operator such as AT&T's satellite business Dish, under pressure from cord cutting.

"The [US] stock market really didn't understand Sky," says Roberts. "The American investor thinks of what they watch at home and their choices. There was a misunderstanding of this market. The very first question I got asked was 'why isn't this like Dish network?'

"We were 10% above Disney's final bid. I don't think that 10% will judge us on whether it was right or wrong.

"You had a 39% stockholder in Fox so you really had to have a margin so everyone could see who was the best offer. Maybe it could have been a little less, but I don't think too much.

"We don't know we are right in our judgement. But we've financed it and we've paid for it. Now it's all about what can we do from here. Time will judge whether we were right or wrong."

NOTES

Chapter 1

1 http://www.thetvfestival.com/wp-content/uploads/2018/03/MacTaggart_1989_Rupert_Murdoch.pdf

2 https://www.independent.co.uk/news/business/profile-mark-booth-a-hand-of-steel-to-hold-up-sky-1142230.html

3 https://www.irishtimes.com/business/first-englishman-to-head-bskyb-knows-business-from-bottom-up-1.197393

4 https://www.telegraph.co.uk/finance/2761773/How-the-Government-failed-ITV-Digital.html

5 https://www.telegraph.co.uk/finance/2832319/Skys-digital-bonanza.html

6 https://www.theguardian.com/media/2002/jan/29/itvdigital.broadcasting

Chapter 2

1 https://www.telegraph.co.uk/finance/2752563/Sky-keeps-growing-as-Kirch-write-off-pushes-loss-to-1.4bn.html

2 https://www.theguardian.com/media/2003/aug/23/bskyb.broadcasting

3 https://www.theage.com.au/national/investors-wary-of-james-in-top-sky-job-20030919-gdwdbr.html

4 https://www.theage.com.au/national/investors-wary-of-james-in-top-sky-job-20030919-gdwdbr.html

5 https://www.theguardian.com/media/2003/oct/13/newscorporation.citynews

6 https://www.independent.co.uk/news/media/murdoch-backs-son-james-as-bskyb-chief-92388.html

7 https://www.theguardian.com/media/2003/nov/12/citynews.broadcasting

8 https://www.theguardian.com/media/2003/nov/15/business.bskyb

Chapter 3

1   https://www.newyorker.com/magazine/1996/09/16/a-grass-roots-murdoch

2   https://www.nytimes.com/2007/06/26/world/asia/26murdoch.html

3   https://www.wsj.com/articles/SB985656802114995176

4   https://www.theguardian.com/business/2003/dec/14/theobserver.observerbusiness3

5   https://www.telegraph.co.uk/finance/2892192/Ad-hoc-Skys-branding-tripped-up-by-its-alpha-males.html

6   https://www.telegraph.co.uk/finance/2892073/The-Sky-is-not-falling-in.html

7   https://www.theguardian.com/media/2004/aug/05/bskyb.citynews1

8   https://www.theguardian.com/business/2004/jun/24/7

9   https://www.theguardian.com/media/2004/nov/18/newscorporation.rupertmurdoch

Chapter 4

1   https://www.theguardian.com/money/2006/jul/19/consumernews.internetphonesbroadband

Chapter 5

1   https://www.telegraph.co.uk/finance/2950994/Branson-goes-head-to-head-with-Murdoch-in-ITV-row.html

2   https://www.telegraph.co.uk/finance/2950994/Branson-goes-head-to-head-with-Murdoch-in-ITV-row.html

3   https://www.theguardian.com/media/2006/nov/22/bskyb.television

4   https://www.youtube.com/watch?v=uLLyPilHAJA

5   https://www.managementtoday.co.uk/world-exclusive-mt-interview-james-murdoch/article/653028

Chapter 6

1   https://www.campaignlive.co.uk/article/skys-darcey-clashes-ofcom-pay-tv-enquiry/668174

Chapter 7

1 https://www.ft.com/content/7c178a76-dec1-11e2-b990-00144feab7de

2 https://www.bbc.co.uk/sport/av/cycling/43292936

Chapter 8

1 https://www.pressgazette.co.uk/reaction-to-james-murdochs-mactaggart-lecture/

2 https://inews.co.uk/news/media/paul-dacre-speech-in-full-four-predictions-a-cry-for-free-speech/

3 https://www.telegraph.co.uk/news/politics/conservative/5757787/Conservatives-review-each-quango-to-see-if-it-can-be-abolished.html

4 https://www.ft.com/content/1de7f24e-d045-11de-a8db-00144feabdc0

5 https://www.theguardian.com/business/marketforceslive/2008/oct/22/bskyb-britishairways

Chapter 9

1 https://www.telegraph.co.uk/finance/newsbysector/epic/bsy/7827991/BSkyB-takeover-Rupert-Murdoch-moves-towards-full-BSkyB-takeover.html

2 http://www.bbc.co.uk/pressoffice/speeches/stories/thompson_mactaggart.shtml

3 https://www.bbc.co.uk/news/business-12050727

Chapter 10

1 https://www.theguardian.com/business/2010/jul/01/bt-vision-sky-sports

2 https://www.telegraph.co.uk/finance/newsbysector/mediatechnologyandtelecoms/10207714/The-BT-man-who-kicked-out-BSkyB-doesnt-think-its-all-over.html

3 https://www.telegraph.co.uk/finance/newsbysector/
mediatechnologyandtelecoms/10051240/BT-Sport-BT-boss-wants-to-bring-sports-
back-to-fans.html

4 https://www.telegraph.co.uk/finance/newsbysector/mediatechnologyandtelecoms/
media/11411992/Sky-chief-we-won-the-Premier-League-auction.html

Chapter 11

1 https://www.telegraph.co.uk/finance/newsbysector/mediatechnologyandtelecoms/
media/10989545/BSkyB-seals-5bn-deal-with-Murdoch-to-create-Sky-Europe.html

2 https://technology.ihs.com/506803/bskyb-confirms-deal-to-buy-sky-italia-and-sky-
deutschland

Chapter 12

1 https://www.telegraph.co.uk/finance/newsbysector/
mediatechnologyandtelecoms/9003338/Netflix-launch-in-UK-starts-price-war.html

2 https://www.theguardian.com/media/2000/may/07/bskyb.newsinternational

3 https://www.telegraph.co.uk/finance/newsbysector/mediatechnologyandtelecoms/
media/12130382/Skys-new-vision-of-home-comforts-more-TV-available-everywhere-
at-a-higher-price.html

Chapter 13

1 https://www.exaronews.com/rupert-murdoch-secretly-admits-i-knew-about-bribing-
officials

2 https://www.ft.com/content/8ad34584-911d-11e6-a72e-b428cb934b78

3 https://www.ft.com/content/a3966692-c2ef-11e6-9bca-2b93a6856354

4 https://www.theguardian.com/business/2016/dec/12/murdoch-sky-bid-schedule-of-
agreement-shareholders

Chapter 14

1 https://www.pressreader.com/uk/the-daily-telegraph/20161210/281505045850139

2 https://www.theguardian.com/commentisfree/2017/sep/01/britain-fox-news-murdochs-uk-media

3 https://money.cnn.com/2018/04/04/media/bill-oreilly-defamation-suit-denied-settlement-under-seal/index.html

4 https://www.theguardian.com/commentisfree/2017/sep/01/britain-fox-news-murdochs-uk-media

Chapter 15

1 https://www.theguardian.com/media/2000/may/07/bskyb.newsinternational

2 http://www.bbc.co.uk/pressoffice/speeches/stories/thompson_mactaggart.shtml

3 https://www.theguardian.com/media/2011/jun/08/bskyb-spend-uk-programming

4 https://www.hollywoodreporter.com/news/miptv-sky-content-boss-gary-davey-talks-original-content-push-competition-netflix-amazon-988228

Chapter 16

1 https://www.cnbc.com/2017/11/06/21st-century-fox-has-been-holding-talks-to-sell-most-of-company-to-disney-sources.html

2 https://www.nbcnews.com/news/us-news/rupert-murdoch-talks-sell-much-his-media-empire-disney-n818146

3 https://www.nytimes.com/2016/11/07/business/media/media-merger-success-comcast-and-nbcuniversal-say-yes.html

Chapter 17

1 https://www.washingtonpost.com/lifestyle/style/nbc-news-faces-skepticism-in-remedying-in-house-sexual-harassment/2018/04/26/7fa8a666-4979-11e8-8b5a-3b1697adcc2a_story.html?noredirect=on&utm_term=.db4f7c41c7bf

2   https://www.telegraph.co.uk/business/2018/05/21/boost-comcast-murdoch-battle-matt-hancock-signals-no-probe-sky/

3   https://www.cnbc.com/2018/05/23/activist-investor-chris-hohn-says-he-would-back-cash-bid-by-comcast-for-fox-assets.html

Chapter 18

1   https://www.managementtoday.co.uk/mt-interview-jeremy-darroch-bskyb/article/1100043